Issues in applied linguistics

Michael McCarthy

CAMBRIDGE
UNIVERSITY PRESS

PUBLISHED BY THE PRESS SYNDICATE OF THE UNIVERSITY OF CAMBRIDGE
The Pitt Building, Trumpington Street, Cambridge, United Kingdom

CAMBRIDGE UNIVERSITY PRESS
The Edinburgh Building, Cambridge CB2 2RU, UK
40 West 20th Street, New York, NY 10011–4211, USA
10 Stamford Road, Oakleigh, Melbourne 3166, Australia
Ruiz de Alarcón 13, 28014 Madrid, Spain

http://www.cambridge.org

© Cambridge University Press 2001

First published 2001

Printed in the United Kingdom at the University Press, Cambridge

Typeface 9.5/13.5 pt. Swift Regular [VN]

A catalogue record for this book is available from the British Library

Library of Congress Cataloguing in Publication data applied for

ISBN 0 521 58487 6 hardback
ISBN 0 521 58546 5 paperback

Contents

Foreword

My partner and I have regular lessons in traditional Irish fiddle playing from an expert teacher. She has a PhD in musicology, and specialises in traditional fiddle styles. Each week she teaches us a new tune or set of tunes. We learn them by ear, with no reference at all to 'theory', no writing down or reading from notes, and they are committed to memory. Occasionally, the teacher steps back from playing and talks about the music, its distinctiveness and character; sometimes she talks about the instrument and what it can do. She encourages us to listen a lot to the great exponents of the tradition. All this teaching is never done in a threatening or obfuscating way. In between lessons we practise our stock of tunes for about two hours daily. Sometimes we take them very slowly, to improve accuracy and intonation, sometimes we blast them out in a carefree way, which helps with overall rhythm, feel and the general pleasure of 'performing'.

The parallels with language teaching and learning strike me regularly and profoundly. In learning the fiddle I am learning a new language, one that has deep historical roots and which expresses the emotions of a people to whom I am only related through my grandparents and through an abiding love of their land and culture. This new language has substance (musical in this case), form (the various structural patterns of jigs, reels, etc.) and meaning (it is dance music, it communicates with and 'lifts' dancers; it generates emotions; it is Irish, not Spanish or Rumanian). Many people – not only Irish people – use it, and play together for enjoyment in pubs, clubs, schools and homes. It is difficult and complex to learn. There seem to be so many things to remember at once. Progress is slow, but very rewarding, and depends on my ability to practise a lot, and my motivation to persevere. Sometimes I wonder if I might have learnt better and faster if I had taken it up at the age of six or seven, so I could dazzle audiences as many young children do in present-day Ireland. Other times I am glad I can bring the wisdom of experience, feeling and understanding to this encounter with a different culture. And so on.

But what has all this to do with applied linguistics? A good deal, I would argue. Applied linguistics is about the relationship between knowledge, theory and practice in the field of language, and my fiddle teacher seems to me to be the epitome of an 'applied language practitioner', though not in verbal language. She knows all there is to know about music in general and the violin in particular. But her task is not to impart that knowledge and theory to me. What she does is to mediate it and use it to inform a very practical task: teaching this typical, stumbling but basically willing learner to play and enjoy the fiddle. Her knowledge and her practice are interdependent, but are not the same thing. She uses her knowledge to solve practical problems, like why I make a squeaky sound at times (perhaps the angle of the bow), why I lack fluency (perhaps my shoulder and wrist are too tense), and how much new input I can take and process at any one time, as well as whether I am covering a wide, useful repertoire to enable me to play with people I've never met before but who share my new language.

In this spirit have I put this book together, as an exploration of what it is applied linguists in the field of language teaching do, why they do it, and purely personally, how I think they should be doing it. I am aware of the near-impossibility of writing a book that covers applied linguistics adequately in its multifarious branches as we tread gingerly into a new Christian millennium, and this book does not claim to be a definitive survey, or even an introduction. It is an expedition into various ways of looking at language and how they influence language teaching. It comes from my own 35 years of involvement in language teaching and teacher education, both as a teacher of English and Spanish, and as a learner of French, Spanish, Welsh, Latin, Catalan, Swedish and Malay, and a lifelong learner of English as a mother tongue, with widely varying degrees of success, and through a wide range of methods and approaches. It also comes from my more recent identity as an academic, when I 'quit the road' and put down roots in British university life.

In recent years I have immersed myself in the academic study of language and language teaching and learning, and have been overawed by the volume of academic work published in relation to our profession. No one can read it all. In this book I therefore refer to what I have read (recall, this is no survey) and what I have found useful, illuminating, sometimes downright irritating, but mostly thought-provoking, and provoking thought, above all, is what applied linguists should be doing for their consumer audiences. This book therefore claims to do no more than this:

to raise questions that have nagged at me over the years and questions which regularly preoccupy the profession in general, and to look at how the academic- and practice-based study of language can help to provide answers to practical problems, or at least point us in promising directions. Much of the ground will be familiar to my peers and betters, though I do invest a personal degree of commitment to the historical dimension of our profession, which is not always so much to the forefront. I hope that younger, and newer, entrants to the community of applied linguists (graduate students, practising teachers given the opportunity to step back from the chalkface and engage in study or research, anyone curious to know what role the study of language plays or can play in language teaching) will find something in it of merit. There are, to be sure, gaps, and all I can do is hope that the works of other scholars will fill those. If serious shortcomings remain in this book after the endless work put into it by reviewers and editors during its development, the blame for these should all be laid fairly and squarely at my door.

Cambridge, June 2000

Acknowledgements

This book has taken a long time to write. Although the background research for it was done mainly in the highly conducive reading rooms of the Cambridge University Library, no book is ever really the product of the solitary scholar. Many colleagues, friends, conference presenters, academic collaborators and professional contacts have influenced me and what I have written here. They are too many to mention. However, as with all my academic work, no one has influenced and helped me more in recent years than Ronald Carter, friend and colleague. Ron is the epitome of the unselfish intellectual, always ready to give and share ideas, to be critical without being carping, to see connections and to push me to think differently. To Ron goes a big thank you for inspiration, support, companionship and collegiality. Other scholars who have had an immeasurable influence on my overall thinking include John Sinclair, Henry Widdowson, James Lantolf, Doug Biber, Amorey Gethin, Mike Hoey, Malcolm Coulthard and the never fading memory of David Brazil. To all these I owe a massive debt. There are also many other colleagues, friends and professional contacts who have contributed directly or indirectly to what is in this book, and who have influenced and inspired me in different ways, amongst whom I would like to extend special thanks to the following: Jens Allwood, Susan Conrad, Guy Cook, Justine Coupland, Zoltan Dörnyei, Carmen Gregori Signes, Martin Hewings, Almut Koester, Koen Van Landeghem, David Nunan, Felicity O'Dell, Anne O'Keeffe, Luke Prodromou, Randi Reppen, Mario Rinvolucri, Helen Sandiford, Diane Schmitt, Norbert Schmitt, Yasuhiro Shirai, Diana Slade, John Swales, Hongyin Tao, Mary Vaughn and Linda Waugh. At CUP, both Alison Sharpe and Mickey Bonin have had input into this book, but Mickey gets special thanks for bearing the irksome burden of guiding me through successive reviewers' reports, scolding me for slowness and encouraging me because he believed in the book, adding his own academic comments and editorial expertise, so that he got his manuscript at long last. And thanks to Cathy Rosario, whose expertise and efficiency in the final editing process removed inelegant sentences, glitches and bugs so that the book could go to press. Finally, I thank my partner, Jeanne McCarten, for her support and inspiration over twenty years, without which I might never have finished one book, let alone this one.

This book is dedicated to the fond memory of my late brother-in-law, Warwick Partridge, an 'applied' man, if ever there was one.

1
Applying linguistics: disciplines, theories, models, descriptions

1.1 Applied linguistics as problem-solving

In their day-to-day business, professionals whose work involves language in some way or another often face problems that seem to have no immediate or obvious solution within the habitual practices which demarcate their professional expertise. One avenue open to those who find themselves in this position is to have recourse to the discipline of linguistics. It is the belief that linguistics can offer insights and ways forward in the resolution of problems related to language in a wide variety of contexts that underlies the very existence of the discipline usually called applied linguistics. Applied linguists try to offer solutions to 'real-world problems in which language is a central issue' (Brumfit 1991:46), however tentative or 'implied' those solutions may be. What, then, might fall within the domain of typical applied linguistic problems? A list of such problems will certainly be wide-ranging and potentially endless, but might include the following:

1 A speech therapist sets out to investigate why a four-year-old child has failed to develop normal linguistics skills for a child of that age.
2 A teacher of English as a foreign language wonders why groups of learners sharing the same first language regularly make a particular grammatical mistake that learners from other language backgrounds do not.
3 An expert witness in a criminal case tries to solve the problem of who exactly instigated a crime, working only with statements made to the police.
4 An advertising copy writer searches for what would be the most effective use of language to target a particular social group in order to sell a product.
5 A mother-tongue teacher needs to know what potential employers

consider important in terms of a school-leaver's ability to write reports or other business documents.

6 A historian wishes to understand the meanings of place-names in a particular geographical area and how they have changed over time.

7 A person constructing a language test for non-native speakers for entry into further education needs to know what the key linguistic or psycholinguistic indicators are of reading ability in a second or foreign language.

8 A literary scholar suspects that an anonymous work was in fact written by a very famous writer and looks for methods of investigating the hypothesis.

9 A dictionary writer ponders over possible alternatives to an alphabetically organised dictionary.

10 A computer programmer wrestles with the goal of trying to get a computer to process human speech or to get it to translate from one language into another.

11 A group of civil servants are tasked with standardising language usage in their country, or deciding major aspects of language planning policy that will affect millions of people.

12 A body is set up to produce an international, agreed language for use by air-traffic controllers and pilots, or by marine pilots and ships' captains.

13 A zoologist investigates the question whether monkeys have language similar to or quite distinct from human language and how it works.

14 A medical sociologist sets out to understand better the changes that occur in people's use of language as they move into old age.

The list could continue, and with professional diversification of the kind common in modern societies, is quite likely to grow even bigger over the years. What all these professional problems have in common is the possibility of turning to the discipline of linguistics to seek insight and potential solutions. If they were to do this, the professionals directly involved would become, even if only temporarily, applied linguists. This is different from saying that there is a community of applied linguists (usually associated with university academic departments) whose job it is to mediate (and teach) linguistics and to suggest applications. That there is such a community is not questioned here; the existence of academic journals such as *Applied Linguistics* and *International Review of Applied Linguistics*, and the provenance of the majority of articles published in them, is ample evidence (for further argument on this aspect of the mediation of theory see Block 1996). But in this book I shall advocate that 'doing applied linguistics' should not be only the responsibility of the academic community.

Over the last few decades, more and more people working in different professional areas have sought answers to significant problems by investigating how language is involved in their branch of human activity. This has been especially notable in very recent years in areas such as (3), (10) and (14) in the list of possible problems above (e.g. the growth of forensic applications of linguistics, see Kniffka *et al.* 1996; the growth of interest in language and the elderly, see Coupland *et al.* 1991). Other areas, such as (1), (2) and (8), have used linguistic knowledge and insight over a much longer period. In the future, even more professions will almost certainly turn to linguists for potential solutions to practical problems: the increasing sophistication of computers is just one obvious example where a correspondingly complex understanding of human language may be beneficial. Thus even more professionals will have the opportunity to become applied linguists.

No one will need to embrace the whole range of the discipline of linguistics to find a solution to their particular problem. Linguistics itself is now an extremely broad discipline, and we shall see in this book just how large a number of interests it encompasses. Furthermore, within this broad discipline, the various compartments into which the subject falls are themselves quite vast (e.g. see Malmkjaer's 1991 encyclopedia of the discipline), and compartmentalisation creates its own problems for the application of linguistics (see Brumfit 1980 for a discussion). What this book will try to do in its limited scope is to exemplify how language teachers and others involved directly or indirectly in language teaching and learning (such as materials writers, syllabus designers, dictionary writers, etc.) may approach their problems via the many and varied aspects of linguistic study. Wherever relevant, I will also mention work done by other, non-pedagogical applied linguists in the spirit of learning and benefiting from their insights and in the fostering of a shared professional identity, which can only be a good thing. The book cannot and does not pretend to offer prescriptions for the solving of every problem. You, the reader, will, it is hoped, see how and where linguistics might rub shoulders with your own professional preoccupations.

1.2 Linguistics and applied linguistics: hierarchy or partnership?

Applied linguistics, I shall maintain throughout this book, is essentially a problem-driven discipline, rather than a theory-driven one, and the community of applied linguists has characterised itself in the historiography of the discipline by variety and catholicism of theoretical orientation. This is in contrast to linguistics, where association with particular schools of thought or theories tends to exert considerably greater centripetal force. Indeed, not least of the questions immanent in a book such as this one are: Can there be a *unitary theory* of applied linguistics, or indeed do theories of applied linguistics exist at all? Is it not a defining quality of applied linguistics that it draws its theory off-the-peg from linguistics; in other words, that it should be understood as what Widdowson (1980) calls *linguistics applied*? One major difficulty in asserting the latter is the viability of the view that linguistics exists as a set of agreed theories and instruments that can be readily applied to real-world language-related problems. Such a view oversimplifies the natural and desirable state of continuous flux of the discipline of linguistics (e.g. see Makkai *et al.* 1977), or of any discipline for that matter, and obscures the two-way dialogue that the academic applied linguistic community has had, and continues to have, with its own community of non-academic practitioners and with its peers within linguistics.

Applied linguistics can (and should) not only test the applicability and replicability of linguistic theory and description, but also question and challenge them where they are found wanting. In other words, if the relationship between linguistics and its applications is to be a fruitful partnership and neither a top–down imposition by theorists on practitioners – admonitions of which are implicit in Wilkins (1982) – nor a bottom–up cynicism levelled by practitioners against theoreticians, then both sides of the linguistics/applied linguistics relationship ought to be accountable to and in regular dialogue with each other with regard to theories as well as practices (see also Edge 1989). Accountability can discomfit both communities, and abdication of accountability is sometimes the easier line to adopt. I shall attempt wherever possible to refrain from such abdication in this book, and bi-directional accountability will be considered an important constraining influence on both the applicability of linguistics and the evaluation of applied linguistic solutions. Accountability will centre on a set of responsibilities falling on the shoulders of linguists and applied linguists in turn. These include:

1 The responsibility of linguists to build theories of language that are testable, which connect with perceived realities and which are not contradicted or immediately refuted when they confront those realities.

2 The responsibility of linguists to offer models, descriptions and explanations of language that satisfy not only intellectual rigour but intuition, rationality and common sense (but see Widdowson 1980 for comments on both sides of this particular coin).

3 The responsibility of applied linguists not to misrepresent theories, descriptions and models.

4 The responsibility of applied linguists not to apply theories, descriptions and models to ill-suited purposes for which they were never intended.

5 The responsibility of applied linguists not simply to 'apply linguistics' but to work towards what Widdowson (1980) calls *relevant* models' of language description (see also Sridhar 1993, who sees applied linguists as generating their own paradigms for studying language).

6 The responsibility of applied linguists to provide an interface between linguists and practitioners where appropriate, and to be able to talk on equal terms to both parties (see James 1986).

7 The responsibility on both sides to adopt a critical position vis-à-vis the work of their peers, both within and across the two communities.

8 The responsibility of both communities to exchange experience with front-end practitioners such as language teachers, psychologists or social workers, who may not have a training in linguistics nor the time or resources to 'do applied linguistics' themselves, but who may be genuinely eager to communicate with both groups.

1.3 Theory in applied linguistics

Posing the question whether applied linguists should have theories and whether the discipline as a whole should seek a unifying and homogenous set of theoretical constructs is, in my view, a misleading and unproductive line to pursue, and one which will be discussed further in Chapter 6. It is difficult enough to establish a set of central tenets that unites the generally pro-theoretical community of linguists (but see Hudson 1988 for an interesting list of such tenets; see also Crystal 1981:2, who takes a fairly optimistic view of the existence of a 'common core' within linguistics), let alone bring under one umbrella the diversity of approach that marks out the domains of operation of applied linguistics. Within linguistics, widely differing theories lay claim to deal with what is important in language: as we shall see, a sentence grammarian may differ fundamentally from a discourse analyst over the question of just what is the central object of study. On the other hand, the sentence grammarian and discourse analyst may unite in distancing themselves from the more speculative claims of those trying to map the invisible and largely inaccessible territory of language and the human mind. However, most linguists would unite in accepting that they have theories and are 'theoretical' in their work (but see Gethin, 1990 for an opposing view).

Perhaps then, the right question to ask is: should applied linguists *be theoretical*? One response is that they can hardly not be, that we all bring to any problem-solving situation a perspective, a set of beliefs or attitudes that may inform, but are separate from, the decisions we take to resolve the problem(s) of the moment. This seems an eminently sensible view of things, but it has its dangers. It could encourage an *ad hoc* and unreflective process that never learns from experience or to induce from varied circumstances – a philosophy that says 'my set of beliefs and established approaches will serve me well in the face of any problem and need not subject themselves to objective scrutiny nor to constant revision; they are accountable to no one but myself'. There is also the risk that action, however manifestly successful, that does not or cannot justify itself explicitly in some set of theoretical postulates is to be frowned upon: this is the critic that says 'that's all very well in practice, but what about in theory?'.

This book will take the line that 'being theoretical' is a desirable thing, but that theoretical *stance* is more useful as a motto than theoretical allegiance, akin to what Widdowson (1984:30) refers to as having 'a theoretical orientation'. Widdowson's (1984:21–27) view that applied linguistics must formulate concepts and theories in the light of the phenomena it is trying to account for will be valuable as long as it retains its plurality. Applied linguists must certainly account for, and be accountable to, the contexts in which they work and the problems with which they engage. An important component of this is not to shy away from stating the beliefs, claims and attitudes that inform their position on any given applied linguistic activity, whether it be solving a language-teaching problem or proposing a socio-political language-planning solution that might have wide humanitarian implications. This is one's theoretical *stance*. The obli-

gation to espouse any particular establishment school of thought or canonical set of beliefs, claims and postulates consistently over time and
across different situations, may be referred to as theoretical *allegiance*,
which Widdowson (1980:21) rightly suspects is 'essentially conformist'.
Thus the question 'What school of thought do you belong to?' or 'What is
your theoretical position?' will likely be misdirected if put to an applied
linguist. 'What is your theoretical *stance* with regard to this problem or set
of problems?' is a question we have every right to ask of our applied
linguist peers. Furthermore, there is a very good reason why stance and
accountability go together: we owe it to our membership of a disciplinary
community to be able to contextualise our particular position in relation
to those of others. In short, the theoretical life-blood of applied linguistics
is not allegiance to theories but is more a commitment to a discourse. This
discourse is the communication of varied positions among peers using a
shared language that enables us to find common ground with the positions taken by others already reported and established, and to recognise
when new ground is being broken (see Crystal 1981:10ff). As Lantolf (1996)
puts it: 'letting all the flowers bloom'. Thus the *rhetoricising* of stance, that
is to say rendering it into an organised, communicable and persuasive set
of claims, arguments, illustrations and conclusions is the way in which the
community accounts for itself member to member and to the outside
world. Being theoretical and being accountable are two sides of the same
coin. Encountering problems and adopting a convincing stance towards
them is what defines applied linguistics as a discipline.

1.4 Approaching problems in an applied linguistic way

It is now appropriate to open up the relationship between the more
theoretical aspects of language study and how they might be applied in
the language teaching context. I shall begin by considering what avenues
within linguistics suggest themselves for approaching two of the problems
relevant to language teaching in the list of 14 above. Let us consider
problem no. 2 in the list: that of the teacher trying to understand why
learners from the same language background are having difficulty with a
particular grammatical structure in English. The teacher's potential recourse to linguistics is likely to involve different areas depending on what
questions are asked (see Figure 1).

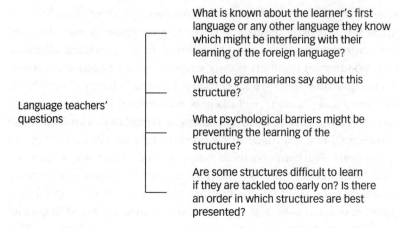

Figure 1: Potential linguistic questions for the solution of a grammatical problem

If we consider another of the problems, that of the dictionary writer looking for alternatives to the alphabetical dictionary, we might imagine a different set of questions, as in Figure 2:

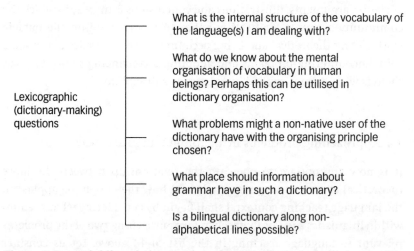

Figure 2: Potential linguistic questions for the solution of a lexicographic problem

The dictionary writer, like the language teacher, confronts the same basic questions: Can linguistics offer an approach or a solution to the problem at hand? If so, which branch(es) of linguistic study, and by what method(s)?

How reliable is the information offered by linguists? How tenable are their theories and models of the language? How willing and ready are linguists to contribute to this kind of practical undertaking? The title of a paper by McCawley (1986), 'What linguists might contribute to dictionary making if they could get their act together', strikes a slightly pessimistic tone in this regard. If there is conflicting information to be had from the findings of linguists, how does one best evaluate which approach is likely to be most useful? Can the non-linguist take on such a task, or is this a job for highly trained specialists?

The concern of this book is therefore to raise to the fore a selection of problem areas in language teaching and learning where knowledge about language plays or could play a major role, to review what it is that linguists do, and to consider whether and how their discipline can be applied, giving as many as possible practical examples of applications. As a conclusion to the book I shall consider broader ideological issues within applied linguistics, and how applied linguists have developed and are developing a sense of a professional community with common interests, as well as the predictable debates, factions and divisions, uncertainties and varied positions that characterise any such community, especially one as loose-knit as that of applied linguists. I shall exemplify across a variety of languages, even though, inevitably, many examples will centre around English, because of the historical fact that a large amount of the output of linguistics and applied linguistics and writing about language teaching has been based on English, and also because English is the language of this book. But it is important to offer examples in other languages in order to underline the universality of the applied linguistic enterprise and the underlying bond that unites the work of practitioners across the world working in a variety of language teaching contexts. It is *language* as a human phenomenon that we are attempting to understand, in the hope that we might teach it more effectively in its many manifestations around the world, and also produce better dictionaries, materials, and syllabuses, or make improvements in whatever our area of preoccupation might be.

1.5 Applying linguistics in language teaching: two examples

Before we enter the more detailed chapters on what linguists do, it may be useful to look more closely at the two examples of linguistics in application briefly touched on above (Figures 1 and 2) as a template for the overall purposes and goals of this book. I shall therefore take the two examples and follow them through to two sets of potential applied linguistic conclusions.

1.5.1 Example 1. Grammar: Why do they misuse *it*?

Many teachers of English as a second or foreign language will be familiar with errors such as the following in their students' written work:

1 A teacher has set an essay entitled 'Traffic in Cities'. An Italian student writes the title at the top of the page:

> Traffic in Cities

And then begins the first paragraph of the essay:

> It is a very big problem nowadays and many cities in the world suffer from it. ... etc.

The teacher crosses out the first *it* and puts *traffic* instead.

2 Another student writes an essay about his specialist university subject – construction engineering:

> This essay will show the increasing development of the insert of Glulam (glued laminated timber). It will help to find the reasons for the present boom in Glulam structures. For it*, it is interesting to look at the history, the properties, the manufacturing process and the types of structures which are possible.

The teacher puts a red mark against the asterisked *it* and suggests saying *this essay* instead of *it*.

These two learner errors are typical of many which prompt the teacher to seek some sort of explanation of the problem, both for their own professional integrity and satisfaction and in order to be able to hand on a useful rule or principle to the learner. Let us consider what questions the teacher might pose and the steps that might be followed:

1 What type of problem is this? Is it:

    (a) a grammar problem concerning a particularly tricky English grammatical choice?

    (b) a problem encountered only by speakers of a particular language or group of languages, or one encountered by most learners?

(c) a problem from that fuzzy area of 'style', to which there is unlikely to be a clear, satisfactory answer and which one may therefore just as well forget?

Question 1(a) is not so simple as it may seem. Many linguists understand the term *grammar* to be limited to questions of the internal structure of *sentences*, and would consider the *it* problem as it manifests itself in the student essays to be outside of the purview of the grammarian and something to do more with *pragmatics*, the study of how things acquire meaning in different contexts (see Evans 1980, for instance). This is one of the consequences of the pronounced theoretical demarcations we often find within linguistics. Others might disagree with shunting the problem out of grammar and into pragmatics, and see this particular problem with *it* as belonging to the recently developed sub-disciplinary area of *discourse grammar*. This is a sort of hybrid way of studying grammar by looking at whole texts and taking contexts into account (see section 5.6; see also Hughes and McCarthy 1998 for examples and applications to teaching; see Carter *et al.* 1995 for further discussion). Therefore, one of the first and most important things for the teacher who would be an applied linguist is to have a good working knowledge of how linguistics is sub-divided and how the linguistics community makes its decisions as to what to include in what. Without this knowledge, it will be even more difficult to answer question 1(b), which concerns whether the problem is likely to be widespread or limited to learners with a particular first language background. Question 1(c), whether to consign the problem to the rag-bag category of 'style', will also depend to a large extent on whether a satisfactory solution can be found within studies of sentence grammar, or pragmatics, or discourse grammar. Then again, the answers to questions 1(a) and 1(b) need not be mutually exclusive and it may be very beneficial to pursue both. Finally, we may indeed conclude that the problem *is* a 'grammatical' one (in terms of the most appropriate label to attach to it), and thus challenge whether grammarians who place it beyond their purview are being properly accountable to their audience. In other words, we might begin to re-theorise the paradigms of grammar from an applied linguist's point of view.

If the teacher decides initially that the *it* problem is likely to be one of grammar, then this decision opens up a further set of possible avenues towards a solution. One set of choices for investigation might be:

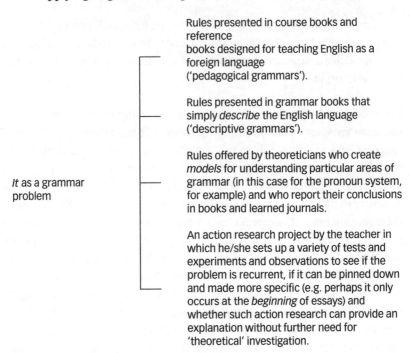

It as a grammar problem

Rules presented in course books and reference books designed for teaching English as a foreign language ('pedagogical grammars').

Rules presented in grammar books that simply *describe* the English language ('descriptive grammars').

Rules offered by theoreticians who create *models* for understanding particular areas of grammar (in this case for the pronoun system, for example) and who report their conclusions in books and learned journals.

An action research project by the teacher in which he/she sets up a variety of tests and experiments and observations to see if the problem is recurrent, if it can be pinned down and made more specific (e.g. perhaps it only occurs at the *beginning* of essays) and whether such action research can provide an explanation without further need for 'theoretical' investigation.

Figure 3: Paths of investigation in solving a grammar problem

Pursuing the problem in terms of question 1(b) (Is it a problem encountered only by speakers of a particular language or group of languages, or one encountered by most learners?) raises yet another set of questions:

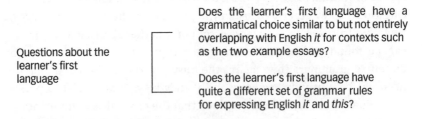

Questions about the learner's first language

Does the learner's first language have a grammatical choice similar to but not entirely overlapping with English *it* for contexts such as the two example essays?

Does the learner's first language have quite a different set of grammar rules for expressing English *it* and *this*?

Figure 4: First-language-related questions

This assumes that the problem is one to do with the learner's first language. Another question might be: Is the learner *transferring* something from the first language (which may or may not be viewed as a positive strategy), is the first language *interfering* in some way (which would usually be interpreted in a negative way), or is it possible that it is not a case of transfer or interference at all, but perhaps a strategic choice the learner has made to solve a particular problem (a positive strategy)?

In turn, these questions open up possible paths for exploration:

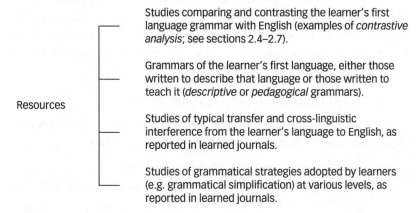

Resources

Studies comparing and contrasting the learner's first language grammar with English (examples of *contrastive analysis*; see sections 2.4–2.7).

Grammars of the learner's first language, either those written to describe that language or those written to teach it (*descriptive* or *pedagogical* grammars).

Studies of typical transfer and cross-linguistic interference from the learner's language to English, as reported in learned journals.

Studies of grammatical strategies adopted by learners (e.g. grammatical simplification) at various levels, as reported in learned journals.

Figure 5: Cross-linguistic resources for the solution of a grammatical problem

We can already see that the pathways into 'doing applied linguistics' lead us into complex fields and a multitude of potential resources, and that the success of the applied enterprise depends on:

1 Identifying and defining problems.
2 Contextualising those problems within linguistic study and developing a theoretical stance.
3 Harnessing appropriate resources for the exploration of possible solutions.
4 Evaluating the proposed solutions.

We shall also see later in this book that real-world problems are best not regarded as divorced from the world outside of the classroom, from the wider socio-cultural and political contexts in which language learning takes place. As with all problem-solving activities, the solutions may not come easily or immediately.

Let us now pursue further the problems with *it* in the student essays and consider what happens if we conclude that we are dealing with a grammatical problem concerning a rather subtle or difficult choice within

English grammar. Our first and most direct resource might be the coursebooks and other books in use in the classroom. It is likely, though, that we shall find *it* dealt with under the pronouns of English, where it is contrasted with *he* and *she* in relation to human or non-human entities. This is also likely to be so in grammar reference books designed for learners, but the better and more detailed ones may also point to the use of *it* in contrast to possible choices such as *this* and *that*, as does this extract from Alexander (1988). Alexander gives us the following rule:

Subject pronouns replacing demonstratives

Demonstratives are replaced by *it* or *they* in short responses when the thing or things referred to have been identified:

Is this/that yours? Yes it is (Not * Yes, this/that is)
Note: An asterisk (*) before a stretch of quoted language indicates an incorrect or inappropriate form.

This illustration may offer a partial solution to the problem, in that it seems to suggest the possibility that *it* cannot be used to refer to *things not already identified*, and this principle could perhaps be extrapolated to the student essays. At this point we are evaluating a linguistic statement, rather than simply taking it on board wholesale, which is perhaps the most crucial phase of all in doing any kind of applied linguistics.

However, the evaluation may well be that the concept of 'things not already identified' is not a very useful (or teachable) one. In both the examples of errors in student essays, the 'thing being talked about' certainly seems to have been *identified* ('traffic' in the first case and 'the present essay' in the second). We might therefore search further afield than pedagogical grammars such as Alexander's to find a more satisfactory solution. One likely area would be the considerable journal literature on student essay-writing which has grown up around the 'college composition' tradition in the United States. Articles within the college composition field do indeed treat such apparently puzzling areas as pronoun and demonstrative usage (e.g. Moskovit 1983; Geisler *et al.* 1985). When we find such studies (either by manually searching indexes or doing key-word computer searches on electronic media such as CD-ROM bibliographies or on-line bibliographical services), we see how they, in their turn, draw on wider areas such as the study of writing as communication, text- and discourse analysis, and the study of reading. In the case of pronouns versus demonstrative and/or full noun phrase, we find writers such as Hofmann (1989) and Fox (1987a and b) having recourse to notions such as *text boundaries, segments, topics* and *focus* in the development of the text, rather than 'sentences' or the 'identification' of things in the real world (see also McCarthy 1994a). These terms are not the familiar ones of sentence grammar, then, but belong to the world of discourse grammar and text analysis. What is crucial, it seems, is not so much whether something can be *identified* in the text, but what its status is as a *topic* in the text from the viewpoint of the interactants (i.e. writer and reader or speaker and listener): Is it the current topic? Is it a secondary or marginalised topic? Is there potential ambiguity or confusion as to what the current topic is? These are quite different questions from: Is it third person? Is it human or non-human?

In the first student essay (on traffic) it seems that crossing the gap from the title to the main text disallows the use of the 'topic-continuing' pronoun *it*, and linguists have indeed argued that the *it* pronoun may not be able to refer back to something separated by a textual boundary such as a paragraph division (e.g. Fox 1987a and b). In the second essay, the use of *it* in the phrase *for it* seems to create confusion as to what we are actually focussing on at that precise moment: is it *glulam* or the essay itself? In other words is this use of *it* a typical grammar problem of *reference* or one of the *structuring of information* within the textual world shared by writer and reader(s)? Linguistic descriptions that offer no insight into what seems to be a crucial distinction may be less than useful for the practitioner seeking an answer to this particular set of problems.

One or two papers on college composition may not, in themselves, be enough to offer a convincing and generalisable solution to the pronoun problem, and the teacher doing applied linguistics may feel the need to explore further in text- and discourse analysis, or may decide to gather more data from learners. In addition, even if the teacher feels that a satisfactory explanation is available, there will still be the problem of how to fashion it into a point for teaching and learning, i.e. the problem of methodology, which will largely remain outside of the remit of this book. However, implicit in what this book describes will always be the belief that teaching methodologies and descriptions of languages should interact to produce good teaching (i.e. that accountability should not end between linguists and academic applied linguists, but should apply between all groupings within the language teaching profession). Good descriptions and practical guidelines should influence methodology and methodological developments should influence the quest for better description and more accessible guidelines for learners.

1.5.2 Example 2. Lexicography: the case of the bilingual thesaurus

Let us turn to another problem mentioned at the outset of this introductory chapter: that of the lexicographer trying to develop an alternative to the traditional, alphabetical bilingual dictionary. Alphabetical dictionaries are useful if the user already knows the word in the target language or has a word in his/her own language to look up. But what if one only has a vague idea of what one wants to say, i.e. that one has a meaning floating round in the mind, but no words whereby to access it, either in the first or the target language? Among the resources available in such a situation will be thesauruses and word-finders of various kinds, and dictionaries of synonyms and antonyms. These types of reference works depart from purely alphabetical organisation and bring words together on the same page according to notions of meaning rather than their orthographical (written-alphabetical) form. The classic model for such organisation is Roget's *Thesaurus* (Roget 1852). Roget brought words together according to their role in describing a philosophically organised world, a model 'almost Aristotelian in character' (Kjellmer 1990), where the taxonomies of the natural and human world are reflected in an orderly vocabulary. And yet we react with mild amusement when we note that Roget included the word *stomach* under the category *container* (along with boxes and baskets); somehow, Roget's classification often seems remote from commonsense, everyday meanings and how words relate to one another.

The lexicographer in search of alternatives for organising the vast meaning-stock of any language has available a range of semantic and cognitive models of meaning. If the thesaurus is, in addition, to be bilingual, then a model which permits the mapping of one language's meaning-stock onto another – with all the problems of lack of one-to-one fit which that entails – will be a desirable basis from which to work. In other words, a merely *descriptive* list of words for each of the two languages in question will not be enough; it is the model that underlies the description that is crucial.

The lexicographic problem's difference from the grammatical one (that of students misusing *it*) is only one of degree. Even though a satisfactory answer may have been forthcoming from pedagogical or descriptive grammars, they in their turn presuppose some model or underlying theoretical view of how grammar functions, whether it be that sentence-level syntactic structures lie at the core, or whether a more context-sensitive, discoursal model is presupposed. Subsequent chapters of this book will explore these competing claims. In the case of thesaurus design, the lexicographer is not unlike the grammarian designing a grammar: the key question is 'What is the model of language and meaning which will drive the organisational structure of the thesaurus?'. In other words, what theoretical stance(s) may be adopted to solve the problem? Though this would seem to place the lexicographer on a higher plain in the applied linguistics firmament than the teacher looking for a solution to a problem of pronoun misuse, this book does not take that line. The teacher applying a grammatical description is doing applied linguistics just as much as the lexicographer applying a model of word-meaning; they are simply working in different ways.

The various models of meaning offered by linguists all have some attraction for the lexicographer. For example, Katz and Fodor's (1963) influential notion of decomposing words into their semantic properties, epitomised in their description of the meaning(s) of *bachelor* in English (see Figure 6), would seem to offer a possible basis for mapping words in

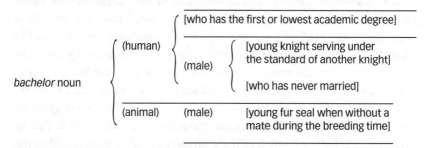

Figure 6: Katz and Fodor's description of *bachelor*

different languages onto one another.

But there is a great deal of semantic overlap and grading in meaning within families of related words, and Katz and Fodor's technique turns out to be severely limited for the lexicographer working with thousands of headwords in a dictionary or thesaurus. The approach to meaning based on such a notion of 'componential analysis' has been superseded in linguistics by other models of meaning, as we shall see, amongst which the lexicographer might gain insight from *frame-theoretical* approaches. In frame theory, the sharp distinction between what we know about language and what we know about the world is broken down (Lehrer 1993), enabling the lexicographer to include socio-cultural information within the 'meaning' of a word (see also Schmid 1993). Such a broader-based model of meaning may well provide a more practical basis for the construction of a bilingual thesaurus and the mapping of two linguistic cultures onto one another in a commonsense and intuitively more satisfying way.

At this point I permit myself to exemplify the applied linguistic outcome from one of my own published works. McCarthy (1995), in a bilingual thematic (thesaurus-type) dictionary for Italian learners of English, attempts to map English words connected with poverty onto Italian words and expressions in the same frame (see Figure 7). In addition to semantic equivalences, the learner is given circumstantial information that is crucial to distinguishing use, as well as advice on appropriate collocations. The particular frame embraces adjectives, nouns, verbs and fixed expressions. The dictionary entry was constructed from a base English list of 'poverty' words, and translated into Italian by a team of experts with native speaker command of both languages. The experts included all the information which would, theoretically at least, enable the Italian user to distinguish accurately among the possible English candidates for an Italian 'meaning' connected with poverty which the user might wish to word in English. The extra information beyond the pure semantics includes degrees of formality, the contexts in which each word normally occurs (e.g. *bankrupt* versus *destitute*), and the word set includes words such as *beggar* and *beg*, which are roles and actions that have a real-world association with poverty. In addition to the thematic grouping, any of the words can be accessed in Italian or English in the alphabetical index, thus enabling the resource to be used either as an alphabetical bilingual dictionary or via the overall theme, as a tool when the learner has a meaning in mind but no clear words as a starting point. The thematic dictionary is as imperfect and flawed as any other enterprise, and I present it here simply as an example of a product that began with a problem. The solution involved an applied linguistic process of starting with the learner (How can he/she get to an English word starting only from a vague notion of a desired meaning?), proceeding to the application of a relevant theoretical model (frame theory), and producing the goods (the dictionary). Its users will be the only proper evaluators of its success or failure as a piece of applied linguistics.

poor *agg* [descrive: es. persona, paese] povero *a poor area of the city* una zona povera della città
poor *s pl* (sempre + **the**) i poveri *charities which help the poor* istituzioni benefiche che aiutano i poveri
poverty *snn* povertà, miseria *to live in poverty* vivere in povertà *a poverty-stricken region* una regione colpita dalla miseria

needy *agg* [più formale di **poor**. Che manca delle necessità basilari. Descrive: es. persona, famiglia] bisognoso
needy *s pl* (sempre + **the**) i bisognosi
penniless *agg* [che non ha denaro] senza un soldo, al verde *The failure of his business left him penniless.* Il fallimento della sua azienda lo ha ridotto sul lastrico
destitute *agg* [formale. Che non ha né denaro, né beni, né casa ecc] indigente, privo di mezzi *The war left many families destitute.* La guerra ha lasciato molte famiglie nell'indigenza. **destitution** *snn* indigenza
bankrupt *agg* [descrive: spec azienda, persona d'affari] fallito *to go bankrupt* fallire, fare bancarotta
bankruptcy *snn/n* fallimento, bancarotta
bankrupt *vt* far fallire, mandare in rovina *High interest*

rates have bankrupted many small firms. Alti tassi di interesse hanno fatto fallire molte piccole aziende.
beggar *sn* mendicante, accattone *The streets are full of beggars.* Le strade sono piene di mendicanti.
beg *vi*, **-gg-** chiedere l'elemosina, mendicare *vedere anche **351 Ask**
panhandler *sn* (amer) mendicante, accattone

270.1 Termini più informali

badly-off *agg*, *compar* worse-off *superl* worst-off [abbastanza, relativamente povero] in ristrettezze *A lot of old people are quite badly-off.* Molti anziani vivono in ristrettezze. *I'll be worse-off after the tax system changes.* Quando cambierà il sistema fiscale le mie condizioni finanziarie peggioreranno.
hard up *agg* [informale. Che ha pochissimo denaro, spesso in via temporanea] a corto di quattrini, in bolletta *I was always hard up when I was a student.* Quando ero studente ero sempre in bolletta
broke *agg* (dopo il *v*) [informale. Che non ha soldi] al verde *flat/stony broke* (ingl) o *stone broke* (amer) spiantato, povero in canna

Figure 7: Entry for *poor* in an English-Italian thematic dictionary (McCarthy 1995)

1.6 Conclusion

One final important area must be addressed before I embark on the rest of this book, for which we need to return to the question of who, precisely, applied linguists are. In section 1.1, I spoke of applied linguists in university academic departments, but distanced myself from equating only those people with the title 'applied linguist' or with the notion of 'doing applied linguistics'. This is important, for the temptation to ring-fence applied linguistics within the academic community leads inexorably to a gulf of suspicion between academics (whether linguists or applied linguists) and practising language teachers 'out there' at the chalkface. Kirby (1991) speaks of a 'growing chasm which separates theoreticians from practitioners' and an 'end of the honeymoon' (a reference to a paper on the subject by Lennon 1988). One of the central problems Kirby identifies is the feeling that applied linguistic research does not address the practical needs of teachers, and much of what he says cannot be denied. But the solution that applied linguists (in the academic sense) and theoreticians must become more sensitive to the needs of language teachers is only half a solution: the position this book takes is that non-academic teachers should *become* applied linguists, not just look to them for guidance. Only when the community of applied linguists itself becomes a broader church will the problems of the current uneasy relationship be able to be properly addressed and moved towards solutions satisfactory to all parties. That is why this book is aimed at language teachers and other language practitioners, not just applied linguists in the academic sense of the term. If it can only speak to this last group, then it has failed.

What I have tried to do in this introduction in considering two quite different language-teaching problems and how they may be solved by having recourse to aspects of linguistics, is to emphasise the multi-faceted nature of applied linguistics, even in just one of its professional branches, that of language teaching and learning, and to begin to explore the various levels on which problems may be tackled. In the first case (the grammatical problem) I stressed the potential of linguistic *description*, that is the sets of observable facts about languages that linguists can offer. In the second case (the lexicographic problem), I stressed the *modelling* of language, that is theoretical constructs that help us to understand how languages (might) work. Behind models lie *theories* – the mental explorations, speculation and argumentation that go to build a set of ideas, beliefs or principles about language. Linguists are in some sense inevitably involved in all three of these activities, though some eschew description of actual language use, for example early exponents of transformational-generative grammar (see section 3.3.2), while others would argue that only looking at real language in use is the proper starting point on the long journey to a theory of language (e.g. Sinclair 1991; see also Chapter 5). Most prefer to move in both directions: the good applied linguist not only starts from day-to-day practical problems and looks for solutions in descriptions, models and theories of language, but also develops his or her own models and theoretical stances. Behind these there usually develops a guiding set of beliefs about language, however rooted in practical concerns and however scornful non-academic applied linguists may occasionally be of those for whom language seems to be an abstract, rather than a concrete, object. The examples we have looked at and the typical procedures followed to get to the roots of the problems have been pedagogical ones, but essentially the same questioning must take place in the mind of any applied linguist who tries to locate his or her particular set of problems within the vast array of linguistic theories and descriptions.

We thus travel in this book across a landscape strewn with different theories, models and descriptions and attempt to build up the complex picture that is present-day applied linguistics with reference to language teaching and learning. The book will consider the description of sounds, words, and grammars, the modelling of how we communicate and create texts, how the mind processes language, and theories of what language is and how those theories shape our day-to-day perceptions and actions as language practitioners. It will also be concerned with how applied linguists engage in discourse with one another and construct their common language and professional identity. No one level of activity will be considered privileged, and the interrelationships between levels of applied linguistic activity will inform the argument throughout.

The lack of a monolithic definition of applied linguistics, the lack of unitary theory and of clear disciplinary boundaries will be regarded as a positive characteristic of the discipline, its very openness to outside influences being its strongest and most enduring quality, and one that has served it well over the decades that the term *applied linguistics* has had currency.[1] All this will take place against the background of a belief that applied linguists and linguists alike owe accountability to one another, principally through the fruits of their work, and that the cornerstone of such accountability is fluent and non-obfuscating communication between the partners in the task of making social sense of phenomena connected with individual languages and language as a whole.

Notes

1 Exactly when the term 'applied linguistics' came to be established is not clear. The term 'linguistics' goes back to the middle of the nineteenth century, although the beginnings of 'scientific' linguistics properly go back further (see Lepschy 1982). The use of 'applied' in the sense of practical applications of sciences can be dated back to at least the middle of the seventeenth century. Howatt (1984) looks back to Henry Sweet (1845–1912) as applying 'living philology', though Howatt dates the first 'public' use of the term applied linguistics to 1948.

2

Language and languages

2.1 Introduction

The title of this chapter suggests a division between a general, abstract view of human language and the study of the different, specific languages spoken by human societies, and perhaps that such a division is related to how applied linguistics operates or should operate. In this chapter I will argue that separating the two preoccupations overmuch is misleading, and that the one should always inform the other as a basis for applied linguistics. This is particularly crucial when we come to pose the question of the relevance to language teaching of the study of similarities and differences between languages, and whether we believe in a 'universal grammar' as a principal driving force in language acquisition, or whether we choose to focus on linguistic and cultural differences that might influence learners. In short, how we address the two concerns affects greatly how we engage in the enterprise of applied linguistics and how we position ourselves professionally in terms of the domains in which we operate.

A historical perspective on the study of language and languages is helpful in understanding how the applied linguistic profession has shaped itself into its present form, with its mix of social concerns, interest in individual languages and a preoccupation with language as a global phenomenon. Nowadays, it is rather unfashionable to see linguistics (or applied linguistics) as a historical discipline, and the emphasis in university studies is generally on the synchronic (the study of language at a particular, usually the present, moment of time). There are dangers in this however, not least an arrogance that only more recent research and insight is relevant, something often reflected in the absence of bibliographical references to anything older than about 20 years in research papers. Another danger is simply that of 'reinventing the wheel', brought about by ignorance of relevant work that may have been carried out decades or even centuries ago. This book, therefore, makes no apology for taking the discussion back over several centuries and paying tribute to our earliest applied linguist ancestors.

2.2 Some relevant history

The degree to which the study of language in general and the study of individual tongues have complemented each other historically has varied over the centuries and has largely been a question of prevailing social forces. The foundations of modern western linguistics laid by the Ancient Greeks and Romans and their interest in language were grounded in philosophical developments of a much more global nature. Robins (1951:18) points out that the initial divisions of language into parts of speech by the Ancient Greeks was made on logical rather than formal grounds, a fact whose influence has continued down the centuries. Thus deep do the roots of some approaches in modern linguistics (and applied linguistics) run. In India, the ancient Hindu grammarians' interest in language was based on religious concerns (Itkonen 1991:6). When the old Roman Empire gave way to the Byzantine period, very practical motivations connected with teaching and teachers guided the Byzantine grammarians, who none the less contributed to the general development of grammatical theory (Robins 1993:25).

In Britain, around the end of the first millennium, the Anglo-Saxon scholar Aelfric took over Roman models for his pedagogical Latin Grammar, and this was a precursor of many centuries of Latin-dominance in English grammar (Robins 1990:80). In the Middle Ages in Europe, Latin grammarians both referred to local vernaculars in their studies and opened up the question of whether there was a universal grammar for all languages which might possibly diversify into 'species', or grammars of individual languages (Fredborg 1980). In Britain, alongside such theoretical concerns, a group who today might be called pedagogical applied linguists, the Oxford Grammar Masters, were led on by very practical matters of teaching Latin in their grammar schools. Among their number was John of Cornwall, who more or less took his theory, ready-made, from the earlier Roman grammarians (Hunt 1980) – an approach in which he was not alone.

Later, during the European Renaissance era, at a time when new areas of the world were opening to trade and cultural contact, the discovery of new individual languages spurred on further the study of universals in the grammar of languages, as well as a search for universals based on

European vernaculars, as epitomised in the work of the Port Royal grammarians (Robins 1990:139; Hughes 1986). In the seventeenth and eighteenth centuries, major efforts were made to classify the apparently huge variety of world languages according to their resemblances, once again combining the study of individuality with that of language as a global phenomenon and seeking universal qualities (e.g. Stackhous 1731; Harris 1751).

Latin continued to hold sway for a very long time, and the history of the notion of 'Standard English' is inseparably linked with the view of Latin as a yardstick against which to describe other languages (e.g. see Watts 1999). But although it is true in the seventeenth and eighteenth centuries that Latin as an ideal often dominated and perhaps obscured the attempt to model language on a wider scale (Latin forming the usual basis for analogy in the description of English and other languages, see for example Hewes 1624),[1] much interesting comparative work did spread its net wider than just comparing an individual tongue with Latin. Indeed, the decline of Latin and the need for better international communication (Hayashi 1978:2) resulted, from the latter part of the sixteenth century onwards, in scholars bringing groups of languages together for practical applied linguistic purposes in the form of polyglot dictionaries, such as Baret's triple dictionary of English, Latin and French (1573), and his quadruple dictionary of English, Latin, Greek and French (1580). This tradition was continued, but without including Latin or Greek, in Howell's quadruple English-French-Italian-Spanish dictionary (1660). These were applied linguists responding to social change and to very practical needs, not essentially different from those in the twentieth century who blazed new trails in the development of learners' dictionaries.

The seventeenth and eighteenth centuries further distinguished themselves in terms of practical solutions with two-way, or 'double' grammars, such as Offelen's (1686) grammar designed 'for Germans to learn English; and for English-men to learn the German tongue'. Similar double grammars existed for English and French (Mauger and Festau 1690), English and Italian (Altieri 1725), English and Portuguese (Castro 1751) and even a triple/quadruple grammar 'whereby the French and Italian, the Spaniard and Portuguese, may learn to speak English well; with rules for the learning of French, Italian and Spanish' (Colsoni 1695). Thus from the eighteenth century onwards, a solid foundation existed for comparative/ contrastive studies of languages both at the level of pairs of languages, such as Elphinston (1756) on French and English, and wider groupings, such as English, Latin, Greek and Hebrew by Baily (1758), and Hungarian, Finnish, Lapp and Estonian by Gyarmathi in 1799 (see Itkonen 1991:279–80), as well as a range of practical products which responded to consumers' needs.

Rasmus Rask (1787–1832), continuing the search for a universal grammar, based his quest on cross-linguistic study rather than philosophical speculation (Itkonen, *ibid.*), until in the middle of the nineteenth century we find comparative studies of the languages of Europe on philological principles (e.g. De Vere 1853) and even one claiming to be based on a comparison of over 60 languages (Barnes 1854). Also in the nineteenth century, the revelation of Sanskrit's ancestral role in the history of European languages produced a new impetus for global studies of language along historical lines (Robins 1990:148ff). Nineteenth-century linguists worked in an environment of social and scientific theories that increasingly questioned the status of human beings in the natural order (e.g. Darwin's theory of evolution). These new ways of looking at human development informed the study of individual languages with a view to classifying them into larger families (e.g. Farrar 1870). Once again, the preoccupation was as much language in general as languages in particular. Then, as the might of the British Empire grew and the world it encompassed seemed to shrink, serious questions were raised as to the possibility of a universal, 'world language' that might serve international trade and communication (Eclectikwn 1846), and, once more, we find linguists asking questions about individual languages with global preoccupations concerning 'language' informing the debates. For instance, in the early part of the present century it was debated whether English or Esperanto was better as a world language (see Long 1919).

In more recent times, Chomsky, although he stated his case and exemplified it in English, had as his concern a universally valid theory of human language, a defining characteristic that marked off humans (Chomsky 1957) – his work having grown out of a society where behaviourism was a dominant scientific paradigm. Also in this century, the continuing growth of contrastive linguistics (James 1980) has led to a huge amount of research comparing individual languages in great detail, and, while such studies may not have the modelling of human language as a whole as their goal, most of them clearly operate within frameworks that take certain facts about human language for granted.

For our purpose, which is the creation of relevant models of language accountable to the needs of language professionals, maintaining the balance between a preoccupation with individual languages and with language as a general human phenomenon is crucial, for without it false trails lie waiting for the applied linguist pursuing solutions to cross-linguistic problems. We shall see that the study of individual languages can be done on many levels, with different applied linguistic implications, and understanding these can be greatly assisted by never forgetting that it is language, and not just languages, which is our concern. Equally, ignorance of individual languages can lead linguists into the trap of over-generalisation, and claims about the existence of 'universals' which are patently not universal; for example, see Gethin's (1999:10) evidence from a number of languages that seriously undermine universalist claims made by Pinker.

The historical perspective on applied linguistics espoused in this book reminds us that scholars of languages and language over the centuries have combined the study of individual languages with comparisons across languages and with debates about language as a whole. The historical perspective also demonstrates how sensitive much of what would today come under the umbrella of applied linguistics has always been to historical and cultural forces that allow the flourishing of theoretical debate, but which also periodically anchor linguistic activity in practical concerns generated by cultural and socio-economic forces of the time. An example of this is how interest in spoken language has waxed and waned over the centuries. It was brought to the fore in Tudor times in Britain, when the need for educated Europeans to communicate with one another in a Europe where Latin had dissolved into a series of vernaculars led to the production of speaking manuals (e.g. Boyer 1694 for the learning of spoken French) and to the use in the English grammar schools of the *Vulgaria*, which were Latin textbooks with an emphasis on speaking Latin (see White 1932; see also McCarthy 1998:16 for further examples). Then in the nineteenth century, renewed interest in spoken language was aroused by European traders' encounters with languages that were very exotic to them such as Japanese (Mutsu 1894; Coningham 1894). It would be wrong to think that our present-day applied linguistics is in any way fundamentally different, and an understanding of the socio-economic and cultural forces that gave birth to and which have impelled our profession, as well as those which are pushing it forward now, is vital to its health, not least in urging a degree of modesty upon us. It is only too easy to think we are the first to tread the ground we walk upon.

2.3 Knowledge of language and knowledge of languages

It is possible to know different languages while knowing little about language as an overall phenomenon. What we *can* know about human language is vast; what it is relevant to know in an applied linguistic context is very much in the hands of applied linguists themselves. While every new direction in linguistics is eagerly seized upon by applied linguists in search of something new to apply, the professional community as a whole would probably agree on a number of key points concerning the nature of human language in general (see Hudson 1988). These may be seen as a core set of tenets to inform what professionals such as language teachers do. They can be condensed into the following:[2]

1 All normal humans acquire a first language with little or no formal tuition.
2 Humans can, with varying degrees of proficiency, learn one another's languages.
3 All human languages have forms and meanings. Forms are reflected in syntax, vocabulary and phonology.
4 All languages are realised in substance, whether sound alone or sound and writing. Languages without their own, indigenous writing systems (the majority) may borrow ways of writing from those that have developed them.
5 All human languages function adequately in their social settings; no languages are more 'primitive' than others, and where languages need new ways of expression, they easily borrow from other languages where the necessary expressions exist (e.g. the way English has plundered other languages over the centuries, and how it, in turn, lends ways of saying nowadays to other languages).
6 All languages function within social contexts. Social actions such as conversations, story-telling, transacting business, forming and consolidating relationships through language, are universal, as is creativity. No language is inherently 'better' at these things than any other.
7 All languages reflect and are integrally bound up with some sort of psychological, social and cultural reality for their speakers. As these realities change so do the languages that encode them and help to decode them.

These points may seem obvious, almost nugatory, and they form the implicit bedrock for most, but certainly not all, modern applied linguistics. However, it is often possible to lose sight of the woods when tangled up in the trees of comparisons between individual languages and the historical baggage of linguistic imperialism that some of the major European languages carry with them. In the past, Latin and Ancient Greek were dominant, and, today, none exerts greater hegemony than English (see Phillipson 1992). Not losing sight of the woods enables us better to understand the types of language study where individual languages are compared or contrasted, and properly to evaluate their relevance to the applied linguistic community. Applied linguistics must embrace knowledge about language as a general human phenomenon, for without it the construction of relevant linguistic models becomes extremely difficult, and comparisons may run the risk of being skewed by prejudice based on a particular language. Knowledge about language and knowledge about languages will be equal prerequisites to the relevant modelling of languages for pedagogical purposes, and the historical lesson of the significance of such a balance in our overall understanding must not be lost.

2.4 Comparing languages: typological aspects

Let us first consider one of the levels that languages are often compared on: the morphological. Morphology has a long history as an important component of linguistic analysis, going right back to the ancient Indian linguists (Robins 1980:155). It has also been important in cross-linguistic comparisons and the study of language typology (e.g. Bloomfield 1933:207), resulting in major works on the classification of the world's languages (e.g. Voegelin and Voegelin 1977). Although it is true that some earlier versions of transformational-generative linguistics in the 1960s denied the status of morphology, it re-surfaced in Chomsky's work in the 1970s and is now widely recognised again as central to language study.

In the study of morphology in the world's languages, it is apparent that, although all languages divide lexical and grammatical forms into units that represent meanings, the notion of a 'word' as it is understood in a language like English may be more elusive for languages displaying 'isolating' morphologies. In such languages, one unit of meaning may be represented by one sound or character, for example Chinese languages, or Vietnamese (Comrie 1981:39). The structuralists in fact rejected the word as an entity and gave central place to the morpheme (see Harris 1946), as did early transformational-generative grammar. Molino (1985) illustrates how different morphological processes such as inflexion (the addition of

	inflexion	derivation	compounding
Arabic	✓	partial	very weak
Chinese	very weak	very weak	✓
English	weak	✓	✓

✓ = typical feature of the language

Figure 8: After Molino (1985)

endings denoting grammatical features such as tense, case, number, etc.), derivation (the creation of new words using prefixes and suffixes) and compounding (the creation of new vocabulary items by combining more than one existing word) are differentially represented in individual languages. English, Arabic and Chinese, for instance, give different weight to each process, as represented in Figure 8.

What do such insights mean for language teachers? Are they relevant facts? If there were evidence that the difference in fundamental morphological characteristics caused difficulties in language learning, such facts would clearly be relevant and may be essential in modelling languages pedagogically. If not, the facts may be none the less fascinating as facts about human language and may contribute to a new understanding at the level of our general knowledge about language (e.g. that although our morphologies may be different, we have sufficient universal commonality to make foreign language learning unproblematic at the morphological level). In reality, there is some (although limited) tantalising evidence that Chinese learners of English experience particular difficulty with polysyllabic English words, which are likely to be polymorphemic too (Meara 1984:234). This may be because of fundamental morphological differences between Chinese languages and English. On the other hand it may be a problem related to reading habits which, in turn, may be conditioned only partly by the morphological characteristics of the mother tongue. This latter hypothesis would introduce a psycholinguistic and cultural dimension to the modelling of the problem. Either way, if the research evidence can be shown to be more conclusive in terms of regular difficulty, a morphological modelling of L1 (first language) and TL (target language) may be relevant and useful, and can be conducted in a way that is fully accountable to language teachers' needs.

Language teaching, though, does not and should not only proceed by means of trouble-shooting, and applied linguistics as a problem-solving discipline should not be equated with being error- and difficulty-driven in its services to language teaching. 'Problems' may also be questions that need evaluating in terms of their relevance, or simply new areas of investigation that open up. For example, we might wish to explore whether language learners' use of the word-formation resources in L2 are influenced by the morphological characteristics of their L1, whether such influence is generally positive or negative, and how persistent such influence might be over various stages of language learning. Broeder *et al.* (1993) report just such an investigation based on subjects from several typologically different source languages (e.g. Finnish, Arabic, Italian, Punjabi), and Germanic target languages. They report that language typology is relevant in learners' ability to construct nominal compounds in the target languages, and that learners use both source-language- and target-language-related information in constructing in L2.

Another, related question that morphology may have some bearing on is whether languages displaying similar morphology are necessarily easier to learn than those displaying basic differences. Geographically neighbouring languages often display common morphological tendencies and morphological modelling across groups of such languages may be relevant to the naturally arising question: Are neighbouring languages easier to learn (see Dušková 1984; Hedard 1989)?

Morphology is not mentioned idly in this book: fashions change, and the 'unfashionability' of morphology as a branch of applied linguistic study in the post-Chomskian era is keenly evidenced in its absence from language teaching syllabuses and materials, at least for the teaching of English, apart from lip-service to the commonest features of derivation. It is also relatively absent from the pages of the most widely read applied linguistics journals. Is it time for morphology to make a comeback? Should applied linguists be concerned with theories of 'universal' morphology (see Dressler 1986), or should we merely be aware that morphological differences between particular L1s and L2s may cause the occasional hiccup in language learning?

Where languages display 'uniform verbal morphology' (e.g. the uniform complexity of verb-inflexions in a language like Spanish), what problems might be encountered in learning a non-uniform language like English (see Hilles 1991)? How should we (or should we at all) account in any pedagogical model of spoken language for the morphological creativity observed in everyday talk, for which Carter and McCarthy (1995b) offer corpus-based evidence from English conversation? What kinds of difficulties might the problem of the application of the concept of a 'word' to Chinese languages, mentioned above, throw up for Chinese learners of a language like English? Should we heed Sampson's (1979) exhortation that decomposing words (including derived forms) may fly in the face of his claim for English that 'the semantic atoms of our language are the same as the items listed in an ordinary dictionary', i.e. whole words (see also the discussion in Chapter 3.4)? This last point is related to the interesting research question of whether learners proceed from decoding whole words to breaking down words into their roots and derivations, etc., for which Aiking-Brandenburg *et al.* (1990) find no conclusive evidence, although they do advocate the teaching of derivational morphology as an aid to comprehension and spelling.

The question of the relevance of morphological theory and description is a complex one. It shares many of the features that other fundamental questions in applied linguistics manifest, that is to say, the existence of a body of scholarship with a long tradition within linguistics offering the potential for applicability, the need to evaluate local and global modelling, the often tenuous and difficult-to-prove relationship between such theories and available evidence of problems in language learning, and the accountability of existing theory and description to the practical needs of language professionals.

2.5 Grammatical issues in cross-linguistic comparison

In the historical discussion in section 2.2, the hegemony of Latin as a model for the description of other languages was mentioned, with a cautionary note as to its influence on the way languages are described. This seems particularly to affect how the grammar of languages is presented pedagogically. The influence of Latin models may be on the wane in current pedagogical presentations of English and other modern languages, but within the last one hundred years, pedagogical modelling of languages exotic to English have frequently been poured into the mediating mould of Latin categories.[3] This has resulted in a set of labels in English that at best obscure the categories of the target language and at worse probably create the kind of learning difficulties many Europeans and others will recall from their schooldays. I personally recall very painfully trying to struggle with the alien categories that Latin threw up, such as the 'ablative absolute'. Figure 9, from a pedagogical Assyrian Grammar, illustrates the kinds of problems exacerbated by 'mediated' cross-linguistic comparisons of this kind.

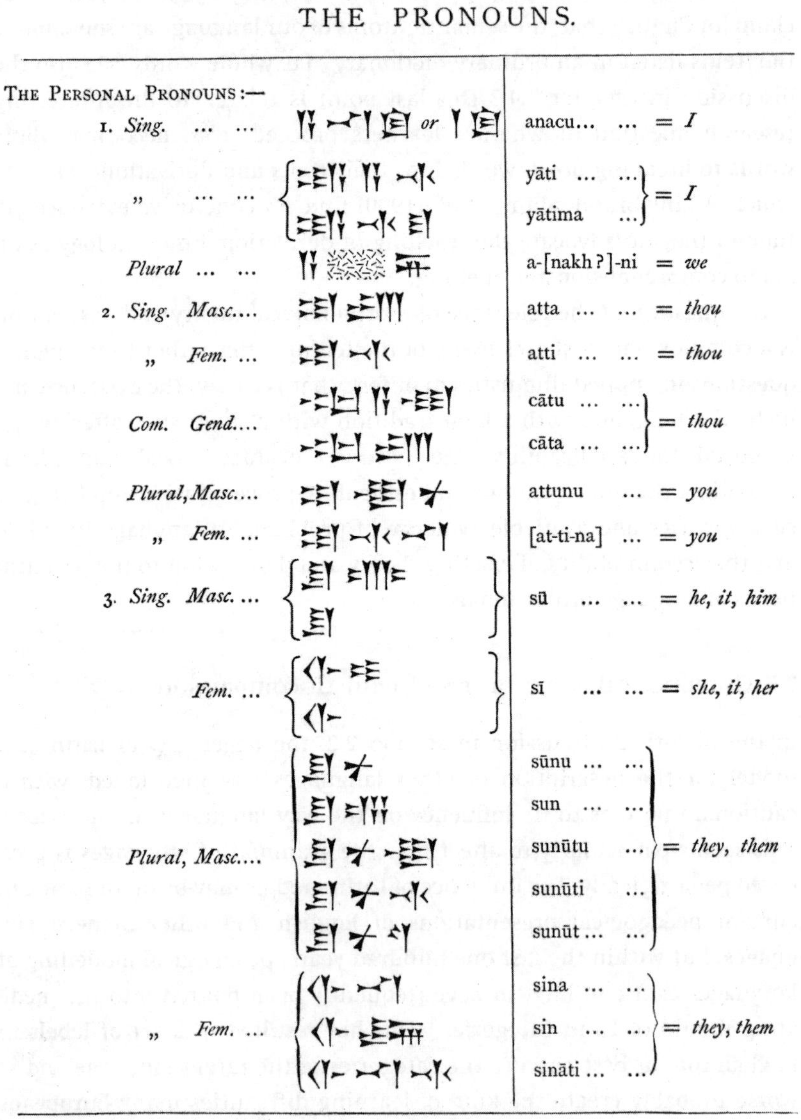

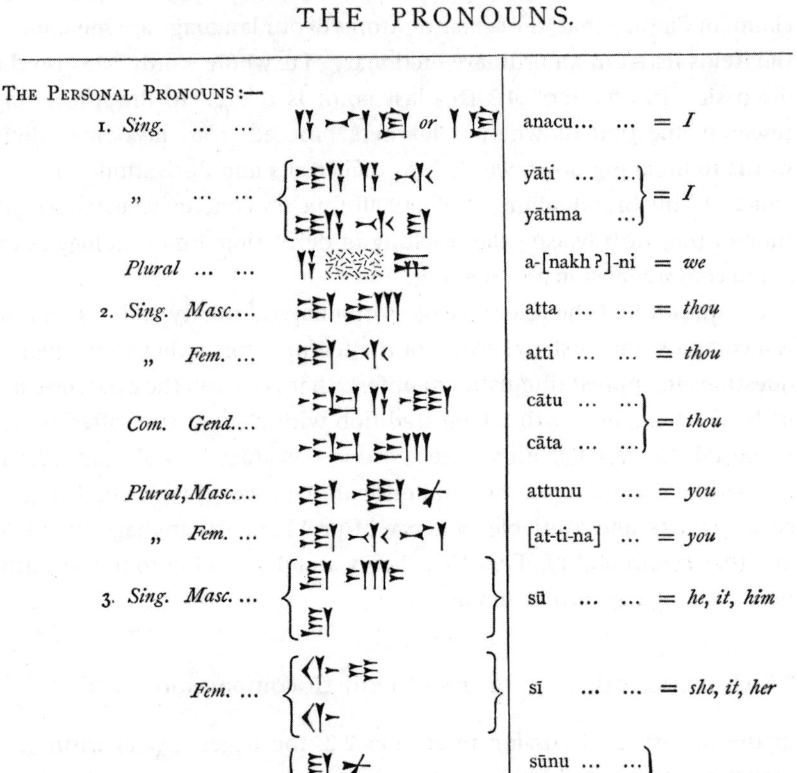
THE PRONOUNS.

THE PERSONAL PRONOUNS:—

1. *Sing.*	[cuneiform] *or* [cuneiform]	anacu... ... = *I*
"	[cuneiform]	yāti ... ... / yātima ... = *I*
Plural	[cuneiform]	a-[nakh ?]-ni = *we*
2. *Sing. Masc.*...	[cuneiform]	atta ... ... = *thou*
" *Fem.* ...	[cuneiform]	atti ... ... = *thou*
Com. Gend....	[cuneiform]	cātu ... ... / cāta ... ... = *thou*
Plural, Masc....	[cuneiform]	attunu ... = *you*
" *Fem.* ...	[cuneiform]	[at-ti-na] ... = *you*
3. *Sing. Masc.* ...	[cuneiform]	sū ... ... = *he, it, him*
Fem. ...	[cuneiform]	sī ... ... = *she, it, her*
Plural, Masc....	[cuneiform]	sūnu ... ... / sun ... ... / sunūtu ... / sunūti ... / sunūt ... ... = *they, them*
" *Fem.* ...	[cuneiform]	sina ... ... / sin ... ... / sināti ... ... = *they, them*

Figure 9: Assyrian pronouns (from Sayce (s.d.):57)

What is confusing here is that three different surface forms (*anacu, yāti* and *yātima*) all seem to be 'first person singular personal pronouns', while *cātu* and *cāta* both seem to be a second person singular common gender pronoun, not to mention numerous formal variations in the third person pronoun paradigm. The paradigm does not fit modern English either, with the grammar having to introduce archaisms such as *thou* to account for distinctions of number in the second person. One suspects that without the influence of these familiar Latin categories, a truly bilateral comparison between English and Assyrian might have been more illuminating of what is obviously a rich system in the latter language. What I advocate in this book is an applied linguistics which (a) understands and pays tribute to its historical roots in classical linguistic study, but (b) respects the equality of all languages in terms of their amenability to description and modelling for pedagogical purposes. These two principles can be followed without having to be subservient to notions of 'ideal' languages and models extracted therefrom, whether classical ones such as Latin or Greek, or currently dominant ones such as English.

The question of neighbouring languages referred to in section 2.4 is a good place to consider another aspect of the role of grammatical modelling in cross-linguistic comparison. Let us take the example of ways of talking about the future in European languages. Several languages apart from English have a way of talking about future events that employ the equivalent of the English verb *to go*. These languages include French, Dutch and Spanish (but not German, Swedish or Italian, for example). Learners of the languages that do have a *be going to* future are often given advice about the usage of the *be going to*-equivalent form that suggests that L2 has something special or different about its usage. King and Lansdell's (1979:33) adult French language course gives the meaning of the *go*-equivalent, *aller + infinitive*, as 'to say what someone is intending to do'. In a later expansion in the same book, the notion of 'probability' is added to the meaning of the form and the learner's attention is drawn to the fact that the examples are all of the spoken language (*ibid.*: 70). Bougard and Bourdais (1994:152) French course assigns to the *aller* construction reference to 'something that is already planned and very likely to happen'. Learners of English are told in Soars and Soars (1987:64) that the *be going to* future expresses 'intention or evidence'. English-speaking learners of Spanish will learn in Halm and Ortiz Blanco's (1988:219) coursebook that the Spanish *be going to* equivalent (the verb *ir + a*) embraces 'the immediate future'. Shettor's (1994:125) Dutch pedagogical grammar says *gaan* (the

Dutch *be going to* equivalent) expresses 'intention'. The Dutch learners' course *Levend Nederlands* (1984:79) assigns to *gaan* the meaning of 'een intentie of een plan'. However, *descriptive* linguistic studies, both of individual languages and contrastive ones, seem to suggest that French *aller*, Dutch *gaan*, English *go* and Spanish *ir* are actually very similar, having perhaps more in common than that which separates them, in that they all relate to the future based in a present state of affairs (on French see Wales 1983; on English, French and Dutch compared, Haegeman 1983; on English Aijmer 1984, Haegeman 1989; on Spanish, Bauhr 1992). The future-in-present meaning offers a unitary explanation, for example, for apparently different English sentences such as 'I'm going to take up golf in the spring' (present state of intention/decision), 'It's going to rain' (based on present evidence), 'I'm going to be fifty next birthday' (based on present age) and 'I'm going to have to replace that door' (based on its present state). If there is evidence that, at least for the four languages mentioned (and probably others), the *be going to* future is very similar across languages, we may actually be confusing learners by suggesting it has a special status with regard to particular features such as 'intention' or 'immediacy' in particular languages, and if difficulties do arise, they may turn out to be pedagogically induced ones.

The real value of the cross-linguistic comparison in the case of *going to* may be in pointing up the potential familiarity with the structure that particular groups of learners may bring from their L1. Once again, the main point is that cross-linguistic comparison should not be seen as merely error- or difficulty-driven, but problem-driven in the true sense that we hope to project applied linguistics in this book, where 'problem' includes curiosity, enquiry, comparison, evaluation and questioning, as well as trouble-shooting errors, obstacles and difficulties, and sorting out failure.

2.6 Lexis and the question of available paradigms for comparison

Contrastive analysis of languages proceeds within the current paradigms of linguistics and so, often, the language teacher has to take what is on offer, and 'linguistics applied' (see section 1.2) determines the scope of comparability the teacher can utilise in building knowledge about languages. The cross-comparison of lexical systems is a good example of this. For a long time, the study of lexis was dominated by the science of semantics and, for many applied linguists, lexical meaning was synonymous with semantic meaning as semanticists described it. This was not necessarily a bad state of affairs, and vocabulary teaching undoubtedly benefited indirectly from developments in the study of semantic fields, as I have argued elsewhere (Carter and McCarthy 1988; McCarthy 1990). Good, contrastive work on semantic fields has been and continues to be done (Lehrer 1969, 1974, 1978, 1985; Miller 1978), and the study of the way languages divide up the available semantic space, how they 'word the world', has been crucial in understanding the difference in general structure of the vocabularies of different languages (see Lyons 1977:253 on the work of Trier).

It was only in the late 1960s that the paradigm of lexical studies began to shift in Western Europe, and more and more energy began to be devoted to collocational meaning in vocabulary, especially among the neo-Firthians (e.g. Halliday 1966; Sinclair 1966), and the study of how words combine (often quite arbitrarily) began to be seen to be as significant as the study of what they meant in denotational or connotational terms. Collocational studies have given us an explosion of applied linguistic activity (not least in lexicography, with pioneers such as Sinclair driving hard from the practical end; see Sinclair 1991) that has a very direct and stimulating relevance to language teaching (see also section 3.4). In this case, probably because of its intuitively immediate relevance, it is often applied linguists 'doing applied linguistics' in the sense I have advocated who have provided hard evidence for the facts of collocation in individual languages, rather than those who have just been involved in 'linguistics applied' (i.e. taking already existing descriptions). Kennedy's (1987a) study of expressions of temporal frequency in English is a good example of this, arising out of a practically motivated analysis of academic English texts. Kennedy considers the arbitrary combinations such as *fairly commonly, very rarely, pretty regularly* and *virtually always* (compare the non-occurring *virtually rarely*, or *pretty always*) and gives a very useful list of appropriate collocations that a language teacher could use directly (see also Kennedy's (1987b) work on quantification, which has a similar practical motivation). In my own work with O'Dell (McCarthy and O'Dell 1999), we have used collocation as a means of presenting differences in synonymous pairs or amongst sets of related words, based on corpus evidence. For example, in considering the closely related adjectives *terrible* and *horrible*, information on their likely co-occurrence with human or non-human nouns was crucial in our decision as to how they should be presented and practised. Table 1 shows how often the two adjectives co-occur with person-related nouns per one thousand words of spoken text, revealing a markedly greater preference for *horrible* to occur with person-related nouns, although both adjectives may occur with such nouns.

Table 1: Collocations of *terrible* and *horrible* with person-nouns (per one thousand words).

	+ pers n. per 1k
terrible	19
horrible	43

Studies of collocation in other languages also exist (notably Russian; see Kunin 1970; Benson and Benson 1993), but cross-linguistic comparisons are relatively scarce:[4] the paradigm has not shifted sufficiently yet. And yet we are at a good point where applied linguistics as a profession seems to be expressing a shared urge for more knowledge, insight and useful description of collocation (whether for lexicographers, materials designers, syllabus compilers or vocabulary teachers), rather than relying on ready-made products and 'linguistics applied', or waiting for semantics to come of age.

2.7 Discourse analysis: new paradigms in cross-linguistic comparison

Where paradigm shifts occur in one area they sometimes influence paradigms in other areas of language study, and the development of discourse analysis, the study of the relationship between language and its contexts of use, is a case in point (see Coulthard 1985; Cook 1989; McCarthy 1991a; McCarthy and Carter 1994). As we shall see below and in Chapter 5, discourse analysis has had a profound effect on how languages are compared, but it has not only offered new frameworks for analysing longer stretches of naturally occurring language, it has also caused traditional areas such as grammar to be re-assessed (e.g. Givón 1979; Monaghan 1987; McCarthy and Carter 1994: ch 3; Hughes and McCarthy 1998). Influences have been felt in phonology, too. Many languages are well-catalogued in terms of their basic pronunciation features, and inventories of phonemes exist which make cross-comparisons of similarities and differences between languages relatively unproblematic (e.g. the phoneme inventories in Campbell 1991). However, in the study of intonation across languages, things are not so straightforward.[5] Traditional models of intonation stress either semantic, 'emotional' and/or 'attitudinal' correlates of tone contours such as rises and falls (e.g. O'Connor and Arnold 1961; Crystal 1969; Lindstrom 1978), which have been very influential in English language teaching,[6] or grammar-related features of intonation (e.g. Halliday 1967; Kullova 1987). This has often made it difficult to have satisfactory cross-linguistic comparisons because of the elusiveness of notions such as 'emotion/attitude' and the need to cross-compare two levels of language encoding simultaneously in grammar-related descriptions.[7]

Discourse-oriented views of intonation (i.e. those which take into account features of the discourse such as participant relationships, state of shared knowledge, etc.) offer the potential of a more universal model of intonation and of more accurate and relevant descriptions for individual languages. For example, Brazil's (1985; 1997) discourse model of English intonation stresses assumptions made by participants in talk about the state of shared knowledge, and whether information is being 'referred to' (i.e. assumed as shared) or 'proclaimed' (assumed to be newsworthy). These categories are likely to be universals across all languages, even if their realisations in terms of precise tone contours may vary. The potential contribution such a theory could make to models for pedagogy is immense, both for individual languages and for cross-linguistic comparisons. As yet, though, little in the way of ready-made comparisons exist using this approach.[8] This, however, is not necessarily a negative feature for our conception of applied linguistics, since we have argued that it is as much the task of applied linguists themselves as it is that of linguists, to create relevant models within their own needs and contexts.[9]

Comparing intonation across languages brings us back to the problem of linguistic hegemony discussed in connection with Latin and English. If we are to compare two languages, especially where one is perhaps already better described than another (as is often the case with intonation), do we just overlay the system devised for one language on to another, or do we simply let the data speak and start from scratch (see Keijsper 1983)? Much depends on whether one follows an instrumental tradition (i.e. of scientific measurement) or a functional one (attempting to assign meanings/ attitudes to forms). If the latter, then attempts at cross-linguistic comparison are likely to proceed on the basis of preconceived models of functional categories and may cause great problems. On the other hand, purely scientific or distributional studies of intonation across languages may provide a mass of data with little gain in interpretation (e.g. Scuffil's 1982 study of German and English[10]), although it may potentially form the basis for language-independent universal models of intonation (Collier 1991).

Most studies of intonation across languages in fact tend to be a mix of semantic/grammatical/attitudinal approaches, suggesting a dominance of the approaches used for 'base' languages such as English (e.g. Chitoran 1981; El-Hassan 1988). Just as we have argued that grammars of languages should be seen on their own terms (both to the benefit of individual description and to the search for universals), studies of intonation should, ideally, do the same. The point in dwelling so long on intonation is that it not only represents many of the age-old problems of linguistic description and how applied linguists should evaluate cross-linguistic study, but also offers new directions resulting from the paradigm shift that discourse analysis represents, and an opportunity to tackle the long-standing problem of looking at intonation in its own right, disentangled from lexico-syntactic and semantic frameworks. However, new paradigms in linguistic study and their applications will not necessarily simplify the very complex interactions that undoubtedly take place between a learner's L1 intonation and the target intonation.[11]

The most significant influence that discourse analysis has had on how we compare languages is in providing a new set of parameters within which to carry out comparisons, which are independent of the traditional levels of analysis such as sentence grammar and semantics (see Marmaridou 1988). Discourse and conversation analysts have focussed on structures and patterns beyond the clause and sentence. They have brought to the study of language notions such as coherence and cohesion over clause and sentence boundaries (Halliday and Hasan 1976), the concept of exchange (Sinclair and Coulthard 1975), turn-taking in talk (Sacks *et al.* 1974), speech acts (themselves borrowing from developments in the philosophy of language), face and politeness phenomena (Brown and Levinson 1987), discourse-marking (Schiffrin 1987; Fraser 1990), and so on. Originally based on the description of individual languages (very many on English), such categories have naturally and rightly been brought into service in the comparison of languages too, and universals of interaction have been observed (House 1985). It is here that fundamental questions and problems arise, questions directly relevant to pedagogical applied linguistics.

Discourse-level studies across languages may be divided into two major types: those which deal with lexico-grammatical phenomena re-interpreted from a discoursal point of view, and those which look not at language forms but at the socio-cultural aspects of linguistic behaviour. These two different modes have fundamentally different implications for language pedagogy, and need careful evaluation as to their relevance in the modelling of languages for pedagogical purposes. The first approach, that based on lexico-grammar, is in many ways more straightforward, in that it extends the understanding of forms that were traditionally problematic or neglected, by looking at their occurrence in real data. Examples here would include word-order phenomena: whereas the typological tradition of conventional linguistics stresses the canonical sentence (usually the neutral, declarative form[12]) and the various possible combinations of subject-verb-object that characterise different languages (e.g. Givón 1984), discourse-based investigations are concerned with non-canonical word-orders, such as fronting of objects and other elements in subject-verb-object languages, and how this relates to topicalisation in different languages (e.g. Källgren and Prince's 1989 study of Swedish and Yiddish). Such studies may reveal interesting formal differences that could merit inclusion in a 'discourse-grammar' of particular languages.

On the other hand, where languages are typologically similar, features of discourse such as disturbances of canonical word-order for topicalisation purposes may be formally identical or very similar across languages and thus raise different questions about their transferability in language learning, ones which are likely to have complex answers (e.g. Trevise 1986 on French and English). Other areas of language form that have come under a more discourse-based approach include ellipsis (e.g. Kuno 1982), questions of various kinds (Anzilotti 1982; Takashima 1989), and clause-types (Dunbar 1982). These studies necessarily involve some kind of pragmatic framework with which to approach grammatical functioning across languages, but often suffer from the lack of a unitary framework for pragmatics.

Turning to the non-formal aspects of language comparison at the discourse level,[13] considerable interest has been shown in how management features of conversation, such as discourse-marking, operate in different languages (see Abraham 1991; Özbek 1995), both in formal terms (i.e. the occurrence and distribution of markers) and in sociolinguistic terms (how they reflect social norms of interaction). Marking seems to be a universal feature, and the potential for modelling individual languages as well as assessing the degree of universality in marking is great. Both viewpoints, as before, raise different questions for language teaching in relation to transfer of forms and transfer of behavioural features.

Even more intriguing are the comparisons made across languages in the performance of specified speech-acts such as apologising, complimenting, requesting, and so on (see Trosborg 1995 for the most complete study), for not only do such studies often reveal different ways of realising such speech acts (in terms of sequencing, frequency, etc.) but they also underpin the cross-linguistic study of interactional styles, and how these may be related to cross-cultural mis-communication and the creation of negative stereotypes. García's (1992) study of responses to requests by Venezuelans and English-speaking Americans, for instance, dwells on an apparent difference between a 'deference'-oriented approach by the Americans and a 'camaraderie'-oriented approach by the Venezuelans, which García attributes to different, culture-bound 'frames' of conversational participation. Similar studies have found speakers of French who come over as 'blunt' compared to speakers of English who come over as 'beating about the bush' (Béal 1994).

How does the applied linguist evaluate the relevance of such non-formal cross-linguistic studies? Is the metalanguage of speech acts sufficiently universal to validate such studies (see Wierzbicka 1985)? Are cross-cultural speech-act problems in fact formal ones in disguise? Form-related problems may well lurk behind cross-cultural studies where subjects are required to perform in L2 rather than their L1; for example, Scarcella and Brunak (1981) suggest that language learners may learn formulaic utterances for such features as politeness in an L2 before they are fully aware of their distributional appropriacy. So, although a difference in behaviour may not necessarily correspond to a deep cultural difference, we may yet evaluate such studies as being very relevant in the arguments in favour of cross-cultural awareness as a necessary component over and above the learning of speech-act forms in the L2.[14] Underlying this kind of discoursal comparison is the global question of what is relevant in language description in general, for unless we take a stand on that, then we cannot evaluate whether clear differences between behaviours across cultures manifested in language performance are in fact matters of 'language' at all. If we follow Harris (1990) in seeing the integration of the linguistic and non-linguistic features of communication as vital to an adequate theory of language (see also Fleming 1995), then non-formal features of discoursal difference across languages are necessarily part of a proper contrastive theory which would lay considerable claim to relevance and accountability to the needs of second language pedagogy. Nor would we wish to stop there, for from beneath the welter of discourse-based studies of individual languages and groups of languages there steadily emerges a feeling that form as such (especially grammatical form) is, as Hopper and Thompson

(1993:357) claim, 'shaped by the entire range of cognitive, social, and interactional factors involved in the actual use of language', and that grammatical regularities, rather than representing 'frozen semantics', come to us as a result of 'sedimented conversational practices' (ibid.).

The advent of discourse analysis has not solved the fundamental problems of contrastive analysis, in that it proceeds in different ways for the different levels of analysis, whether syntactic, lexical, phonological or discoursal (Fisiak 1983). However, discourse analysis (and the cross-cultural rhetoric studies that concentrate more on written text structures across languages; e.g. Kaplan 1966, 1983; Bar-Lev 1986) help satisfy the desire in language teachers to include the learner and his or her cultural starting point in any relevant modelling of language for pedagogical purposes. A contrastive analysis that does not situate languages in their socio-cultural contexts of use is less likely to yield the kinds of relevance and accountability we need, and is less likely, ultimately, to provide an adequate view of communication through language as a universal phenomenon.

2.8 Conclusion

We have dwelt long on problems and levels of comparability in this chapter, because comparing languages is never far from the applied linguist's mind, especially in second-language pedagogy. We have also argued that a view of language as a whole is a pre-requisite to good applied linguistics, as it has been recurrently throughout history. While we have hovered back and forth between theoretical and practical aspects of contrastive analysis, we would not wish to make too much of a distinction between 'theoretical' contrastive analysis and 'applied' contrastive analysis (Fisiak 1983), for central to this chapter and this book is the notion of taking a theoretical stance. Our argument here is that applied linguists need to adopt a stance both on the differences between languages and the relevance of such differences to their professional area, whether it be pedagogy, lexicography, language planning or whatever, and how language as a whole should be studied and understood. Recently, for example, Malmkjaer (1997) has taken the rather unfashionable line of arguing for an enhanced role for translation in foreign language learning, integrating it with the other language skills, and seeing it as a way of focussing learners' attentions upon both L2 and L1. She admits, though, that competence in translation and general linguistic competence do not necessarily go in tandem, and that translation may cause cross-linguistic interference. Malmkjaer has taken a stance, and argued persuasively for it, based on historical, linguistic and pedagogical evidence, in other words, good applied linguistics.

In this chapter we have considered some broad questions arising from the relationship between different languages and language as a global phenomenon. We have seen how, historically, the two notions have been in dialectal relationship, against different socio-economic backdrops. But another central dialectic has underlain the development of applied linguistics, and that is the perspective from which language and languages are viewed. In Chapter 3, we look at two extremes along the spectrum of models of language: that which views language as an abstract system, and that which views it as inseparable from its contexts of use.

Notes

1 The dominance of Latin as the framework for the analysis of other languages goes back much further. Fredborg (1980), for instance, sees it as operating to the detriment of the study of the European vernaculars in the 12th century. Latin models are certainly never far from the surface in the attempts to categorise English parts of speech down to the eighteenth century, for example Gill (1619), Jonson (1640), Cooper (1685), Priestley (1761) and Lowth (1762).

2 The points listed here are a convenient shorthand for the purposes of this chapter, and I would not wish to suggest that there is not great disagreement among linguists as to what the basic tenets are and what is significant or relevant to a linguistic theory (e.g. see Gethin 1990 and 1999 for a radically different view from the mainstream of what is central in linguistic argument).

3 The belief in Latin as an ideal model language, however, is very resilient. In the last stages of revision of this book, a campaigner for the promotion of teaching Latin in British primary schools stated in a BBC radio interview that one of the desired aims was the teaching of English grammar through Latin. The interviewee remained unchallenged as to why this should be preferable or necessary rather than teaching English grammar through English (BBC Radio 4, *Today*, 23 May 2000).

4 One early exception is Mitchell (1975:10), and a recent excellent example is Newman (1988) on Hebrew and English collocations. A brief selection of Swedish collocations may be found in Gellerstam (1992). Also in recent years, work has commenced on various computer-based projects across languages, using sophisticated databases (e.g. Heid and Freibott 1991; Thomas 1993; Fontenelle 1994), and such projects may be assumed to increase in scope and importance in the near future.

5 There have been attempts at 'intonational typology' for the world's languages, for example Romportl's (1973) grouping into four major types, though these are not isomorphic with typologies based on morphological traits.

6 Cook (1979) has a focus that includes more functionally oriented categories such as asking for and checking information, degrees of positiveness, etc., but the attitudinal approach has generally been very influential in English language teaching (e.g. Roberts 1983).

7 Chitoran (1981) takes up some of the issues involved in cross-linguistic syntactic and semantic comparisons in the study of intonation.

8 But see Mansfield (1983) for its application to Italian.

9 Brazil's is not the only discourse-sensitive account of intonation. Schaffer (1983, 1984), for instance, matches intonational choices with discourse features such as turn-taking and topic management, while Selting (1992) looks at the role of intonation in oral narrative.

10 This may be compared with Trim's (1988) study of German and English which relates the distribution of tones to sociolinguistic aspects such as the creation of negative stereotypes.

11 The complex nature of intonational traces of L1 in L2 is discussed in Lepetit's (1989) study of Japanese and English learners of French.

12 See Keenan (1976).

13 These non-formal levels of language behaviour are parallelled in what Lehtonen and Sajavaara (1983) call the 'interpersonal' level of comparison, though they would seem to include psychological factors too.

14 There is certainly no shortage of cross-linguistic studies of features such as politeness, e.g. for Thai see Khanittanan (1988); on Spanish and English: Haverkate (1988); English and Arabic: El Sayed (1990); English, French, Hebrew and Spanish: Blum-Kulka (1989).

3

Modelling languages: the raw material of applied linguistics

3.1 Introduction

In Chapter 2, I dwelt in some detail on the relationship between a general view of language and the study of individual languages in relation to one another. This enabled us to gain a historical perspective on the development of applied linguistics as a professional discipline, and to remind ourselves of the inherent socio-economic and cultural boundedness of our discipline. But it should also serve to remind us that, whenever we are studying a particular language, either as the starting-point for language learning (the L1) or as the target language (the L2 or L3, etc.), our view of that particular language is likely to be highly conditioned by our view of language as a whole. In this chapter I shall investigate further how views of what constitute language data, and of what constitutes relevant data with regard to teaching–learning processes, influence the way applied linguists 'do' their professional activities. I shall take a look at the core linguistic levels of grammar, morphology, lexis and phonology and see how different attitudes towards language as a whole have affected the way their role in language learning and teaching have been perceived. In Chapter 4 I shall look closer at how such views have affected research paradigms in the study of language acquisition, and especially at the nature of input in second language acquisition research.

3.2 Language as abstract system, language as social phenomenon

One position that has remained strong in the discipline of linguistics over a long period is that language as an object of investigation can best be modelled by viewing it as an abstract system, existing independently of its contexts of use, or, in Di Pietro's (1977: 4) words, as associated with 'mental constructs' rather than 'sociological factors'. In general, linguists who take this view would argue that such features as social and cultural influences, individual variation in language use, the effects of immediate context, and so on, are best excluded from the study of language, and that, what matters are the universal, underlying phenomena, which may be summarised as follows:

- That all normal human beings acquire human language of some sort, while other animal species do not. Linguistics must therefore address this innate capacity.
- That beneath the externally different forms of different languages, there lie universal features. Relating these universal features to the individual characteristics of languages is a central task of linguistics.
- That adult native speakers can say of their own language(s) what is grammatical and well-formed and what is not, by recourse to intuition and introspection.
- That externally observable language behaviour (often referred to as *performance*) is only an imperfect guide to the internal knowledge of a language that any individual possesses. This internal knowledge (often called *competence*) is amenable to scientific investigation.

Such an idealised view of language is most readily associated with the classic Chomskian paradigm as displayed in Noam Chomsky's earlier writings (e.g. Chomsky 1957; 1965), but many linguists who are not necessarily loyal disciples of Chomsky would also find themselves at ease with most of these general principles. For example, the discipline of semantics has certainly proceeded upon the assumption that words and their meanings can be discussed by recourse to linguists' intuitions, and that different systems of meaning and the different lexicons of languages none the less operate in universally consistent ways which can be explicated and displayed without reference to the social contexts of use (see Nida 1975; Lyons 1977). When semantics began to move more towards centre-stage in Chomskian linguistics, it was at that time mainly concerned with the componential structure of words and the compositional meaning of syntactic forms in combination in sentences (Katz 1977: 2). Contemporaneously with the development of Chomsky's linguistics, case grammar, while committed to a more functionally oriented account, in contrast to the belief in the autonomy of syntax espoused by early versions of Chomsky's linguistics, still eschewed reference to real contexts of use (Fillmore 1968). Similarly, psycholinguists have long believed that the meanings of words are acquired by young children in an internalised, systematic way, that children's performance can offer a window on the internal development of their semantic competence, and that such phenomena as the acquisition of the phonology of languages are subject to universally valid principles (Jakobson 1968; Hawkins 1991; Aitchison 1994: Chapter 15). Underlying the whole approach to language as an abstract code or system is a commitment to rationalism, often referred to via its historic links with the philosophy of Descartes as 'Cartesian' linguistics (Chomsky 1966).

Beaugrande (1997) draws attention to the methodological consequences of such a position: the linguist becomes a 'homework' linguist, as opposed to a 'fieldwork' linguist (p. 280). Similarly, Di Pietro (1977) reminds us that the linguist working within this general paradigm only needs to refer to his or her own language, and not that of any other user, inevitably leading to insoluble disputes over what is grammatical and what is not. Perhaps the most striking consequence, observable in much work in second-language acquisition, is that human subjects may come to be treated as laboratory subjects, as readily when it is a question of investigating language as when investigating the common cold, or the memorisability of complex digits, or the ability of rats to find bits of cheese in a maze. But more subtle effects may be seen in how language learning materials are designed and in advice and prescriptions offered to teachers resulting from such laboratory-style 'treatments'.

It would be a gross over-simplification to lay the responsibility of viewing language as an abstract system solely at the door of Chomsky and his followers. Robins (1979:205) notes that:

> In the European linguistic tradition, the conception of syntax as
> a theory of sentence structure embodying its own specific
> elements and relations can be regarded as part of the legacy of
> the Middle Ages.

Furthermore, the classical tradition of the study of dead languages such as Latin and Ancient Greek, because of the general inaccessibility of real speakers and contexts of use, has contributed greatly over the centuries to the view that languages can be systematised, displayed and taught in all their glory without reference to individuals and to real occasions of use. This heritage was not always confined to dead or inaccessible languages: in Great Britain, until the 1960s, the teaching and learning of the Welsh language in Wales itself often followed the same pattern as the teaching of Latin, and, in the English-speaking urban areas of Wales, only a privileged few high achievers were given access to real speakers and real contexts for use, even though such contexts were living and available nearby. I need no points of reference beyond my own, personal experience as a schoolboy in Wales in the late 1950s and early 1960s to vouch for these claims.

More directly relevant to recent philosophical influences in second language pedagogy is the development of speech-act theory (Austin 1962; Searle 1969). Although the study of speech-acts would seem on the face of it to be definitely concerned with language in use (to use Austin's own title, with *How to do things with words*), most of the initial theory and discussion of speech acts proceeded with intuitive data, invented phrases and sentences corresponding to what linguists' intuitions accepted as prototypical ways of making requests, apologies, etc.[1] It is true that more recently, speech-act studies have come to be based on real language use (e.g. the study of complimenting, see Manes and Wolfson 1981, and the study of the performance of speech-acts such as apologies and requests by language learners, see Trosborg 1995), but it is also true that much speech-act research, and a good deal of what in general passes for 'pragmatics' (i.e. the study of how meaning is achieved in use), has based its statements on highly abstracted data (e.g. Grice 1975; Leech 1983). As a balance to this, Oller (1977: 50) sees pragmatics as 'the dynamic interaction between the speaker's knowledge of the world (including immediately perceived information, relationships between speakers, and the like) and the syntactic-semantic dimensions', and further adds that the dimensions 'are by no means independent' (*ibid.*). Thomas (1995: xiii) promises that her book 'accords a central place to the roles of both speaker and hearer in the construction of meaning and takes account of both social and psychological factors...'. Speech-act theory had a direct affect on language teaching in the early days of the communicative movement, with proposals for syllabus design by applied linguists such as Wilkins (1976) being firmly rooted in inventories of abstracted data, and teaching materials offering learners intuitively grounded formulae for the achievement of speech-acts such as apologies, interruptions, complaints, etc. (e.g. Abbs and Freebairn 1980: 53; Jones 1984:36ff; Soars and Soars 1987: 54–5).

The other side of the coin is the view that language cannot properly be studied as an abstract phenomenon. Again, no single school or linguist can be said to be the origin of this perspective, though sociolinguists such as Dell Hymes (Hymes 1967) have had a great influence on many branches of applied linguistics, including language teaching. The view of language as a social phenomenon is, broadly speaking, based on the view that language *only* exists for social purposes, and that, logically, its study must address and encompass those social purposes. Its tenets may be sum-marised as follows:

- The forms and meanings of languages have evolved in social contexts, and are constantly changing and evolving in response to social and cultural developments.
- Language itself contributes to construct social and cultural realities, and is not neutral in the part it plays in our perceptions and articula-tions of our social experience.
- Language is acquired in social contexts; language acquisition is one feature of socialisation and acculturation.
- 'Performance' constitutes *the* most important evidence for how lan-guage works and what it is; it is not simply a veil obscuring underlying 'competence'.
- Performance is best observed in real language phenomena such as written texts and conversations; it cannot properly be studied under laboratory conditions.
- Linguistic evidence is *external*. The linguist's intuition is no longer the primary evidence. External evidence means that issues such as correct-ness and standards will no longer be absolutes. For a global language like English, since many of its highly competent users will not be native-speakers, the native-speaker as the sole source of evidence for use also becomes displaced. I shall return to the issue of the primacy of the native-speaker in Chapter 6.
- 'Meaning' is only an abstraction from the actual communicative achievements of participants in written and spoken interaction. Mean-ing is *emergent* in language forms, rather than immanent.

The two broad views of language are unquestionably a simplification of a quite complex cline of beliefs and approaches in current applied linguis-tics, and I shall try to do some credit to that complexity in this book. None the less, underlying the eclecticism that is generally accepted as healthy to the applied linguistic profession, the two views can be observed operating dialectically, creating a tension that occasionally surfaces in debates be-tween strong advocates of one line or the other. It is, as such, a powerful thread in the fabric of the discourse of applied linguistics (see Chapter 6 for applied linguistics as a professional discourse).

The view of language as social phenomenon undoubtedly has much to commend it to language teachers in comparison to the notion of language as abstract system: it seems more real, visible, amenable to verification or falsification, and seems to chime in more with learners' needs to *use* second and foreign languages rather than just to *know* them or *know about* them. However, it too has its problems. Just what does 'social context' mean? How does one systematise context? What features of language use, over and above the phonological and lexico-grammatical variations that reflect socio-cultural features such as formality and informality should be included in our modelling of a language? If language really is individuals interacting with other individuals in unique contexts, how can we ever build enough information into our model of a target language to capture such variability, and is not at least some degree of abstraction desirable, and inevitable (Larsen-Freeman 1997)? How much abstraction? Why not go the whole hog and take language right out of the messiness of real contexts and simply present it as a system to be learnt in the abstract and only later applied to situations of real communication?

The degree to which these questions are real ones for applied linguists is reflected in the different schools of thought that have contributed to the broad field of 'discourse analysis', generally seen as a sub-discipline firmly on the social end of the cline of language study, and currently enjoying a surge of interest within second-language pedagogy (see Cook 1989; McCarthy 1991a; McCarthy and Carter 1994). In the British discourse analysis school as exemplified by the work of Sinclair and Coulthard (1975), their observations of the language used between teachers and pupils led to a model of spoken discourse at quite an abstract level of generalisation (see section 5.4). On the other hand, in the strongest versions of American conversation analysis (which has also contributed to defining the general field of 'discourse analysis'), fine-grain investigations of individual conversations often content themselves with illustrating how unique individuals achieve unique goals on unique occasions. In this view, there is little generalisation about language forms, since their force and meaning are argued to be contingent upon their particular placement in that particular discourse, how participants respond to them, etc. (see Heritage and Watson 1979; Atkinson and Heritage 1984; Bilmes 1988; Pomerantz and Fehr 1997). It is difficult to see how the kind of conversation analysis completely embedded in individual pieces of data without any generalisability could be 'applied' in pedagogy, although there have been calls for the 'sensible' incorporation of findings from conversation analysis into communicative language teaching (Celce-Murcia *et al.* 1997: 144). Similarly, van Lier (1989) sees conversation analysis as having a positive role in assisting our understanding of what interviews are, in the context of oral proficiency interview tests. It must also be acknowledged, though, that in the practice of language teaching there have been negative consequences flowing from the strong view of language as a social phenomenon, with teachers in the early, heady days of the communicative movement often made to feel guilty if their learners were not constantly using and 'outputting' language in contexts and activities designed to ape as well as could be done the 'real world'.

Thus the picture is complex, with neither end of the cline between language as abstract system and language as social phenomenon offering a trouble-free route for application in language pedagogy. However, understanding how these views have influenced the construction of grammars and the descriptions of lexis, morphology and phonology that underlie teaching materials and classroom activity, and that have formed the input for language acquisition studies is crucial, whichever end of the spectrum our sympathies ultimately incline towards. I shall now consider some examples of language description in terms of how they reflect a view of the nature of language study.

3.3 Grammar and grammars

3.3.1 The sentence: friend or foe?

If you studied any grammar at all at school or as an adult, whether of your first language or that of a second language, it is highly likely that the grammar you learnt was modelled on classical languages such as Latin and Ancient Greek, for in most parts of the world such models still dominate, though their influence may not always be obvious on the surface. If you studied at a university, it is possible you were introduced to academic models of grammar which may or may not have ever been applied in language pedagogy. For example, you may have encountered the transformational-generative grammar of Chomsky and his followers (see section 3.3.2), the case grammar promoted by Fillmore (1968) and Anderson (1971), or the systemic grammar of Halliday and his followers (Halliday 1985; Downing and Locke 1992). What the traditional classical model and most of the others in circulation will have in common is some notion of a core unit, usually the sentence (though Halliday's grammar tends to see the clause as more core-like; see section 3.3.2). It is worth dwelling a little on the nature of the sentence, for it is not simply an artefact used by grammarians. As we shall see in Chapter 4, a good deal of second language acquisition experimentation uses sentences as the input, and very few language teachers would ever claim to do their job without recourse at some time or other to the sentence as a vehicle of illustration, whether for grammar or vocabulary or some other feature such as intonation.

Behind the use of the sentence as a theoretical and descriptive unit lie a number of basic assumptions, not necessarily all shared by all grammarians, but recurring across many different models and in descriptions of many different languages:

- That sentences have meaning; they are often traditionally defined as 'completed thoughts' or units of meaning. This meaning can be apprehended from the sentence alone, without recourse to further information about context, who said it or wrote it, etc.
- That sentences express fundamental meanings found in all languages (e.g. subjects doing things to objects, people and things acting in time and space, events and ideas logically relating to one another). In other words, the sentence is a universal of human language. Thrushes, dolphins and dogs may have vocal signals that carry meanings, but they do not have sentences.
- That sentences are formed in individual languages according to rules. Native speakers acquire and know these rules, and can tell when a piece of language corresponds to or violates the rules.
- That sentences are formed from other, lower-level grammatical units such as phrases and clauses; they are the highest level of grammatical structure – beyond them lie texts and contexts.
- That sentences exist in both spoken and written language, however imperfectly they may be realised in the real-time performance of spoken language.

Most language teaching accepts these assumptions. It is assumed that sentences can be used as vehicles to illustrate how any language expresses meanings, that their construction is systematic, and that learners will be familiar with them as units of meaning and as objects of study, and will expect them to be used in class and in materials. It is also generally assumed that what has been written and practised as a sentence will transfer unproblematically to speech, given the right amount and type of practice. The fundamental beauty of the sentence in pedagogy is its ability to act as a vehicle for the *illustration* of language, rather than as a vehicle of communication. The sentence as a unit in fact fits very well with a view of language as an abstract system, since sentences are simply slabs of language, fenced off from the messiness of context and individual users; they are ideal containers for illustrating rules, patterns and meanings in a clear, non-distracting way. They can be brought together according to their similarities in structure (e.g. ten sentences all containing past tense verbs), regardless of whether their meanings and contexts are coherently related to one another. What is more, in using sentences as a way of investigating acquisition, we can approximate better the language user's underlying *competence* in any language, since their response in experiments is likely to be oriented to the abstract features of the form and meaning of the sentence rather than to the distractions of any unique occasion of actual use. In laboratory 'treatments' of subjects, sentences can be controlled, and offer the possibility of stable, replicable input for the experimenter, free from the vagaries and caprices of real, unpredictable language. Finally, the sentence can be seen as the crowning achievement of the manipulation of morphemes, words, phrases and clauses in the L2, which the learner can progress to, stepwise, through exposure, practice and production, and feel the satisfaction of that achievement (see Hughes and McCarthy 1998 for a further discussion of the pedagogical value of the sentence).

The sentence, though, clearly does not sit so easily alongside a view of language as a social phenomenon. The problems of situating a description around the unit of the sentence in such an approach could be summarised as follows:

- Meaning is not independent of context. When people process sentences, what they are really doing is imagining a context for them, however minimal.
- Rules about well-formedness are not absolute; something may be unacceptable to a native speaker in one context but pass unnoticed and be perfectly acceptable in another. Individual judgements will vary greatly.
- Judgements of grammaticality are likely to display fuzzy boundaries; any set of sentences will rarely produce a unanimous *yes* or *no* response from native-speaker informants.
- Issues of well-formedness and acceptability are socio-culturally and politically influenced and are not innate. Schooling and social identities condition people's perceptions of well-formedness as much as natural acquisition processes do, and such conditioning will vary historically and be subject to fashion and the persuasiveness of dominant rhetorics.
- Much everyday speech (by far the bulk of language output in any society) seems to function perfectly adequately without a predominance of

well-formed, complete sentences. A lot of spoken language is characterised by single-word or short, phrasal utterances, false starts, wandering
structures, strings of clauses and phrases often without any obvious
starting or finishing point.

- In conversation, units that look like sentences (e.g. a main clause and
  an associated subordinate clause) may often be produced jointly
  by speakers rather than as a construction by one voice (see Tao and
  McCarthy in press for some examples).
- Well-formedness is clearly less important to interlocutors than communicative appropriacy and efficiency: notions of typicality and lack
  of problematicness are more useful than an abstract notion of well-
  formedness.
- Some sentences in written and spoken texts are complete units of
  thought or meaning; others depend on preceding or subsequent sentences to make any sense at all.
- Children do not necessarily acquire sentences as the most primitive
  units of communication; in early stages of acquisition, children communicate effectively with single words, or phrases, or fixed, unanalysed
  clausal units (Jespersen 1964: 113; Peters 1983).

In language pedagogy, the sentence may be less than useful, even irrelevant, in performing mundane speech acts such as greetings, suggestions,
thanks and apologies, not to mention in the extended performance of
spoken collaborative tasks. In the very earliest stages of communicatively
oriented language courses, beginner-level learners may well achieve more,
faster, if the sentence as a unit does not surface at all, and many successful
courses focus in the early stages on the acquisition of useful formulae,
with only implicit attention being paid to putting together entities such as
subjects, objects and clauses (e.g. Richards 1994).

3.3.2 Models of grammar and their applicability

When it comes to applying grammar models in second language teaching
(or indeed in other applications, such as the automatic grammatical
tagging of computerised text), the traditional, classical-based model has
its attractions, and it is no mere act of historical chance that its influence
has been so tenacious and resilient. The traditional model proceeds on the
basis of the study of syntax and morphology, syntax being principally
concerned with the rules which allow the arrangement of words into
well-formed structural configurations, and morphology being concerned

with 'items and paradigms' (see McCarthy 1991b), that is the way individual words (e.g. nouns, verbs), inflect or combine to create the paradigms of tenses, number, person, etc. An example of a paradigm was given in section 2.5, for Assyrian pronouns, where it was argued that at least one of the problems of the classical-based approach is the imposition of the paradigms of Latin on to languages that operate in quite different ways. That is not to say that one should never create paradigms, or that they are not useful, but simply that they should be formulated on their own terms, with attention to the relevance for the learner, whose task it will be to map L1 paradigms and L2 paradigms onto one another. Paradigms need not be seen as entirely abstract artefacts, and much can be learnt about social and cultural structures from them. For example, if we just take three European languages, and build paradigms for their human-subject-pronouns in relation to one another (Figure 10), we see important sociocultural differences in the ways that familiar and distant relationships are (or are not) discriminated. For a Spanish-speaking learner of English, the Spanish paradigm can be greatly reduced and simplified, especially in terms of distant versus familiar relations in the second person (shaded English boxes) and in terms of gender. For the English-speaking learner of Swedish, *you* has to be discriminated into *du* and *ni*, not only on the basis of number, but also on the basis of familiarity and distance (shaded Swedish boxes). For both the Swedish-speaking and English-speaking learner of Spanish, the system in both L1s has to be discriminated to accommodate masculine and feminine plurals (shaded Spanish boxes), though Swedish does at least discriminate familiar and distant second person.

Meaning	Spanish	English	Swedish
1st singular	*yo*	*I*	*jag*
2nd singular familiar	*tú*	*you*	*du*
2nd singular distant	*usted*	*you*	*ni*
3rd singular masculine	*él*	*he*	*han*
3rd singular feminine	*ella*	*she*	*hon*
1st plural masculine	*nosotros*	*we*	*vi*
1st plural feminine	*nosotras*	*we*	*vi*
2nd plural masculine familiar	*vosotros*	*you*	*ni*
2nd plural feminine familiar	*vosotras*	*you*	*ni*
2nd plural distant	*ustedes*	*you*	*ni*
3rd plural masculine	*ellos*	*they*	*de*
3rd plural feminine	*ellas*	*they*	*de*

Figure 10: Human-subject-pronouns in Spanish, English and Swedish

The item and paradigm approach thus has a good deal of usefulness in modelling languages in relation to one another, as long as one is careful not simply to try to fit everything into a Latin strait-jacket. It also systematises visually for the learner an array of forms which might otherwise be confusing, and may serve as a useful mnemonic, especially for those learners with strong visual or diagrammatic orientations in their learning styles. A pronoun paradigm such as Figure 10, if constructed and dealt with in a humanistic way, can remind us, in Di Pietro's words, that 'The pronouns of a language are more than grammatical forms which somehow replace nouns. They mark the many relationships between speaker, hearer and referent which grow from the social status of the parties involved, the setting of the speech act, and even the visual orientation of the speaker' (Di Pietro 1977: 8). It is not, therefore, the paradigm itself but the linguistic assumptions that underlie it and the use to which it is put that matters.

The weakness of the item and paradigm approach is that it does not always bring together into formal paradigms items that learners may have to make genuine choices from when constructing real texts. McCarthy (1994a) and Hughes and McCarthy (1998) have argued, for instance, that the pronoun *it* occurs in regular opposition in texts to the demonstratives *this* and *that*, such that in the following two (concocted sentences), the anaphoric (backward) reference to the first sentence presents a genuine grammatical choice to do with topical focus (see also section 1.5.1):

> *Freda told me about Sally's problem.* **It?/this?/that?** *grabbed my attention immediately.*

It, *this* and *that* would be unlikely to be brought together in most traditional grammatical paradigms, where *it* would probably be found in a pronoun paradigm such as in Figure 10, indicating a non-human or impersonal pronoun, in contrast to the human ones, while *this* and *that* would be locked into their own demonstrative paradigm with *these* and *those*, to the exclusion of other items. The implications of such choices for a view of language as a social phenomenon are that considerable rethinking of what the relevant paradigms are may be necessary, based on the evidence of real contexts rather than using off-the-peg paradigm frameworks largely inherited from the classical languages, or based solely on formal grounds. Here we see that the relationship between one's view of language and how one models it for pedagogy influences the very basics of the linguistic raw material with which the learner will be presented or which the researcher may adopt as experimental input. Grammar does not exist in a vacuum, with its categories pre-ordained, independently of the use to which it is put by applied linguists, who shape it according to their underlying perspectives and who interpret its effects in practice.

Much the same can be said of traditional views of syntax. If the abstracted sentence is the unit of description, then an English sentence such as:

> *Thought it was Jim, but couldn't be sure.*

would not only be ambiguous, but would fall down on the requirement that English clauses must have a subject, or that the subject must at least be retrievable (as in imperative clauses). Who 'thought it was Jim', and who 'couldn't be sure'? Our example sentence can only be considered unambiguous and well-formed if we create a context for it; in other words, if we transform it from a sentence into an *utterance*, and imagine a situation, with a subject such as *I* or some other person, in a context where ellipsis of the subject is normal and unproblematic. For this reason, such ellipsis is often referred to as *situational ellipsis* (Quirk *et al.* 1985:895); we need a situation, or have to create one, in which the identity of the subject is obvious (e.g. a speaker telling a first-person narrative). How this affects grammatical description is that in a sentence-based view, there is something *missing*, and ellipsis is seen as a special set of cases where grammatically obligatory items may be 'missed out', since the sentence cannot be processed unless certain items can be 'retrieved' or 'restored'. In a socially embedded view of language, where utterances are always studied in contexts, nothing is 'missing' from the utterance, and there is no reason to believe that the notion of 'restoring' or 'retrieving' the subject has any psychological reality for speakers and listeners. Nothing is missing since the subject is there in front of the listener or is simply obvious and/or current/salient in the context. We might therefore wish to re-cast our account of ellipsis in a grammar embedded in social contexts so that items such as subjects are considered to be 'added' when they need to be stated explicitly for the benefits of participants. A parallel can be seen in lexis, which is often highly implicit in face-to-face spoken language (see Cheng and Warren 1999), but explicit when required (Cruse 1977).

In sum, sentences place requirements on grammatical forms that contextually embedded utterances may never need to make. In language acquisition experiments where sentences are the raw input for grammaticality judgements, we may simply end up testing those requirements rather than knowledge of or competence in the processes of ordinary communication.

Transformational-generative (TG) approaches to grammar locate themselves firmly within sentence-based schools of thought, though they represent a departure from the item and paradigm approach of classical-based grammars. The interests of TG grammarians include not only the processes whereby structures are as they are in particular languages, but also the ways in which grammars correspond to universal linguistic features and to the innate competence of native speakers. The main purpose of a transformational-generative grammar is, as its name suggests, to describe the basic transformations necessary to generate the permissible sentences in any given language. So, for example, in early TG descriptions of English, explaining how passive voices in the surface structure of sentences (i.e. the final product as written or spoken) are arrived at by 'transforming' basic active-voice structures with a prior existence at a deep level, or how embedded relative clauses derive from combining underlying matrix clauses in the deep structure according to specified rules, is considered to be a central aim of the grammatical description (Chomsky 1957). What is more, the purposes of the description must extend not only to saying how an infinite number of correct grammatical structures may be generated, but also to the formulation of rules that will automatically forbid the generation of incorrect, ungrammatical sentences. Thus a sentence such as *The woman (who[m]) I met was Irish* would be deemed to be well-formed in terms of the transformations it has undergone from the two matrix or 'kernel' sentences *The woman was Irish* and *I met the woman*, through deletion of *the woman* in the embedded clause, movement of that clause to a position after the head of the subject noun-phrase, and the (optional) addition of *who(m)*. This is necessarily a brief and superficial account of the complex evolution of TG theories (see Matthews 1979 for some of the key theoretical changes that evolved among TG adherents in the 1960s and 1970s), but it does exemplify TG's faithfulness to the pursuit of the underlying rules of syntax that are believed by its apologists to drive the construction of sentences and which are the goals of acquisition. The earliest versions of TG were not even concerned with meaning, although later versions saw semantics as an essential part of the grammar of a language, while still excluding anything about use in the real world, as Oller (1977) reminds us.

Chomsky never saw TG (or linguistic theory in general) as having any relevance for language pedagogy. In fact the whole of the debate on language acquisition in his *Cartesian Linguistics* emphasises that grammar is a question of explaining the universal inborn human capacity for language acquisition as a prerequisite to the acquisition process, and he rejects notions of 'training' and 'institution' (Chomsky 1966:63). None the less, such a systematic view of sentence construction is appealing, and was not without its adherents in second language teaching materials designers in the 1970s, as those of us who taught with highly successful courses such as O'Neill's *Kernel Lessons Plus* will recall. O'Neill's title itself was a tribute to TG, and its exercises in the creation of features such as relative clauses instructed the learner to 'transform' simple sentences into more complex ones. The cognitive aspects of learning are foregrounded. In the rationale for the teacher, O'Neill and Kingsbury (1974:iii) state:

> Contextualisation, by itself, is often not enough. An additional
> and more formal approach has been found desirable for adult
> students. However, this 'approach' keeps the use of formal
> terminology to a minimum. The aim is *not* to make students
> name parts of speech or to parse. The aim *is* to give students a
> cognitive grasp of the patterns and an insight into their
> transformations and the part they play within the whole system
> of English (this is the function of the exposition) and *also* to
> provide the sort of exercises that promote real fluency in the use
> of these patterns (this is the aim of the exercises).

In fairness to such an excellent textbook author as O'Neill, his courses went far beyond the mere manipulation or 'transformation' of sentences, but his work remains as an example of at least the partial influence of TG, and the power of the independent sentence as raw material in language pedagogy, even in a course where other elements such as extended narratives and notional-functional components were also present.

Also in the immediate aftermath of Chomsky's impact on linguistics, we see attempts to apply the transformational model to cross-linguistic comparisons of the type discussed in Chapter 2 of this book, and there was one attempt to apply a three-way contrastive analysis on transformational principles between relative clauses in Hindi, Arabic and English to the prediction of error and difficulty for learners of English from the first two L1s (Fox 1970). As we shall see in Chapter 4, such straight comparisons and predictions were destined to founder on the evidence of real language learners' performance, but for as long as contrasts between languages rested on comparisons of isolated sentences, the transformational-generative model probably served as well as any.

Grammars with a social orientation include functional grammars such as Halliday's systemic grammar (Halliday 1961; 1978; 1985) and discourse grammars (e.g. Givón 1979). For Halliday (1977:16) functional theories of language are 'not concerned with language as object but with language in the explanation of other phenomena'. Halliday's grammar is highly elaborated, and deserves more attention than it has received in second language pedagogy (a notable exception to this neglect being Downing and Locke 1992). In Halliday's model, the clause, rather than the sentence, is seen as the crucial hub around which language turns. Rather than explaining functions of the clause in purely morpho-syntactic terms (positions of subject and object, lists of tense inflections, etc.), the clause is seen as the nexus of basic choices (or systems) which represent the *meaning potential* of any given language. The choices speakers and writers make from these systems are socially motivated.[2] The choice of including or not including a modal verb in the verb phrase, for example, is seen as a matter of the interpersonal relationship projected between participants in the act of communication; the choice of a transitive verb rather than an intransitive one, or vice versa, is seen as a choice among potential representations of the relationship between the participants and processes encoded in the clause itself (Berry 1975). Thus a clause such as *The letter might have got lost* would be seen as arising from choices within the systems of tense, aspect and voice motivated by social concerns such as presenting one's statement as tentative, choosing not to name or blame an agent for the loss of the letter, distancing onself from the event (c.f. the immediacy of *The letter may be lost*), and using *get* as a characteristic passive marker of emphasis on (often unfortunate) end-results rather than agent or process (Carter and McCarthy 1999). The Hallidayan grammar does consider combinations of clauses (to all intents and purposes 'sentences'), but notably prefers to call them 'clause complexes' (Halliday 1985:215–6), and the clause remains as the central object of interest. Even orthographic sentences in extended texts are not treated as independent units, but must be related to one another in the grammar by the processes of above-sentence *cohesion* (Halliday and Hasan 1976), involving such features as pronoun reference across sentence boundaries, textual ellipsis and conjunction.

Halliday has proved that it is possible to elaborate a grammar in which the sentence is not paramount, and in which social concerns can be addressed. Another, by no means insignificant consequence of Halliday's view of the clause as socially grounded is that the distinctions between deep structures and surface structures, and between competence and performance, are no longer requirements of the model. Also central to Halliday's view is that social-semiotic structure (i.e. how societies organise their systems of meaning into symbolic representations) and language structure reflect and condition one another. Put simply, this means that an artefact in language (e.g. a text) can tell us much about the social relations that brought it into being, and a context of situation (i.e. the specification of conditions such as relationships between interlocutors, purpose of communication, mode of communications, etc.) can tell us much about what language is likely to occur. The relationship between language and social semiotics is bi-directional. It is difficult to see, therefore, how one might use a Hallidayan grammar in a laboratory-style investigation of language acquisition, since for Halliday, acquisition as well as use is not independent of social contexts and motivations (Halliday 1974; 1977).

The present account of grammars and their applicability is necessarily sketchy and brief, but is meant to illustrate the ways in which views of language from opposite ends of the theoretical spectrum can shape the modelling of grammar, and how grammarians' attitudes to the relationship between their data and social concerns (whether they exclude them or embrace them) can result in quite different priorities in the description of languages. The end product, what the applied linguist has for potential application, will either fit or misfit the applied purpose, and for that reason, awareness of where grammatical models start from is crucial to doing applied linguistics successfully. The same is true for models of the lexicon.

3.4 The place of lexis in different views of language

It may not be so immediately obvious that models of vocabulary are just as sensitive as are models of grammar to the decision to view language as an abstract system or as a socially embedded phenomenon. The issue is not to be confused with the long-established tradition of the historical study of vocabulary change (e.g. for English, see Hughes 1988), which is usually based on socio-historical evidence. The debate we must address for the present chapter is whether more is gained or lost by bringing to centre-stage the users of language, and how words 'mean' in real contexts, than by looking at words in their citation forms, out of context, as most dictionaries and a good many vocabulary learning manuals do. In this regard, a few general points may be made at the outset:

- Even in linguistic sub-disciplines with a strong social emphasis such as discourse and conversation analysis, lexis has been the poor relation of features such as turn-taking, exchange structure, discourse-marking etc., to which much effort has been devoted, and even of discourse grammar, which is a rapidly growing area of interest.
- Lexis has had something of a struggle to establish itself as an independent, yet systematic level of linguistic encoding. Often it has been viewed as subsumed within semantics, or even relegated to the level of a disparate set of 'irregularities'. Chomsky (1965:84) speaks of the lexicon as 'an unordered list of all lexical formatives', in contrast to the well-behaved and generative world of syntax, and it is the 'idiosyncratic' properties of words that relegate them to the lexicon (*ibid*. 87).
- Under both structuralist and notional-functional approaches to second language pedagogy, vocabulary was usually seen to be a lower priority than, respectively, the learning of structure, and the practising of speech-acts. Structural approaches focussed on grammatical forms, while notional-functional approaches emphasised the holistic meaning of speech-acts, rather than the individual words that composed them. This accounted for the Cinderella status vocabulary was perceived to occupy by applied linguists who refused to leave it alone in the 1980s (e.g. Meara 1980; McCarthy 1984; Carter 1987; Carter and McCarthy 1988; Nation 1990).

Semantics has provided applied linguists with useful frameworks for systematising meaning and relations among words (Nida 1975; Lyons 1977). For example, notions such as *synonymy, antonymy, connotation, denotation,* etc., have been widely used alike in the teaching of vocabulary and in lexicography (recall the discussion of thesaurus-design in Chapter 1.5.2). Applied linguistic research on vocabulary teaching (e.g. Channell 1981) and acquisition (Schmitt and Meara 1997) has often based itself wholly or partly on semantic principles. Even the somewhat abstract realm of componential analysis (analysing words into semantic 'components' such as + human, + male, + young for *boy* in English; for examples, see Leech 1984) has prompted direct applications in vocabulary-teaching materials (Rudzka *et al.* 1981). However, keeping the study of lexis penned within the world of semantics makes any proposal to develop a lexical model in harmony with a socially embedded view of language difficult.

Several relatively recent directions oriented towards context in the study of lexis have led to significant new applications within lexicography and language teaching (as well as stylistics and the teaching of literature) and shifts of emphasis in applied linguistic research, offering the possibility of a socially sensitive theory of lexis:

- The Neo-Firthian approach to word meaning, which stresses meaning in context. Firth (1935) argued against the notion of meaning 'chiefly as a mental relation or historical process', that is to say meaning as represented either in pure semantics or in the philological tradition. He proposed that the meaning of a word was as much a matter of how the word combined textually with other words (i.e. its collocations) as any inherent properties of meaning it possessed of itself: *dark* was part of the meaning of *night*, and vice-versa, through their collocation with each other (Firth 1951/1957). Collocations are clearly not absolute or deterministic, but the outcome of repeated combinations created and experienced in text by language users. We talk of a *happy marriage* in preference to (but not absolute exclusion or prohibition of) a *content marriage*; meanwhile a *gay marriage* has acquired its specialised sociocultural meaning (and thus its pragmatically specialised collocability) only recently.

- Key discussions of the implications of a theory of collocation may be found in Halliday (1966), Sinclair (1966), and in Halliday and Hasan (1976), where collocation is seen as part of the process of the creation of cohesion in extended texts. Both Halliday and Sinclair in their early papers on collocation foresaw and spearheaded the development of the large-scale analysis of lexis using massive amounts of text.

- The Neo-Firthians are not the only ones to be interested in lexis as an independent area of study; the general field of phraseology and the study of idiomaticity (e.g. Makkai 1972), both in the West and (in parallel and often unknown to Western linguists) in the former Soviet Union (see Kunin 1970; Benson and Benson 1993), has long worked within a framework not dominated by syntax.

- The growth of corpus linguistics (see Chapter 6; see McCarthy 1998: Chapter 1 for a historical sketch). Computer technology has enabled the vast stock of 'irregularities', that vocabularies of languages were often perceived as, to emerge as anything but 'irregular' (e.g. the lexicogrammatical regularities in verb behaviour evidenced by Hunston and Francis 1998). What is more, studies of large corpora by linguists such as

Sinclair and his associates (Sinclair 1991) have shown lexis to be a far more powerful influence in the basic structuring of language than was ever previously advocated. Corpora are essentially social artefacts; they are snapshots (some bigger and covering a wider landscape than others; some more fine-grained and carefully composed than others) of the output of chosen groups of language users. What they can show us are the regular, patterned preferences for modes of expression of language users in given contexts, and how large numbers of users separated in time and space repeatedly orient towards the same language patterns when involved in comparable types of social activities (or *genres*; see McCarthy 1998: Chapter 2 for an extended discussion of corpora as a way of investigating language genres). What corpora can show us with regard to lexis, amongst other things, is that much lexical output consists of multi-word units; language occurs in ready-made chunks (especially in speech) to a far greater extent than could ever be accommodated by a theory of language wedded to the primacy of syntax (see below; see also Moon 1997, 1998). These developments have occurred in tandem with non-corpus-based studies of lexis in context.

• The study of lexical units in text and interaction. This trend, not necessarily dependent on large corpora, focuses on two main areas: (a) the incidence of multi-word units (e.g. Bolinger 1976; Cowie 1988; Nattinger and deCarrico 1992; Lewis 1993; Howarth 1998) and how they have developed pragmatic specialism in regular contexts of use, and (b) the study of how lexical meaning is emergent in interaction (McCarthy 1988, 1998: Chapters 6 and 7) and how lexical items construct the discourse process (e.g. Hoey 1991a; Nyyssönen 1992; Drew and Holt 1988; 1995).

In terms of a framework for applied linguistics, recent lexical findings within the headings above have far-reaching implications. If lexis is indeed an important agent in the organisation of language, then an over-emphasis in acquisition studies on syntax may be misguided, just as an over-emphasis in teaching and in materials on single words out of context may leave second language learners ill-prepared both in terms of comprehension of heavily chunked output such as casual conversation as well as in terms of fluency. Indeed, fluency can hardly be operationalised at all as a useful concept within applied linguistics without recognition of the part which knowledge and retrievability of ready-made lexical chunks must necessarily play within it.

There are direct implications here, too, for that aspect of morphology that deals with word-formation (principally, derivation and compounding).[3] Rather than seek a set of underlying rules whereby derived and compound words are generated, the mental lexicon can be seen as a complex site of multiple connections. These embrace both open, creative possibilities for using and decoding the word-formation resources strategically in real discourse, and already-lexicalised exceptions to general rules, as well as a large number of off-the-peg, immediately retrievable, derived items and compounded chunks (see Aitchison 1994: Chapter 11, also 165-6).[4] Teaching word-formation rules has not had a high priority in recent approaches to vocabulary pedagogy, though McCarthy and O'Dell (1994; 1999) have included limited practice in the use of prefixes and suffixes. With regard to the investigation of the creative use of word-formation resources by native-speakers in real spoken and written data, Carter and McCarthy (1995b) provide corpus evidence for its everyday occurrence and advocate the exposure of learners to such data. Lewis (1997) has also attempted to take the implications of a lexical view of language into practical applications.

The work done on lexis in interaction has suggested that the abstract relations of meaning delineated by semanticists undergo considerable local adaptation or 'instantiation' in interaction (McCarthy 1988). Lexical meaning seems far less absolute and fixed, especially in face-to-face conversation. Work in this area points to some general findings:

- Categories of meaning such as *synonymy, hyponymy, antonymy*, etc. are local achievements, projected by speakers and subject to negotiation and joint construction with interlocutors (Cruse 1977; Jones 1999).
- Lexical categories display a good deal of fuzziness. Speakers use vague category markers such as *and things like that, or something* and hedges such as *a bit* and *like* to reinforce the indeterminacy of categories (Channell 1994; McCarthy 1998: Chapter 6).
- Delexical words such as *get, do, thing, stuff*, which combine with content lexical words to create collocations such as 'get up', 'do a painting', are extremely frequent in spoken language and express meanings difficult to capture in conventional semantic terms yet which function efficiently and unproblematically in real communication.
- Chunking is ubiquitous, and chunks are not only opaque idioms. Chunks may be quite extensive in the number of words they contain, often up to, but rarely exceeding, six or seven words. On the 'magic'

number of seven as a psychological limit, see Miller (1956).

- Lexical chunks may not necessarily be coterminous with grammatical units: *I can't get over how* ... is a frequently occurring chunk in British English, but it extends over a clause-boundary (patterning runs out after *how*, with numerous 'open' possibilities thereafter, such as ... *how kind they were,* ... *how quickly it all happened,* etc.).

As with grammar, a socially embedded view of lexis changes the landscape in terms of how and what one might apply in any practical domain. It certainly suggests that assumptions learners bring with them to vocabulary learning that words will have precise meanings (and that teachers will know them!) need to be carefully de-nurtured and a new kind of awareness raised. This equally applies to the usual assumption learners bring to the task that the vocabulary of a language is a list of single words. Lexical strategies in communication become as important as cramming words in a vocabulary pedagogy with a social orientation, and not only in spoken contexts. Studies of lexical cohesion in written texts (Halliday and Hasan 1976) suggest that considerable lexical manipulation is involved in the creation of text in terms of the interplay between lexical repetition and variation (see also McCarthy 1984). Once again, the lessons learnt from a socially embedded research agenda in lexis should not be ignored in the consideration of input and output in first and second language acquisition investigations.

3.5 Phonetics and phonology

Most language teachers at some time or another engage with the problems of teaching pronunciation and intonation, but in practical manuals and coursebooks, there is perhaps less direct influence from developments in linguistics than in other areas such as grammar and lexis. Pronunciation and intonation teaching is generally rather conservative in its approaches and methods. For most of us, the reliable inventories of phonemes for the L2s we teach, the sets of minimal pairs of words that enable learners to practise the discrimination of meaning-carrying sounds, and a knowledge of the basics of place and manner of articulation of L2 phonemes is sufficient raw material to equip us well for the kinds of tasks learners will be engaged in and the difficulties they are likely to encounter. If we are lucky enough to teach an L2 where the description of intonation has been codified, we may additionally have recourse to such information if and when we attempt to refine learners' L2 intonation. For a language like English, given what we know are likely to be the difficult sounds and sound-sequences for many learners (e.g. see the useful tips for different languages in Swan and Smith 1987), efficient training, whether of minimal-pair discrimination (e.g. Baker and Goldstein 1990) or in more communicative contexts (e.g. Hewings and Goldstein 1998) has always seemed to be best practice. And yet problems remain. Stubborn difficulties persist despite our best efforts to get students to co-ordinate the lips, tongue and teeth in complex harmony with the release of the air stream. We still get *zis* and *dis* when we want to get *this*, and some sounds just seem to refuse to be learnt properly until the learner is ready for them.

Phonetics and phonology have not stood still as areas of linguistic study. Nádasdy (1995) very clearly illustrates how a quiet revolution has taken place both in phonetics (the study of sounds) and in phonology (the study of the sound systems of languages). These shifts of focus reveal contact points with views of language as a social phenomenon inseparable from its use, many of them being moves away from the description of phonological systems *per se* towards questions of production and comprehension between speakers and listeners and the non-linear, real-time parallel processes of articulation of segments (or 'autosegmental' theories of phonology). A good many questions remain unanswered vis-à-vis the practical consequences for language teaching, but it is true that an applied linguistic theory wishing to ground itself in a social view of language learning should certainly not relegate phonetics and phonology to mechanistic aspects of language. Similarly, in the study of intonation, things have moved on from both the out-of-context, introspective accounts of intonation and emotion or 'attitude' (for a critique see McCarthy 1991a: Chapter 4) and from modelling intonation within mainly grammatical parameters. Recent discourse-based studies have looked at intonation choices as reflecting interactive concerns of speakers and listeners, such as projected states of shared knowledge, marking of extended discourse segments, etc., and tried to apply them in practical contexts (see especially the work inspired by David Brazil: Bradford 1988; Hewings and Goldstein 1998).

3.6 Conclusion

This chapter has focussed on the way opposing views of language, on extreme ends of a spectrum whose limits represent the presence or absence of a social orientation, have direct implications for applied linguistics and how linguistic insight is characteristically applied in language pedagogy. The chapter has focussed on the core practices of linguists in the theorising and modelling of grammar, morphology, lexis and phonology, but the philosophies that underpin abstract versus socially embedded views of language have implications for the way we approach our learners in the pedagogical enterprise. The view of language that I have characterised as 'abstract' is also essentially rationalist, even positivist. The socially grounded view I have opposed to it is essentially relativist and humanist. For this reason, applied linguists often identify with either a 'hard-science' approach to their subject or a 'social-science' approach. Nowhere is this more apparent than in the study of second language acquisition, to which we turn in the next chapter.

Notes

1 Katz (1977: xi), in an attempt to weld a transformational framework to speech-act theory, comments that Chomsky and his followers 'paid as little attention to speech acts as the Austinians paid to transformations', reminding us of the independent schools of linguistics which separately and contemporaneously pursued sentence-based concerns.
2 Halliday is one of the Neo-Firthians, or disciples of J R Firth. Firth, as long ago as the 1930s, was advocating a 'sociological linguistics' (Firth 1935). On Firth's work and influence in general, see Mitchell (1975).
3 For a full account of English word-formation processes, see Bauer (1983). What is claimed here for derived words and compounds could equally hold true for other word-formation phenomena such as acronyms, initials, clippings (e.g. phone instead of telephone), etc.
4 Halle (1977) argues convincingly from a generative viewpoint for the independence of morphology from either syntax or phonology, and, although abstractly based in general terms, none the less adds support to the arguments here for a lexically driven model of fluency.

4

Language acquisition: methods and metaphors

4.1 Introduction

The use of linguistic frameworks in the modelling of first language acquisition has a long pedigree, and has influenced the kinds of frameworks applied to the study of second language acquisition (see Stern 1970:57ff; Brown 1980:58–61). Many of the issues prominent in the study of one kind of acquisition continue to overlap with those in the other. But whatever the initial influence first language acquisition studies may have had, or continue to have, on second language studies, there is no doubt that second language acquisition (SLA) has developed in its own right as a branch of applied linguistics. In many respects, SLA may claim to be a classic example of applied linguistics, in that its proponents have fought hard battles to establish its independence both from a one-way dependence on linguistics (Widdowson's 'linguistics applied'; see section 1.2), and from being seen merely as a branch of educational psychology. Some of its most faithful adherents see it as a rationalist, scientific enterprise, with its own theoretical base and its own avenues of enquiry, in which methods associated with the natural sciences play a major role, for example, laboratory-condition experiments (see the special issue of *Studies in Second Language Acquisition*, 1997, 19 (2), and section 4.2). But also, of late, debates have raged over the status of SLA investigations. By no means everyone agrees that SLA should model itself on the hard sciences, and many see SLA's future as bound up with more humanistic and holistic approaches. Some question whether SLA has contributed anything at all in a real, practical sense to second language pedagogy.[1] In this chapter we shall examine the broad evolution of SLA as a sub-field within applied linguistics and try to relate the debates that fuel its progress to the fundamental issues raised in the previous chapters. This introductory chapter cannot do full credit to what is a very large, complex undertaking; a fully comprehensive survey of the field of SLA can be found in R. Ellis (1994).

4.2 The emergence of SLA

The notion of 'acquiring' a second language through the mediation of an efficiently ordered methodology is not new. For centuries, language pedagogues have claimed to offer the most effective methods for acquiring foreign tongues. In the seventeenth century, Jeremy Taylor's (1647) Latin primer promised:

> A new and easie [sic] institution of grammar: in which the labour
> of many yeares [sic] usually spent in learning the Latine [sic]
> tongue is shortned [sic] and made easie [sic].

Likewise, Mauger (1679) published a French grammar for English-speakers:

> ... enriched with new words, and a new method, and all the
> improvements of that famous language as it is now flourishing
> at the court of France: where is to be seen an extraordinary and
> methodical order for the acquisition of that tongue, viz. a most
> modish prononciation [sic], the conjugation of irregular verbs,
> short and substantial rules ...

The tradition continued in the eighteenth century, with Bridel's (1797) *An Introduction to English Grammar*, which was:

> ... intended also to assist young persons in the study of other
> languages, and to remove many of the difficulties which impede
> their progress in learning.

These endeavours were usually aimed at an orderly presentation of rules of syntax and pronunciation, along with a vocabulary list and, sometimes, model dialogues. McCarthy (1998: Chapter 1.7) traces the development of interest in the acquisition of spoken language from the sixteenth-century *Vulgaria* Latin textbooks, seventeenth- and eighteenth-century manuals of rhetoric and pronunciation, through the nineteenth-century interest in newly encountered (for Westerners) 'exotic' tongues such as Japanese, to the twentieth-century influences of new media and expanded communicative needs. All along, pedagogues have had notions such as removing difficulties, streamlining and speeding up learning, efficient acquisition of rules and items, etc. at the forefront of their efforts.[2]

In more recent times, studies of the effectiveness of different methodologies in language teaching have raised wider issues that have become central concerns in the quest for rigour in SLA studies, such as the control and influence of extraneous variables, the reliability of sample populations, the time-span studied, the relationship between explicit and indirect forms of instruction, the effects of corrective feedback, the type of input, etc. Parallel with these methodological debates, higher-level theoretical concerns have emerged, such as the differences between first and second language acquisition, whether conscious 'learning' is the same as 'acquisition', the theoretical modelling of linguistic input and output and the universality or otherwise of SLA findings.

One early debate in the study of contemporary SLA was whether traditional grammar methods were less, more, or as efficient as audio-lingual approaches. Audio-lingual language learning arose out of behaviourist psychology, which held that learning took place in a stimulus–response–feedback pattern, and that repetition and habit-forming were crucial to acquisition. Learning speech habits was supposed to be an effective spur to acquiring good general competence in a second language. In practical terms this meant much listening, drilling and repeating, often in language laboratories, with little attention to meaning or any cognitive effort in the apprehension of rules. It was a well-established methodology when I entered the ELT profession in 1966 as a Berlitz-method teacher, using the 'blue-book' Berlitz manual familiar to anyone who taught within the Berlitz organization at that time. Learners listened and repeated, and produced structural patterns based on platitudinous sentences (*This is a pen; It is red*, etc.). The method was not without many stunning successes – mind-numbing though it was for the teacher or for more curious learners.

The behaviourist philosophy had many critics, foremost among them Chomsky, with his famous critique of B F Skinner's *Verbal Behaviour* (Skinner 1957; see Chomsky 1959). Applied linguists thus set out to debate and test the rival claims of audio-lingual approaches and opposing, traditional 'cognitive' approaches, in which the acquisition of rules was considered paramount (Smith 1970). Conflicting evidence emerged. Agard and Dunkel (1948) reported a school survey in the USA, where students had been exposed either to traditional methods or to audio-lingual methods. The students studying with audio-lingual methods certainly seemed to be able to reproduce learnt dialogues and patterns with ease, but were poor at speaking on unrehearsed topics. However, their overall proficiency in speaking and pronunciation remained robust (pp. 287–8). Students taught with traditional methods were better at reading. Such findings raised as many questions as they were intended to answer. How reliable are findings that only look at relatively short-term exposures to different methods? How reliable are the methods of post-testing applied in such studies? Do they really test the success of the method, or something else (e.g. ability to do tests, or short-term memory)? What controls were exercised during the experimental period? Were the sample populations (a) representative, and (b) comparable? A more controlled attempt at comparing audiolingualism and traditional methods, with better screening of populations, more rigorously controlled input, more sophisticated testing, etc., was carried out by Scherer and Wertheimer (1964). The results were again mixed, with some fairly predictable gains for audio-lingual students in speaking and listening, but less promising progress in the written aspects of language use.

Overall, the audio-lingual studies were inconclusive but were suggestive, and they did influence practice, in the sense that early optimism towards the technology of such media as language laboratories and the then ubiquitous strip-film projectors faded in the face of poor results and lack of strong supporting research evidence to encourage professionals to persevere with them. Most of all, the audio-lingual studies set off a tradition of concern with experimental studies involving large populations, controlled input and statistical analysis, as well as longitudinal evidence. Also, in relation to our concerns in Chapter 3, the audio-lingual studies represented a clash of cultures in language pedagogy; more than techniques were involved, and beliefs about the nature of language and language learning informed the debates, no less than they have continued to do since then.[3]

The audio-lingual studies were also unfolding against a backdrop of lengthier, broader debates over the possibility of a scientific basis for the study of language and language pedagogy that had been ongoing since the beginning of the twentieth century (e.g. Sweet 1899; de Saussure 1916/1964; Palmer 1924). This, along with the appearance of the new journal *Language Learning* in 1948[4] was all part of the general emergence of a sub-discipline that eventually received the name Second Language Acquisition. As with so many other sub-disciplines in applied linguistics, its adherents came to it from different starting points and endowed it with its persistently eclectic character. By the mid-1970s, the field of SLA had certainly sufficiently come of age for a critique to be published of its methods and their relevance to language teaching (Tarone *et al.* 1976).

4.3 Basic questions and issues

Among the central questions SLA researchers attempt to find answers to are:

• Is second language acquisition like or different from first language acquisition? In some respects the task would seem to be similar, regardless of which language one was acquiring. On the other hand, second language learners have the advantage of previous linguistic experience, and the potential disadvantage of interference from an established first language (see Brown 1980: Chapter 3 for a good discussion). Equally interesting is the question of the acquisition of third or further languages (e.g. see Ringbom 1985).

- Is conscious 'learning' the same as 'acquisition'? Can the first lead to the second? Much debate has been generated over this question, arising from claims made by researchers such as Krashen (1981), and Gregg (1984). For many chalkface, practising teachers it is a non-issue, and yet there are related questions that refuse to go away, such as why well-practised and rehearsed language features still seem not to 'stick', despite best efforts.

- Are there universal features of second language acquisition, regardless of which L2 is being learned? Are there 'natural' orders or sequences in which things will be acquired, regardless of the sequence in which they are taught (Krashen 1981)? First language acquisition points to the existence of regularities in the order of the acquisition of sounds and syntax, independent of the individual or the learning setting.

- What role do the first or other languages play in the ease or difficulty encountered when learning a second language? Are languages from the same families easier or more difficult to acquire successfully (Hedard 1989)? What part do learners' subjective or culturally conditioned perceptions play in cross-linguistic difficulties, aside from objective differences that might exist between languages (see Kellerman 1986)?

- What non-linguistic factors affect SLA, for example, age, gender, motivation, previous learning experience, individual aptitude, etc. (see Skehan 1989)? Can one ever generalise, when, in the final analysis, learners are always individuals?

- What is the difference between SLA in a naturalistic setting (e.g. living and working in the L2 community) compared with a formal setting (e.g. a classroom)? Is the classroom, the street or the laboratory the appropriate site for the investigation of SLA processes?

- Can learners' language be described systematically at various stages of development, or is learner language erratic and unsystematic? What kinds of learner data are relevant, and how should one interpret such data?

- Can aspects of acquisition be studied discretely or atomistically, or should the whole person always be the focus of attention, i.e. a holistic approach to SLA?

- Should acquisition of a second language be measured against monolingual standards, or should second language learners be viewed as language users who can use more than one language, and not as 'failed monolinguals' (Cook 1997: 46)?

- Is there a different outcome from explicit instruction as opposed to more indirect ways of teaching language features? Does corrective feedback help or hinder acquisition? How long do the effects of different types of instruction last?

- Are there significant differences in the way grammar is acquired as compared with vocabulary or pronunciation? Is language acquisition knowledge of 'universal grammar and a language-specific lexicon … in essence a matter of determining lexical idiosyncrasies?' (Larsen-Freeman 1997:88). In other words, is the study of the acquisition of grammar rules in some way more fundamental than the study of vocabulary acquisition, or is this simply a blinkered and misguided perspective on the nature of language and the learning enterprise?

- Should SLA consider the acquisition of social and cultural competencies as well as purely linguistic ones? Since learning normally takes place in social settings, and not in glorious isolation within the learner's head, what value is an approach to SLA that ignores the social and cultural context?

- Are language skills such as listening and reading transferred from the L1, or do they have to be learnt afresh in the L2? Are they 'linguistic' skills as such, or are they best viewed within a framework of cognitive psychology? What social and cultural factors affect acquisition of a skill such as reading?

- Are discrete aspects of acquisition testable as measures of general competence or proficiency, e.g. the relationship between possessing a large vocabulary and success in other aspects of language proficiency; see for example Schmitt and Meara (1997)? How reliable are tests when it comes to interpreting what has been achieved in an SLA experimental setting?

It should not surprise us that responses to the questions posed above are usually mediated through different perspectives on the nature of language and the relationship between language as a whole and individual languages, such as we have discussed in Chapters 2 and 3, and by differing views on the accountability of SLA to its consumers, as foregrounded in

Chapter 1. Views are certainly divided on the answers to the questions listed above; even whether it *matters* that pluralism and different paradigms reign in SLA is a matter of ornery and splenetic debate (Block 1996; Gregg *et al.* 1997). Here we shall consider how far and in what ways SLA has attempted to address some of the more central questions, and how such investigations have influenced the general field of applied linguistics and language teaching.

4.4 Cross-linguistic influences and 'interlanguage'

Perhaps the most stubborn issue that refuses to go away in SLA is the influence of the first or some other language on the acquisition of a new language. Gass and Selinker (1993) note that in the late 1960s, the notion of cross-linguistic transfer was marginalised but that, at the time of editing their book, transfer was firmly back on the agenda, with the need for a reconciliation of differing perspectives. They conclude that transfer 'is indeed a real and central phenomenon that must be considered in any full account of the second language acquisition process' (p. 7). While there is no doubt that a simple cross-linguistic comparison of two languages is insufficient to explain and predict performance in a second language, accounting for features of second language performance is by no means easy. One possibility is that there are universal orders of acquisition that cannot be overridden by pedagogical intervention: the learner will not acquire something until he or she is ready to, regardless of teaching, and not until certain other conditions have been met. For example, evidence suggests that there are regularly occurring orders of acquisition among learners of English negative constructions with auxiliary verbs, such that progression from the affirmative form *can* will likely include intermediate forms such as *I no can* and *I don't can* before the target-form *can't* emerges (Cancino *et al.* 1978).[5] Recurring evidence of this kind has led some to the view that learner language is systematic (Corder 1967), and that it is possible to talk of a learner's *interlanguage* (Selinker 1972; 1992), i.e. a systematised approximation to the target language, a series of organised way-stages, based on hypotheses, on the road to mastery of the TL. Such systematicity does not presuppose that all the rules in a learner's interlanguage correspond to TL rules. The interlanguage view removes the responsibility for performance features away from the leaden and mechanistic influence of L1, and places the focus more on the actual learner and his or her cognitive processes. This view has some attraction, since it can offer an explanation for features of performance which seem to be independent of the L1 (see Tarone 1988). However, if interlanguage exists, then it is unlikely to be in the form of lock-step stages that can be frozen in time and observed in any meaningful way by researchers, and is more likely to be in continuous flux, with hypotheses being constantly under revision, sometimes dissolving, sometimes consolidating, re-cast, thrown out, revived, put on ice, different depending on who the learner is interacting with, when and where, and so on. If this is true, then interlanguage may be an interesting, but largely useless, theoretical construct.

Recent debates over the status of variation in learner performance are relevant to the question of interlanguage. Is variation in learner performance free, or is it systematic, or are both kinds present (R. Ellis 1999)? In other words, if a learner uses a feature (say, for example, the English definite article, or the French subjunctive mood) unpredictably in similar linguistic environments, what does this mean? R. Ellis (ibid.) sees free variation as evidence of learners using items that have been acquired but not yet organised into systems (tying in with associative views of acquisition; see section 4.7.1). Ellis accepts that some facts of learner performance that appear erratic and unstructured can often be shown to be systematic, at least in terms of probability of co-occurrence with particular linguistic environments. He quotes a study of his own (R. Ellis 1988), where learners were more prone to omitting the copula when preceded by a full noun subject than when the subject was a pronoun. The learners were thus working with some kind of systematic set of associations rather than randomly floundering among various possibilities.

Where there is variation that does not correlate systematically with any environmental factors, one can either dismiss it as just that – random, and irrelevant to a theory of interlanguage (e.g. Schachter 1986) – or one can build a model of interlanguage that has free variation as a component. This R. Ellis does, examining evidence of cases where two forms occur in the same linguistic and discoursal contexts and carry the same illocutionary meaning; in other words, all other things being equal, cases where there seems to be no apparent reason why two different forms should occur. Ellis brings into play the notion of 'expressive need' (ibid.), which corresponds to human urges towards variety, curiosity and free choice. In this view, free variation may be short-lived, rapidly giving way to systematic variation as a result of sociolinguistic needs and pressures. In settings where such sociolinguistic constraints are reduced or absent (and Ellis suggests classrooms may be just such settings), free variation may persist and only become systematised in the longer term.

Ellis's view is attractive, and introduces a humanistic and sociolinguistic component to modelling interlanguage that enables apparently random facts to assume the status of relevant data. There are, none the less, problems with such a view. Firstly, there is by no means universal agreement, as we have argued throughout this book, as to what sort of evidence would constitute sufficient context in which to adjudge something as 'free' of all constraints except individual creativity and curiosity. Is a cursory description of the situation in which an utterance occurs enough? Or does one need the strongest possible version of a micro-level conversation analysis, in which every possible feature of context is recorded and transcribed? What status do learners' own accounts of their usage have in such analyses? Equally, if 'expressive need' exists, could it not also be seen as a personal, affective, but externally targeted sociocultural act connected with the learner's desire to create an identity for him or herself in interaction, or to engage in meaning creation, rather than just curiosity? If this last conceptualisation is viable, then, mapped on to a socially oriented view of language, variation is not 'free', and does not need to be explained as such, since learners' voluntary actions are seen as constitutive of the acquisition process. Learners are never conceptualised as mere passive receptors of 'acquisition' in such a view. One thing is clear: good, contextualised corpora of learners in interaction (as natural as possible, given Ellis's caveat about classrooms) would seem to be the way forward. The more sensitive a theory of interlanguage is to the conditions in which we observe it, the more likely it is to generate a true image of the processes underlying the progress from L1 towards proficiency in L2.

One of the reasons why applied linguists felt unhappy with simplistic comparisons of different languages as a way of explaining and predicting learner performance is that blaming the L1 for difficulties and problems in learning an L2 reflected a rather negative and passive view of the learning process. Just as the L1 might *interfere* with the acquisition of L2, might it not also have a *positive* influence on L2 acquisition? The metaphors for talking about cross-linguistic phenomena thus shifted from negative terms such as *interference* and *L1-induced errors* to more positively oriented metaphors such as *cross-linguistic transfer* and *interlanguage strategies* (Odlin 1989; Kellerman 1995). This is a good example of the discourse of applied linguistics and its role in defining our professional profile – a theme to which we return in Chapter 6. The newer metalanguage takes into account the fact that simple comparisons between two languages cannot explain why a structural possibility might be wrongly over-generalised from one language to another. For instance, for an English-speaker learning Spanish, indirect object structures in English, such as *I gave her/Sally the message* may be over-generalised, based on the evidence of similar word-order for full noun objects in Spanish to include pronoun objects (*Yo di ella el mensaje*), which in Spanish must be either before the verb or preceded by a dative-marker preposition. However, the reverse, i.e. Spanish speakers producing *I her gave the message*, may not occur at all, because there is no evidence forthcoming in the English the learners are exposed to that such a possibility exists (for further discussion see Zobl 1980). In other words, a contrastive analysis of two languages lacks the kind of predictive power needed; we must include learners' positive strategies of transfer. In this case, where evidence from L2 supports transfer, transfer is more likely; where supporting evidence is absent from L2, transfer need not take place.

However, Kellerman's work (Kellerman 1983; 1986) suggests that learners may play an even more active role in what and how and when and where they transfer features between L1 and L2, and that aspects such as their perception of how prototypical a feature is might affect their willingness to transfer (e.g. a reluctance to translate metaphoric and idiomatic extensions of words into L2). What is more, transfer may depend on the perception of their role at any point in time by learners. Kellerman (1995) notes that his own Dutch students may consciously transfer more Dutch features into their English when they are communicating with peers with whom they identify as fellow-sufferers than when performing 'on air' for the teacher. All this suggests that the richest context in which to study the influence of L1 on L2 might be real interaction rather than constructed experiments, which might provide no more than a shrunken and impoverished picture of normally complex behaviour. Good case studies of individual learners attempt to capture as many relevant contextual influences as possible and to appreciate learners' individuality (Kellerman cites two studies, by Giacobbe and Cammarota 1986, and Giacobbe 1992, which probe individual transfer in depth).

4.5 Inside the laboratory

Some of the key questions listed in section 3.1 have led researchers to seek answers by conducting experiments under laboratory conditions. These include the question of type of instructional input (e.g. explicit teaching versus more implicit input, the effects of error-correction and other types of feedback), type of linguistic input (e.g. real utterances, invented languages), the effects of time (short-term and long-term retention of input), and so on. In a recent survey of such research, Hulstijn (1997) tackles both the problems and prospects for laboratory studies. It is quite often difficult, Hulstijn points out, to conduct empirical research in natural language-learning settings such as classrooms and workplaces, because there will always be a 'great number of potentially interfering variables in such natural environments' (p. 131). This is undeniably true, but whether one considers this a problem that has to be overcome at all costs depends on one's view of language. If language is an abstract system that can be adequately apprehended outside of any real context of use, and if acquisition is a question of absorbing the system at a 'deep' level, it should indeed be possible to strip away the distracting variables inherent in real contexts and get at what has or has not been acquired at the deep level. In the laboratory, this implies having as 'clean' an input as possible for language experimentation. For example, if one had a group of subjects individually receiving the same instructional input, then we would not want subject number ten to suffer from the tired, bored voice of an instructor who was enthusiastic one hour earlier when addressing subject number one. The researcher, in this case, in order to guarantee a consistent input, might expose all subjects to a pre-recorded voice, or to the dispassionate and imperturbable screen display of a computer (e.g. N. Ellis and Schmidt 1997). Likewise, such research might lean more towards words or sentences as input, since they offer a window, or so it is believed, on the subject's competence by means of grammaticality judgements. The 'messiness' of real contexts might sully the enterprise with considerations such as social appropriateness and communicative adequacy, distracting the subject from judging an item's well-formedness or from acquiring a rule. Quite telling in this regard is Hulstijn's (1997) use of the term 'interfering variables'. If one's view of language is that it is always embedded in its social contexts, and has no meaningful existence outside of them, variables do not 'interfere' with performance or competence, nor with the apprehension of underlying rules and patterns, since the system, and one's competence in its use, has no existence outside of how it communicates in complex, variable-laden situations. Variables, in a socially embedded view, become a positive factor in the investigation rather than a nuisance. On the other hand, laboratory experiments where such variables are not allowed even to exist, for example by using artificially created languages that carry the guarantee that subjects will not have had any prior experience of them, run the risk of demotivating learners through asking them to learn a language that has 'no native speakers and no apparent use', to quote Yang and Givón (1997).

To be fair to Hulstijn, he recognises the need for research in naturalistic contexts, and raises all the proper concerns about laboratory studies in his indispensable and well-balanced survey, as do N. Ellis and Schmidt (1997). He notes, too, that laboratory experiments should be based on proper theoretical questions for investigation, and by and large such questions are apparent in most studies. For example, the effectiveness or otherwise of simplified input, and the enhancement of input (i.e. in some way making important target items salient and more noticeable) are central, practical and important theoretical questions which most language teachers have pondered on at some time or other, and laboratory studies would seem to be a genuine attempt to address them. What bedevils such studies, though, are the metaphors that carry over from the science laboratory into a domain which many feel is quintessentially humanistic. Laboratory studies, as I have self-consciously done above, frequently refer to their human participants as *subjects*, to the input the 'subjects' are invited to participate in as *treatment* and to the attempt to understand outcomes as *testing* (e.g. pre-tests and post-tests). The label 'subject' casts the learner as powerless recipient, and the researcher as administrator-cum-observer, for example, the animal psychologist observing and recording the behaviour of monkeys from a darkened cubicle in the corner of a laboratory.[6] 'Treatment' evokes notions of expert-driven therapy, and 'testing' suggests some sort of objective metering of behaviour. This is not to say that those who carry out laboratory experiments are soulless manipulators: participants are always volunteers, and the overwhelming majority of researchers are ethically concerned practitioners who have pursued research in response to proper pedagogical concerns. None the less, the professional discourse and terminology of any community of scholars reflects and (re-)shapes its paradigms of investigation. Success in SLA is thus measured by some according to the degree to which it works within the paradigms of the hard sciences and the language of the laboratory. This is clearly only one side of the story.

4.6 Classrooms and other settings

Those persuaded by a more socially oriented view of language are likely to look at settings other than the laboratory as appropriate arenas for their investigations. Most obvious and ready to hand of these is the language classroom. In classroom studies, learners can be seen as more than recipient vessels processing input from an expert. What is more, where a socially oriented view of language has been translated into a communicative pedagogy, communication (whether between teachers and learners or learners with one another) can become the focus of interest and the 'window on acquisition', rather than decontextualised sentences. Above all, the teacher can become his or her own researcher, without the need to have recourse to outside experts. Pioneers of this approach include Fanselow (1987:12), who addresses himself to teachers who are 'fascinated by observing, keen on generating alternatives on your own, interested in classifying communications to discover rules, have a compelling desire to explore teaching, and believe that ultimately we can depend only on ourselves to learn and develop'.

More recently, task-based classrooms have offered researchers prepared to take on the messiness of real teaching situations opportunities to study their learners interacting to solve problems that simulate real-world tasks (however imperfectly), and glimpses into learners' communicative competence in different task environments (an excellent example of which is Foster 1998; see also Nunan 1989). Thus variables become ways of observing and interpreting communicative abilities in the target language, rather than hindrances to measuring underlying competence. Such studies are usually at their best and most persuasive when their arguments are not simply based on objective statistical measures, but on the plausible interpretation of data. That is not to say that statistics can play no part in unravelling the effects of variables in context. Recently, for example, the possibility of harnessing the power of computerised expert systems in coping with large numbers of variables in predicting language learning achievement, in the way that medical doctors use computer software to assist with, but not replace, diagnosis, has been seriously mooted (Wilhelm 1999). But the classroom, with its variety of human participants, with, ideally, the teacher-as-researcher (a role combined with that of participant in many studies), and the inherent variability of the learning and teaching process, is a place where tendencies, trends, exceptions and their plausible interpretation can become as valid as 'significance' in the purely statistical sense.

However, one problem with such studies is that the researcher is only in a position to observe the products of acquisition (usually in the form of linguistic output related to particular input), rather than the acquisition process. For researchers such as N. Ellis and Schmidt (1997), this is a crucial weakness of many SLA studies: a truly useful theory of SLA should be based on apprehending the learning process, not just its end-points, and for N. Ellis and Schmidt, this means careful, controlled laboratory experiments. The point is a forceful one: N. Ellis and Schmidt assert that we would need a complete log of the learner's exposure to language input and intake, a record of their attentional focus during the period of instruction, etc., of such mind-boggling detail that would render near-impossible the task of making a proper observation of the processes learners go through. Instead, what we usually have are tantalising snapshots of learning waystages captured on the hoof in class. Such snapshots cannot adequately illustrate the central processes in language acquisition, but a combination of observation of the linguistic environment and participation frameworks, along with the study of feedback (e.g. correction) and attention to learners' introspective data is probably the best way forward within the limitations imposed by the nature of classrooms (see Gaies 1983 for an excellent survey along these lines).

People acquire second languages outside of classrooms, too. On the simplest level, one can itemise the differences in the kinds of encounters classroom learners and learners in non-classroom settings have with the target language, as Lightbown and Spada (1993:71–3) do, in terms of degrees of contact with native speakers of the L2, amount of corrective feedback, time spent confronting the L2, exposure to different discourse contexts, etc. (but see Rampton 1999 for a trenchant critique of such a dichotomous view of acquisition within and without the classroom, and its importunate influence on SLA thinking). However, in line with the social orientation of much of the argumentation throughout this book, the study of acquisition both in and out of class cannot ignore the wide gamut of social and cultural factors that may affect progress in L2. Immigrant communities, for instance, often have ambivalent attitudes to the host-country language, which can affect acquisition both in community settings and in the host-country school system (see Lambert and Taylor 1996 for an excellent study addressing some of these issues). McGroarty (1998) notes that, in the US setting, there is no way of predicting the balance of language use in bilingual communities, and language users may have quite a complex pattern of use of L1 and L2 depending on who they are interacting with: learners are not mono-dimensional, and orient towards multiple identities and social roles. Also censuring the tendency to over-simplification and stereotyping of how individuals interact in society, Holliday (1999) presents cogent arguments for a redefinition of 'culture' to embrace what he calls 'small cultures'. Small cultures are small groupings of individuals orienting towards cohesive behaviours, if only temporarily, and Holliday proposes such groupings as a more appropriate arena for research than traditional, reductionist views of cultural groups. This would seem to be particularly relevant to the complex realities of individuals in non-institutional language-learning settings, such as immigrants (although Holliday's conceptualisation necessarily forces us to re-think notions of 'cultures' in the classroom too). McGroarty (1998) warns against the snapshot tendency of classroom research to focus on short spans of time (a lesson, a semester), and advocates attention to learner biographies, which would seem to be especially important in non-classroom and informal settings where acquisition takes place. Indeed, it is hard to see how a decontextualised, abstract view of SLA can contribute much to the real-world concerns of understanding the deluge of cultural and social challenges faced by the immigrant in non-institutional settings. Anyone who has lived in a foreign country and struggled with its language and culture outside of a formal classroom knows too well what the real issues are in relation to coping with and mastering L2.

4.7 Competing and converging metaphors in the study of SLA

4.7.1 Associative approaches to learning

In recent years, the metaphor of 'deep structure', meant to capture the concept of internalised rules, facilitated by the human predisposition to acquire languages, with its concomitant metaphor of the 'language acquisition device' (Chomsky 1965; McNeill 1966) has been challenged as a model for SLA. The fundamental problem with the notions of deep structure and a language acquisition device is that they are invisible and virtually irrefutable. They do not really 'explain' or 'account for' anything, since they simply remove the problem to a more obscure level of investigation. In a way, the domain of debate is rather like the apocryphal medieval Christian theological debates over how many angels could sit on the head of a pin: the whole debate is meaningless unless you can first demonstrate that angels exist. One of the benefits that N. Ellis and Schmidt see in the sort of controlled laboratory experiment that they report in their 1997 paper is that observing the unfolding learning process can be supported by more probabilistic or associative models of acquisition, rather than symbolic, rule-based models. The basis of such associative models, often discussed within the general metaphorical construct of 'connectionism', is the idea that important information about language can be extracted from 'probabilistic patterns of grammatical and morphological regularities' (*ibid.*). The mind makes connections among multiple nodes of processed information; the more connections, the stronger the trace in acquisition. The concept of rule or exception or constraint is not essential to such a theory. In Chapter 5 we shall see that recent developments in corpus-based grammars also depend on probabilistic models; the possibilities of combining the external evidence of corpora with the internal evidence derived from cognitively oriented probabilistic models of acquisition offer an immense potential for integrating two sometimes supposedly opposite approaches to the study of language that has hardly been explored.

But connectionist approaches do not only help to explain emergent approximations to target behaviour. Important work by Shirai (1992) suggests that connectionism can illuminate cross-linguistic transfer, bringing us back to one of our stubborn issues noted above in section 3.2. If SLA is not rule-based or driven by principles of universal grammar, then doubt is cast on notions such as a 'natural order', and the kinds of connections made between L1 and L2 and the ways in which learners use cross-linguistic information may be a more fruitful line of investigation to explain learning difficulties. Shirai (*ibid.*) argues that connectionism poses new questions and revives old ones about language transfer. Unlike the old behaviourism, connectionism is interested in cognitive processes, not just responses to stimuli, in the same way that N. Ellis and Schmidt (1997) argue for its usefulness in observing emergent acquisition. The nodes that 'fire' in the brain are stimulated by a variety of external phenomena, and repeated firings create stronger connections, which constitute learning. Shirai gives the examples of how a conversational setting might display different semantic content, different interlocutors, different cognitive pressures of the moment, etc., all sparking off different activations.[7] When new languages are encountered, the existing representations of L1 are activated and reshape L2 incoming information. In language transfer, complex factors interact, including language distance (see section 2.3), cognitive load, attention, sociolinguistic factors, etc. Lexical transfer is likely to be strong, since associations of words and meanings across languages are likely to be strong, with repeated activation of appropriate nodes. Grammatical information may involve somewhat different kinds of connections across languages. The connectionist approach also considers the learning environment, and how such things as input-impoverished environments are likely to fire translation-type associations, with a more likely occurrence of transfer errors. Connectionism might also help account for difficulties in acquiring languages resulting from age: the most salient problem is usually that of pronunciation, where a connectionist approach would account for increasing difficulties experienced by older learners in terms of robust connections in the L1, strengthened by the passage of time.[8]

Connectionism is no mere dustbin for uncomfortable facts of language learner behaviour. As we stated in section 4.4, the simple comparison of two languages was never likely to be enough to explain errors in perform-ance and difficulties in learning, and connectionism offers the potential of a multiple perspective necessary for examining the complexity of transfer phenomena without recourse to the notion of rule-governed behaviour. Shirai (1992) notes that a large database would be necessary to investigate fully learner transfer from a connectionist viewpoint, and, once again, the probability built into the model would seem to lend itself to a learner-corpus-based approach, where multiple aspects of contextual variability could be studied. Connectionism certainly has much to gain from a fundamental view of language as a social phenomenon, with its leanings towards contextual variation, real-time processes of production and com-prehension and its preference for patterning over rule. Above all, it offers a rapprochement between learners, learning and the social and cognitive contexts in which acquisition unfolds, rather than just seeing the lan-guage learner as a vessel for the internalisation of deterministic rules, with the success of input being measured solely in terms of output.

4.7.2 Socio-cultural approaches

One of the most intractable metaphors that SLA investigators work with is that of 'the mind'. We all know we have one, but what is it? How is it constituted? Is it synonymous with the neurological activity of the physi-cal brain, which our present-day inadequate scientific knowledge has not yet apprehended? Is it something more, that embraces slippery concepts such as 'free will', 'creativity', 'motivation' and 'intention'? Is it an internal 'empty vessel' soaking up external stimuli like a sponge? Is it internal, but in some way genetically 'primed' to make sense of particular kinds of sensory input (e.g. human language)? How one constructs the mind clearly has a direct bearing on one's theory of second language acquisition and one's approach to researching it. McLaughlin (1990) has this to the fore in his critique of the notion of 'conscious' versus 'unconscious' learning, arguing that without an adequate theory of mind, statements about whether mental states are conscious or unconscious have no scientific validity.

Well-entrenched views of second language acquisition, implicitly or explicitly, are often based on the notion of the mind as an individual organism that receives input, processes it and then outputs communication reflective of its own changed state. This is basically an internalist, somewhat Cartesian account of the human mind. In this view of the mind, processing happens 'inside the head'. However, within philosophy, externalist views of the human mind, where the mind is seen as inseparably linked with the environments within which it acts, are promoted with equally convincing evidence (e.g. Rowland, 1999). The internalist metaphor may be argued to underlie a modelling of second language acquisition such as that espoused by Krashen (1981; 1982), which, in its day, enjoyed considerable acclaim (including national promulgation in Great Britain via an edition of the BBC TV populist *Horizon* documentary programme in the mid-1980s), and echoes of which are still apparent in the design of many SLA investigations. Krashen claimed that language was acquired by the acquirer 'receiving "comprehensible input"' (1985:2). Already the notion that meaning resides in something 'received' by the learner precludes much of what a socially oriented theory of meaning would wish to foreground (for example that all meaning is constructed interactively rather than 'received'). This comprehensible input depends for its comprehensibility on being just beyond the learner's current competence (the so-called $i + 1$ model, where i is where the learner is in terms of knowledge of rules, and $+ 1$ is the next stage of acquisition for which the learners is poised). The outcome of receiving comprehensible input is change of state to the next rule or stage of acquisition the learner is ready for, as determined by natural orders of universal grammar. Because this movement from one stage of acquisition to another is both individual and pre-determined by natural orders, the cultural context in which it occurs and the unfolding of its occurrence is largely irrelevant to the theory.

The inherent mental determinism of such a position inevitably led

Krashen and his followers to be suspicious of the value of conscious attention to learning and of pedagogical intervention that in any way strayed beyond the bounds of simply providing comprehensible input. Widdowson (1990), however, takes a different view, and sees language pedagogy as precisely circumventing any supposed 'natural' acquisition; for him, 'the whole point of language pedagogy is that it is a way of short-circuiting the slow process of natural discovery and can make arrangements for learning to happen more easily and more efficiently than it does in "natural surroundings"' (p. 162).[9] Pre-empting such criticism, the dichotomy of 'learning' versus 'acquisition' was set up as a necessary component of the Krashen theory, but only because the theory constructed the mind in the way it did (see the reference to McLaughlin's arguments earlier in this section). There would seem to be no absolute or logical reason why a learning-acquisition distinction has to be made in a theory with a different construction of 'mind' and a different starting point as to the nature of language. A social-semiotic theory of acquisition such as Halliday's, for example (on Halliday's approach to language in general, see section 3.3.2), needs no such distinction to explain the relationship between voluntary action, attention to form, etc., and the emergence of adult-like functions of language in first-language acquisition (Halliday 1974). In Halliday's model, the need to communicate comes as much from the child as from outside agents, and the child's own voluntary language and attention to meaning is as concerned with achieving 'comprehensible input' for the world around him/her, as is the input provided by the adults who care for him/her, and both are only achievable in dyadic interaction.

Krashen's model essentially cast the language learner as 'a loner who possesses a Language Acquisition Device (LAD) that does all the acquiring for the individual' (Dunn and Lantolf 1998:423). It is true that later versions of the input-output metaphor that was the foundation of Krashen's theory admitted voluntary action on the part of the learner in the form of 'negotiation of meaning' (which embraced actions such as comprehension checks, clarification questions, etc.) (e.g. see Long 1983). However, such views of meaning are somewhat simplistic, and ignore the fact that meaning is a constantly negotiable and negotiated aspect of real discourse, as we shall explore in Chapter 5. The notion of local negotiation by means of checks, clarification requests, etc. (see also Pica 1988), is simply a short-cut, emergency procedure for problem-solving in the continuous process of negotiation that drives all linguistic interaction. The way the notion of negotiation has been classically interpreted in SLA studies manages conveniently to keep intact some underlying allegiance to a notion of 'meaning-as-input' via some kind of conduit, that occasionally gets clogged, like a kitchen drain.

Not all approaches to SLA view the mind as a 'black box' within the head, and, as has been noted with regard to Halliday's model of first-language acquisition, a distinction between conscious action (whether linguistic or non-linguistic) and language development is by no means a pre-requisite of a theory of acquisition. Recently, perspectives drawing strength from the works of Vygotsky have offered a radical departure from the metaphor of the learner as 'lone receptor', and are based on quite a different notion of 'mind'. So different is a Vygotskian approach that two of its proponents have argued that it is profoundly 'incommensurable' (i.e. incompatible) with Krashen's theory (Dunn and Lantolf 1998). The Vygotskian approach rests on two central notions that distinguish it sharply from conventional approaches to SLA: mind as socially constructed, and the notion of the 'zone of proximal development' (ZPD). If the mind is not 'in there' in the child's or second language learner's head, the only way we can understand mental development is by reconstructing the role of instruction and learning so that they are conceived of as activities that 'do not ride on the tail of development but instead blaze the trail for development to follow' (Dunn and Lantolf 1998:419). This would seem to be the very reverse of Krashen's view, where instruction serves the purpose of leading the learner to the next, predetermined stage of development.

In the Vygotskian paradigm, instructors (or peers) and their pupils interactively co-construct the arena for development; it is not predetermined and has no lock-step limits or ceiling. Thus any 'learning–acquisition' distinction necessitated by the separation of voluntary action and pre-determined outcomes is obviated. Learning and development are in unity in the ZPD. The ZPD is the distance between where the child is developmentally and what she or he might achieve in interaction with adults or more capable peers (Vygotsky 1978:86). Meaning is created in dialogue (including dialogue with the self) during goal-directed activities; it is not 'inside the head', as conceived in the 'conduit' metaphor of meaning. 'Mind' thus only has any reality in its social manifestations (such as planning, deciding, acting, etc.). Applied to language teaching contexts, the roles of teachers and learners are re-cast from inputters and lone receptors into a relationship of joint constructors of the territory in which meaning can be co-constructed in language the learner does not yet know (Artigal 1992).

For Vygotsky, the division between language as representing the individual psyche and language as a social phenomenon is broken down (see Emerson 1983 for further discussion). Thus in a Vygotskian view of SLA, what is relevant data also shifts: learners' own accounts of their learning are as valid as the researcher's observations, and both are data for interpretation, rather than 'findings'. Equally, learner–learner interaction data (for example while performing tasks) becomes important not just as a window on language competence, but in terms of how learners construct the task for themselves and harness it for their learning needs (see Brooks and Donato 1994).

Vygotskian approaches, firmly based on socio-cultural theory (SCT), clearly marry better with socially oriented views of language as we have conceived them throughout this book, and are quite opposed to the abstract, rule-governed views we have reviewed. SCT, according to Lantolf and Pavlenko (1995: 116):

> ... erases the boundary between language learning and language using; it also moves individuals out of the Chomskian world of the idealized speaker-hearer and the experimental laboratory, and redeploys them in the world of everyday existence, including real classrooms.

Vygotskians gain nothing by looking at decontextualised sentences. Indeed, if the adherents of SCT within SLA might forge alliances with any other branch of applied linguistics, it would seem that corpus linguistics offers the best way forward, and notions of language as genre, with their emphasis on the inseparability of language choices, social activity, the construction of relationships and the pursuit of goals, would seem to link in most effectively. We shall explore further such links in Chapter 5.

4.8 Conclusion

This chapter has considered the emergence and growth of SLA within the framework of opposing views of language. That is not the same as a survey of SLA in its totality, nor does it claim to be. What I have tried to demonstrate in this chapter is that, even in SLA, which perhaps more than other sub-disciplines within applied linguistics often lays claim to be scientific, the paradigms within which researchers conduct their studies and debates are infused with quite opposite basic views of what constitutes relevant language data. Not to ask the question of what should constitute data for understanding SLA, and not to refer that question to basic ideological issues of what language is and what the object of study of linguistics should be sits badly with our notions of bi-directional accountability to theory and practice that we outlined in Chapter 1.

A complete theory of SLA of course embraces more than this one chapter can hope to achieve. Issues not directly addressed in this chapter also play a major role in how SLA theories are shaped and changed, such as immersion-learning (e.g. Cohen and Swain 1976; Cummins and Swain 1986; Genesee 1987; Swain and Lapkin 1990), content-based language instruction (Mohan 1985), the study of bilingualism and multilingualism (e.g. Cummins 1991; Schreuder and Weltens 1993), the understanding of real-world cognitively demanding abilities such as competence in translation and interpretation (Schweda and Nicholson 1995), and the effectiveness or otherwise of methods of testing and assessment in relation to what they can tell us about SLA. This last issue is by no means a simple matter of efficient and objective metrics: social and cultural factors and the ideological aspects of testing contexts raise very fundamental questions about the use of testing as a measure of second language acquisition (Shohamy 1997; Larsen-Freeman 1997:90), and alternative methods of testing may fit better with socio-culturally oriented approaches to SLA (see Hamayan 1995 for an interesting discussion). What is more, a complete theory of SLA would need to account not only for language acquisition but also for language *loss*, as perceived by those who do not use their L1 or L2 for a long time (including myself, whose once-fluent Swedish is, to say the least, 'rusty' from lack of use for 19 years). Although an under-researched area, what studies are available suggest that less is lost than users might think. While immediate availability of language items may suffer, language can be revived by short periods of immersion, and language users develop strategies for counteracting loss. Somewhere in memory, the items and structures are still stored, but social need does not call upon them. Such findings, as with most findings, can be interpreted in different ways. If things are still there 'somewhere' in memory, then perhaps rule-oriented, universal grammar models are right, but if they shrink through lack of use, equally this could be seen as evidence for the socially driven view of acquisition (we 'unlearn' what we don't need), or for associative models of language (neural nodes not 'fired' regularly lose the strength of their network connections). But that language loss is an important area of applied linguistic study should not be doubted, as de Bot and Weltens (1995) demonstrate: there are implications not only for language pedagogy but for broader issues of language planning too.

SLA is, therefore, a complex discourse in which different voices play out their parts. Differing views of language project differing views of learners, whether as information processors whose development can be picked to pieces and examined in experimental settings, or as whole beings acting in social settings with a consequent demand on holistic methods of observation. It is the epitome of applied linguistics as a catholic discipline, in which opposing paradigms co-exist in continuous dialogue: as long as we are prepared to let 'all the flowers bloom', in Lantolf's most memorable (1996) image of the field, the kind of dynamic applied linguistics we are promoting in this book will continue to flourish. In the next chapter, we look at the notion of language as discourse, and more closely at spoken and written differences, and how these have shaped the activities of applied linguists.

Notes

1 Indeed, one wonders whether much has changed since Tarone *et al.*'s (1976) admonitions concerning the shortcomings of SLA research and the resultant lack of direct applicability in teaching. Many recent SLA studies still lack the kinds of focus that Tarone *et al.* rightly highlighted as crucial to a proper understanding of acquisition.

2 The front-matter of antiquarian language-learning textbooks include claims to provide: 'a most plain and easie way of examining the accidence and grammar by questions and answers arising directly out of the words of the rules: whereby all schollers may attain most speedily to the perfect learning, full understanding, and right use thereof, for their happy proceeding in the Latine tongue: gathered purposely for the benefit of schools and for the use and delight of masters and schollers' (Brinsley 1647); 'a plain introduction into the rules of syntax ... very much facilitating the translating English into Latine, to the great ease of both master in teaching and scholar in learning' (Huish 1663); 'some improvements to the art of teaching, especially in the first grounding of a young scholar in grammar-learning: shewing a short, sure, and easy way to bring a scholar to variety and elegancy in writing Latin' (Walker 1717); 'a short, but clear and sure direction for the true pronunciation, accentuation and compleat acquisition of the English tongue' (Arnold 1718); 'an attempt to make the learning of Hebrew easy' (Bate 1756), etc.

3 In the 1960s the audio-lingual method came under attack from Ausubel (1964), who criticised its lack of attention to meaning, and for its simplistic notion of cross-linguistic interference.

4 The British-based *English Language Teaching* (Oxford University Press; better known by its later name *ELTJ*) had already appeared in 1946. *Studies in Second*

Language Acquisition first appeared in 1978 – an indication of how the field of SLA research was beginning to find its feet by this time.

5 See also Huebner (1985) and R. Ellis (1988) for studies purporting to show such regularities in acquisitional stages.

6 See the reference to Holliday's (1996) critique of the researcher in Chapter 6.

7 Shirai (whose L1 is Japanese) notes the interesting autobiographical example of his own proclivity to confuse the /l/ and /r/ sounds when under cognitive pressure to discuss difficult concepts, using English as his medium of teaching, even though he knows very well the difference in manner of articulation of the two phonemes, and can distinguish them perfectly well in other, more relaxed contexts (*ibid.*).

8 Though one should note that there is by no means universal agreement that older learners cannot acquire native-like pronunciation; see Bongaerts *et al.*'s (1997) study of Dutch learners of English, where some learners, especially those who had intensive training in the sound systems of English, were able to receive ratings on their English pronunciation comparable to native speakers. Anyone who has taught older learners knows that considerable variation in achievement occurs, just as in younger learners, and that it is dangerous to over-generalise on older people's ability to learn second languages. Wagner (1992) notes a distinct lack of research concerning older second language learners. The age question with regard to SLA and young learners is addressed in McLaughlin (1978). More recently, serious doubt has been cast on the whole 'critical age hypothesis' (i.e. that beyond a certain age, usually corresponding to puberty, language learning becomes more difficult) in an important survey of all the evidence by Marinova-Todd *et al.* (2000).

9 That teaching could or should follow the natural orders is by no means axiomatic to their (supposed) existence is also discussed in van Els *et al.* (1984:236–9).

5

Language as discourse: speech and writing in applied linguistics

5.1 Introduction

In the previous chapters, the discussion hovered around the dichotomy of language as an abstract system and language as socially embedded. That preoccupation will not be relinquished in this chapter, but the primary emphasis will be on the differences between language in its common written forms and language in everyday speech. However, in the history of applied linguistics, it is apparent that the influence of the written code and the predominance of abstract views of language have fed off one another, while those whose research focus has been speech have tended more towards socially oriented theories of language. This is inevitably a simplification of a complex picture; applied linguists such as Hoey (1983; 1991a) and Swales (1990), although working with written texts, have a socially and culturally embedded concept of language that is far removed from the abstractions of a Chomskian approach. Equally, as was illustrated in section 3.2, speech-act theory, and a good deal of what comes under the heading of 'pragmatics', although overtly committed to including the study of speech and language in use, have none the less displayed a fondness for invented data and abstracted language as the basis of discussion.

The importance of examining both written language and spoken language is three-fold. Firstly, it has implications for so-called 'skills' approaches to language teaching, in which the four primary skills (reading, speaking, writing and listening) are constructed around a written–spoken dichotomy. Secondly, the descriptive picture, in terms of lexis and grammar, changes considerably depending on the source of one's data, whether written or spoken. Thirdly, the units of acquisition, such as clauses and sentences, the 'rules' underlying them, for example word-order and complementation patterns, and the metalanguage used to talk about them, are also brought into question. As always, the relationship between these factors and how one 'does' applied linguistics is of great importance, for, as in any discipline, questions of data, hypotheses, methodology and interpretation are interlinked.

5.2 Speech and writing

It is generally agreed that there is no simple, one-dimensional difference between speech and writing (see the discussion of relevant factors in Hughes 1996:6–15). The most useful way to conceive of the differences is perhaps to see them as scales along which individual texts can be plotted. For example, casual conversation tends to be highly involved interpersonally (detachment or distancing oneself by one speaker or another is often seen as problematic). Public notices, on the other hand, tend to be detached, for example, stating regulations or giving warnings. *Tend* is the key word here: we have all experienced detached conversational partners and have deliberately distanced ourselves from difficult conversational situations. Equally we have all seen written notices such as *Don't even think of parking here!*, which seem oddly personalised and 'in your face', with an unusually high degree of author-involvement. Another feature that differentiates speech and writing might be the tendency to be explicit in formal written texts, while informal chat tends to be more implicit, leaving a lot unsaid. It is not uncommon, for instance, for conversational partners to pause and say *Still, you know, ...* and nothing more; such a remark will be easily processed by a listener meshed into the talk, but would be out of place in many written texts (except perhaps in a chatty letter or e-mail to a friend). What is more, speech is most typically created 'on the hoof' and received in real time. Writing is most typically created at one time and place and read at another time and place, and there is usually time for reflection and revision (exceptions would be rehearsed and pre-recorded speeches, and real-time e-mailing by two computers simultaneously on-line to each other). Textually, written discourses tend to display greater tightness and organisation or integration; talk can appear rather fragmented and disorganised, though this may be merely a perception of the researcher, and may not correspond at all to how participants experience a conversation. These and other possible scales enable us to plot the characteristics of different types of discourse as 'more or less' typically written or typically spoken. We might illustrate the process thus:

- ◆ typical chatty letter to a friend
- ☐ typical casual, intimate conversation
- ■ academic textbook

involved	detached
implicit	explicit
real time	lapsed time
fragmented	integrated

In this way we avoid over-simplified distinctions between speech and writing but still bring out key areas in which discourses may be differentiated. Understanding these differences is a useful step on the road to better organisation of skills-based language teaching, offering a window into the immense variety of discourse-types that exist in our complex societies. Scales like this have been used by linguists such as Chafe (1982) to capture the different possible modes of expression.

In a similar vein, Biber (1988 and 1995), using computational techniques, looks at how linguistic and contextual features cluster in different discourses, and also offers a delicate, variation-sensitive framework for plotting spoken and written differences. Biber's underlying hypothesis is based on the notion that linguistic features co-occur or cluster in texts because they serve a similar basic communicative function (1988: 101), and his analyses show that in written and spoken discourses of differing types (e.g. romantic fiction, spontaneous and prepared speeches, telephone conversations, personal and professional letters, etc.), the clusters of linguistic features are distributed differently. One of the most important applications of this work has been to show how certain English written styles have 'drifted' towards more oral characteristics over the course of several centuries (Biber and Finegan 1989).[1]

Such findings are of importance not merely to philologists; our assumptions about the relative roles of speaking and writing in our societies, and their consequent influence on priorities in language teaching may have to undergo considerable re-thinking in a world where oral styles and oral communication itself are increasingly taking over in global communication. In recent years, applied linguists have advanced critiques of a purely linguistic approach to explicating the differences between speech and writing, and have tried to locate them in a more relevant way both historically and socially. Stubbs (1980), for instance, rejects the Bloomfieldian structuralist tendency to see writing simply as parasitic on speech, and traces how writing has acquired a social and cultural identity of its own. Roberts and Street (1997), in a critique of approaches associated with figures such as Chafe, Tannen and Halliday,[2] argue that spoken–written differences can only properly be understood within the context of the status of literacy and oracy in societies. Thus linguistics accounts of speech and writing are challenged from applied linguistic bases.

Coming from a totally different angle from that of Biber, Fairclough (1995:167ff), working within critical discourse analysis (see section 5.4), has spoken of the 'conversationalisation' of political discourse over time. In short, we can by no means assume that the relationship between speech and writing in our society is a constant one, and language teaching may have to adjust itself to new realities. When I entered the language teaching profession in the 1960s, learner needs were often related to belletristic academic study or professional contexts such as secretarial work and high-powered business communication that was most often written, with oral skills added for good measure. I am not sure that that framework would still be as widespread globally as we step into the new Christian millennium.

The intermingling of styles, in which writing borrows from features normally associated with speech (e.g. e-mail discourse, 'user-friendly' information brochures, advertising copy, etc.), and in which the wider spread of literacy and job opportunity gives greater access to features associated with written styles (e.g. professional presentations, 'eloquent' speech, etc.) have led some to abandon a straight-down-the-middle view of speech versus writing as a model for pedagogy. McCarthy and Carter (1994: Ch.1) prefer to talk of *modes* of communication (which might be more or less speakerly or writerly), as distinguished from the *medium* of communication (which is either spoken or written). Such a view suggests a blending of the traditional four skills in language teaching, in which writing tasks might be very 'spoken' in their mode, and, vice-versa, where spoken tasks may explore a variety of different levels of detachment, planning, integration, etc. Also significant is Widdowson's (1984:81–94) re-positioning of the normal dichotomy of reading/writing versus speaking/listening in the four skills paradigm, focussing instead on the difference between being a reader and a *speaker*. Readers can allow themselves to be carried along by the text, or can challenge its cognitive schemes, while speakers have to enter a more negotiated process in real-time face-to-face talk. These acts of blurring or integrating the separate skills has direct implications for language teaching methodology, suggesting a breaking down of the compartmentalisation that often takes place in syllabuses and timetables.

5.3 Text and discourse

The terms *text* and *discourse* are often used interchangeably to refer to language 'beyond the sentence', that is to say the study of any utterance or sentence or set of utterances or sentences as part of a context of use. But equally a distinction is sometimes made between *texts* as products of language use (e.g. a public notice saying *Cycling forbidden*, or a novel, or an academic article, or indeed a transcript of a conversation), and *discourse* as the process of meaning-creation and interaction, whether in writing or in speech. A further complication is that the terms *text linguistics* and *discourse analysis* have, respectively, become strongly associated with the study of either written texts or spoken recordings or transcripts. Both approaches have made significant contributions to applied linguistics, and both go beyond the notion of language as abstract system to examine language in social contexts, that is to say attending to the producers and receivers of language as much as to the language forms themselves.

A long tradition of text linguistics has persisted in Northern Europe, beginning with attempts to account for how sentences are linked together using linguistic resources. Werlich's (1976) description of how linguistic features characterise strategies used in different text types (narrative, descriptive, expository and argumentative) was enormously influential among German teachers of English in the 1980s, and is a classic 'text grammar'. Likewise, the Prague school and its followers, among whom was Michael Halliday, focussed on how the construction of individual sentences in terms of their theme (their starting point or topic) and rheme (what was being said about that topic) contributed to the larger patterns of information in extended texts (see Fries 1983; Eiler 1986; Francis 1989; Firbas 1992). Thus in the sentence *Werlich was enormously influential among German EFL teachers*, the theme (or starting point – usually the grammatical subject) is *Werlich*, and the rheme is what is said about him (that he was influential). Different ways in which themes can be repeated over a number of sentences, or ways in which the rheme of one sentence can become the theme of the next, are among the preoccupations of the Prague school linguists, and they represent a major strand of functional (as defined in Halliday 1997: 16[3]) approaches to text.

The school of text linguistics associated with Northern European scholars such as de Beaugrande and Dressler (1981) and van Dijk (1972; 1980) addresses questions concerning the cognitive processing of extended written texts, which has influenced views of reading, along with schema theory (Rumelhart 1977), and applied linguists have not been slow to see the relevance of such studies for the more effective fostering of reading skills (Carrell 1983). If we take the following opening lines of a short British women's magazine text, for example, certain features of the reader's real-world-knowledge have to be activated if we are to make sense of the text:

> Supermarkets are on a mission to change the way we think
> about – and buy – skincare products. They're stocking the
> shelves with more of their own-label products than ever before.
> Sainsbury's, Marks & Spencer and Waitrose have all launched
> new skincare ranges in the past two months.
> (B: November 1998: 110.)

Firstly we need to activate a necessary schema (or mental representation) of how British supermarkets operate, with their 'own brands' (i.e. products displaying the supermarket's own name as manufacturer) often enjoying a less glamorous status than national and international designer-brand products. We also have to infer (if we do not know it) that Sainsbury's, Marks & Spencer and Waitrose are all names of supermarkets, rather than designer-brand manufacturers, since this is not stated explicitly. Then there is the meaning of we, again, not explicit, but dependent on how the reader interprets it (The readership of the magazine? All British women? Those who shop at those supermarkets? Anyone and everyone?). In all these questions, cognitive approaches to text analysis emphasise what readers bring to the text: the text is not a container full of meaning which the reader simply downloads. How sentences relate to one another and how the units of meaning combine to create a coherent extended text is the result of interaction between the reader's world and the text, with the reader making plausible interpretations.[4]

Similar approaches to text analysis may be found in the school of rhetorical structure analysis, where the emphasis is on how units of meaning relate to one another in a hierarchy, and how such rhetorical features as exemplification, summary, expansion, etc. build on core propositions to construct the complex artefact of the finished text (Mann and Thompson 1988). This approach owes much to the text linguistics of Grimes (1975) and Longacre (1983). Applications in reading pedagogy and in the study of writing have been envisioned for these approaches (see

O'Brien 1995 for an example of a study of student mother-tongue writing). Also influential amongst British applied linguists and language teachers has been the very practically oriented types of text analysis that originated in the work of Eugene Winter (Winter 1977; 1982), usually referred to as clause-relational analysis. Working with everyday written texts, disciples of Winter such as Hoey (1983) and Jordan (1984) have demonstrated how culturally common patterns such as the *situation* → *problem* → *response* → *evaluation* → *solution* sequence in texts is constructed by the reader in interaction with the logical relations between clauses within the text and by processing the overt lexical and grammatical signals of the pattern employed by the author.

Hoey's work, in particular, is a good example of an approach which sees texts as interactive arenas for the creation of meaning, in which sentences only have any status in relation to one another. The clause-relational school and the other cognitively oriented models discussed can be seen as attempts to break out of the sentence-internal view of language inherited from traditional models, with their origins either in intuition or in the study of written language alone. Cognitive text-linguistic models are necessarily subjective in their interpretations of meaning in texts, but subjectivity may not necessarily be a negative quality (see Reddick 1986 for a discussion), and the levels of inter-subjectivity that can be achieved by using groups of informants can often reveal remarkable consistency of interpretation. In attempting to re-construct the cognitive processes readers go through, they are seen as offering practical ways in which classroom methods can be adopted, such as pre-text activities in the reading class designed to activate background knowledge, or student analyses of their own texts as a step in process approaches to writing skills (for an extended survey of such applications of text linguistic methods, see Connor 1987).

Also influential in shifting perspectives away from sentence-internal preoccupations have been the studies of textual cohesion associated with Halliday and Hasan (Halliday and Hasan 1976; Hasan 1984, 1985), again overwhelmingly based on written texts, but with a strong social motivation (see the summary of Halliday's socially oriented view of language in section 3.3.2). The study of cohesion is concerned with surface linguistic ties in the text, rather than cognitive processes of interpretation, and thus its categories are grammatical and lexical ones. The categories include reference (e.g. how pronouns refer back and forth in texts to people and things in different sentences), substitution and ellipsis (how reduced grammatical forms such as co-ordinated clauses without subject-repetition can be none the less interpreted textually), conjunction (how the finite set of conjunctions such as *and, but, so,* etc. create relations between sentences), and lexical links across sentences (e.g. repetition, collocation). Hasan's work on cohesion, in particular, has an applied educational emphasis, using the framework of analysis to evaluate children's writing and to reflect on the relationship between linguistic links across sentences and textual coherence.

Thus have the various schools of text linguistics taken the study of language beyond the sentence and brought readers and writers to the fore, laying emphasis on the text as an intermediary between sender and receiver rather than as a detached object in which meaning is somehow 'stored'. Above all, these approaches see sentences as interacting with one another, and perceive no value in examining them in isolation; language has become discourse (i.e. an interaction between sender and receiver) rather than an abstract object.

5.4 Discourse analysis

Although Zelig Harris published a paper in the early 1950s entitled *Discourse Analysis* (Harris 1952), which was concerned with the distribution of linguistic elements in extended texts, and links between the text and its context, discourse analysis as a general approach to language and as an influential force in applied linguistics did not really emerge until the early 1970s, and since then has predominantly been associated with studies of the spoken language. In the 1960s, considerable interest was building up in the sociologically embedded study of language, with Hymes' work (Hymes 1964), springing from ethnography and anthropology as much as from linguistics, providing a grounding for a socially responsive modelling of spoken language. Also in the 1950s, Mitchell had published a seminal paper on the relationship between speech and the situation of utterance, including factors such as participant relationships and roles, and the physical settings in which talk occurred (Mitchell 1957). Discourse analysis emerged in this climate of growing interest in the process of meaning creation in real situations, where texts alone were insufficient evidence for the linguist, and settings, participants and goals of interaction came to the fore. It is this broader emphasis on settings and other non-linguistic features of interaction that sets discourse analysts apart from text linguists, although in recent years, with the emergence of genre analysis and critical discourse analysis, distinctions between (predominantly written) text analysis and (predominantly spoken) discourse analysis have blurred somewhat, and the situation at the time of writing is one of considerable cross-fertilisation between the two tendencies.

A very important and influential study of spoken discourse was that carried out by Sinclair and Coulthard (1975), who tape-recorded mother-tongue school classrooms and found recurring patterns of interaction between teachers and pupils. Teacher- and pupil-behaviour were both constituted and reinforced by the setting (generally large classes) and the institutional roles. These roles were typically marked by the teacher as knower and source of input, as evaluator of pupil response and as controller of topics and the divisions of the lesson itself, with the pupils as receptors and respondents, communicating with the teacher, not their peers. The goals of the interaction were primarily the transmission of knowledge through question and answer sessions or through controlled discussion, the display of key knowledge and the testing of its reception. All this was reflected in structural features, in the sense that regular configurations recurred in predictable contexts and sequences. For instance, *teacher–question → pupil–answer → teacher–feedback* occurred repeatedly as a sequence, while other possible configurations were proscribed, for example an evaluating utterance by a pupil aimed at a teacher's utterance.

Sinclair and Coulthard's analysis also underscored basic communicative functions of teacher–pupil talk in the traditional, teacher-fronted classroom, such as the teacher asking questions to which she or he already knew the answer, or the teacher withholding feedback until the desired correct answer was proffered. Many second language teachers will recognise their own instinctive behaviour here when faced with a large group of learners cramming for an exam, or when resources militate against more imaginative dispositions of the classroom space. Sinclair and Coulthard's work clearly struck direct chords with those of us active in language teaching in the late 1970s and early 1980s, and their work played an important role in underwriting the communicative revolution of the 70s and 80s. Their model for the interaction between teachers and pupils was a structural one, built upon a hierarchy, or rank scale, with smaller units of interaction such as *moves* (a 'move' could be, for example, a teacher question, or a pupil answer) combining to form *exchanges* (most typically completed sets of *question–answer–feedback* moves). Exchanges in turn combined to form larger units within the lesson, termed *transactions*, to reflect their goal of transmitting key chunks of knowledge to the pupils.

Very soon, the Sinclair-Coulthard model was extended into the world outside the classroom (e.g. Hoey 1991b; Francis and Hunston 1992), and since its early days it has enjoyed continuous attention by those interested in analysing second language classrooms. Second language classroom studies have further extended the model, including a notable attempt to interpret teacher-pupil interaction patterns within a Vygotskian perspective (see section 4.7.2) of supportive learning (Jarvis and Robinson 1997), applicability of the model to student interaction in group-work (Hancock 1997), and the use of the model to analyse student-computer interaction in computer-assisted language learning (CALL) sessions (Chapelle 1990). In direct applications in language teaching materials, one can often see the Sinclair-Coulthard basic notion of the exchange, with its three parts of *Initiation → Response → Follow-up* reflected in very practical illustrations for learners, of real day-to-day contexts in which such exchanges might occur, as in this text book for learners of Burmese, where following up after a reply is practised:

S1:	ဒါ ဘာလဲ။	What ⟨is⟩ that?	Da ba-lèh?
S2:	ဒါ ပြတိုက်ပါ။	That's a museum.	Da pyá-daiq-pa.
S1:	အော်။ ဘာပြတိုက်လဲ။	Oh. What museum [is it]?	Aw. Ba-pyá-daiq-lèh?
S2:	ဗိုလ်ချုပ်ပြတိုက်ပါ။	[It's the] Bogyoke Museum.	Bo-jouq Pyá-daiq-pa.
S1:	ဗိုလ်ချုပ်ပြတိုက်။	The Bogyoke Museum.	Bo-jouq Pyá-daiq.

Figure 11: (From Okell 1994: 21)

Sinclair and Coulthard's work above all showed that it was possible to jettison the sentence but still to retain the notion of language structure, within a socially motivated linguistics. Their data was, admittedly, relatively well-ordered and tightly constrained by the classroom setting, but even those who have taken the Sinclair-Coulthard model out into the real, messy world of casual conversation have found that the core structural elements of moves and exchanges remain robust, albeit configured in more complex and chained sequences than those found in the classroom (see especially Hoey's 1991b study). However, within a short time of the publication of Sinclair and Coulthard's influential model, Politzer (1980) was suggesting that its 'objectivity' (in the sense of sequential, structural analysis) was inadequate to the task of properly describing classroom interaction, and that a more sociolinguistics-inspired approach was required.

5.5 Conversation analysis

The Sinclair-Coulthard model was concerned with apprehending the structure of spoken language beyond the sentence, but there are other ways of looking at talk that focus more on the local aspects of interaction, and the joint efforts that participants put into conversation to make it work. In its institutionalised and rather ritualised context of the classroom, the talk that Sinclair and Coulthard examined appeared to progress steadily and relatively smoothly: teachers knew more or less what they wanted to say, and pupils were constrained to respond only in ways permitted by the teacher–pupil relationship. Casual and spontaneous talk between equals does not seem to occur in the same way. It appears, on the face of it, to be a rather precarious exercise, wandering first this way and then that, subject to interruptions, diversions, competition between participants for the floor or control of topics, indeterminate in its duration, unpredictable in its outcomes. Krauss *et al.* (1995) make a comparison between talking and walking: walking appears to flow fluently; in scientific fact it is 'a kind of co-ordinated lurching' (p. 124), with constant 'mid-course corrections' (*ibid.*). This is even more remarkable in everyday conversation, where the real-time adjustments made are in terms of 'the interdependent social behaviour of two or more people' (p. 125). Talk, therefore, is an achievement rather than a pre-ordained object that simply spills out, and it is this sense of work towards that achievement that conversation analysts try to capture.

Conversation analysis (CA) is mainly (but certainly not exclusively) associated with American sociolinguists and sociologists of language. Good illustrations of the approach can be found in the works of figures such as Schegloff and Sacks (1973), who look at how participants close down conversations, Sacks *et al.* (1974), who study turn-taking in talk and how it is smoothly achieved, Pomerantz (1984) on the way participants agree and disagree locally, and in the many studies of oral narratives that have developed within the sociolinguistic and CA perspectives (Labov 1972; Jefferson 1978; Polanyi 1981). There are also more general works and collections of papers covering the field and its methods (Atkinson and Heritage 1984; Boden and Zimmerman 1991; Pomerantz and Fehr 1997). Conversation analysts study local events in detail, for example, how pairs of adjacent utterances constrain each other (adjacency pairs), how speakers use discourse markers to signal interactive features (Schiffrin 1987), how they sum up the gist of the conversation at regular intervals using 'formulations' (Heritage and Watson 1979), and so on. Transcription is very narrow, indicating as many aspects as possible of the way talk emerges, including speaker-overlaps, stutters and re-cast words, changes in loudness, drawled syllables (typically indicated by colons), pauses, laughter, sighs, non-verbal vocalisations, '*ohs* and *uhms*', etc. Conventional punctuation such as commas, full stops and underlining indicates not sentence features but intonational features. An example taken from Drew (1984) will illustrate a typical CA transcript. A complete description of the transcription system is given in Atkinson and Heritage (1984:ix–xvi):

```
E:  ... and I had to have my foot up on a pillow
    for two days, youknow ┌and- hhhmhh
N:                        └Yah?
E:  But honey it's gonna be alright I'm sure,
N:  Oh I'm sure it's gonna be alri:ght,
E: Yeuh,
→N: Oh:: do:ggone. I ┌thought maybe we could┐
→E:                  └I'd  l i k e  to  get  ┘some
    little slippers but uh,
```

Conversation analysts prefer to work with individual conversations analysed in depth rather than multiple conversations analysed more quantitatively (which a corpus linguist might do: see section 6.3). In this latter respect, one might hesitate to envisage easy, straightforward applications of CA in language pedagogy, since the generalisability of such analyses is not always apparent. The fact that features such as turn-taking are achieved locally in individual, unique conversations on the one hand, but that general principles or 'rules' of turn-taking are, on the other hand, so general, commonsensical and obvious (e.g. that normally only one speaker speaks at a time, that speakers may nominate the next speaker, etc.), might be seen as a weakness of CA. But others have seen its techniques as a strength, enabling the linguist to get new perspectives on things taken for granted, and indeed offering convincing applications to language teaching problems. An exemplary study of this last kind is Aston's (1995) investigation of the use of *thank you* in service encounters in English. Many English language teachers will recognise themselves in the classroom vainly attempting to square the desire to teach typical service encounter features such as requesting goods and services and the various *pleases* and *thank yous* that punctuate such events in the typical Anglo-American context. Often students protest that such florid and gushing behaviour is unnecessary and something that sticks in their craw when asked to perform in a target-language fashion. What Aston's study shows, with its careful attention to placement and sequencing of *thank you* in service encounters is the important way in which *thank you* marks the phases of the encounter for the participants, that it is far from being a decorative token or a badge of obsequiousness. A better understanding for the teacher, resulting from meticulous analysis of language features such as *thank you*, is the first step on the road to better ways of dealing with them in class, and more satisfying explanations for learners uneasy with their conventional conceptualisations. In the context of mother-tongue usage, too, CA studies can help to remove prejudices about spoken language, for instance that use of markers such as *like, you know, sort of* and *see* are evidence of sloppy conversational habits (see Watts 1989 for an excellent study and discussion). Not only can such items usually be shown to be part of the regular vocabulary of even the most educated of speakers, but studying their placement and role in talk in the fine detail of a CA approach can often show that they are far from superfluous, fulfilling important functions like projecting and checking the state of shared knowledge and softening what might otherwise be too blunt and possibly threatening to the listener.

The significance of the emergence of discourse analysis and CA for our overall discussion of approaches to language in this book is that both schools showed that it was possible to incorporate social dimensions into language study, and to account for the creation of meaning without reference to syntactic rules, sentences, and elusive qualities such as 'deep structure'. Additionally, both schools worked with a terminology that was largely independent of that elaborated over the centuries for the study of written language, and it is this latter point that is most immediately relevant for the present chapter. With a ready-to-hand metalanguage for talking about spoken language, the stage was set for a more principled approach to curricular targets such as 'speaking skills' and 'oral proficiency', and applied linguists began to publish books and papers exploring the possibilities of translating discourse analysis and CA into pedagogical guidelines, teaching materials and practical classroom tasks (e.g. Bygate 1987; Cook 1989; McCarthy 1991a; Hatch 1992). Richards (1980), in an early example of taking on board insights from CA, stresses the importance of 'strategies of conversational interaction' (p. 431) in the development of conversational competence, and refers to CA studies to back up his arguments. Soon more specific areas of language teaching activity began to come under scrutiny using CA as a means of evaluation. Van Lier (1989) is one such study which takes to pieces the oral proficiency interview and draws on CA insights to answer the question of whether or not conversation should serve as an appropriate model for oral assessment. More recently, some scholars have detected a major shift in approaches to communicative teaching, and a growing orientation toward the bottom-up content of communicative competence, with discourse and conversation analysis playing a central role in the re-thinking of what teaching input should be (Celce-Murcia *et al.* 1997).

5.6 Discourse grammars

The move away from the sentence as the unit of linguistic investigation by text grammarians and discourse and conversation analysts had profound effects on the study of grammar. Linguists began to question not only the validity of many of the rules sentence grammarians elaborated, but the very meanings of grammatical forms, so long taken for granted, were now up for re-interpretation. Semantic meaning (in the sense of inherent qualities of grammatical configurations, for example that in English the *-ed* forms of verbs denotes pastness) came to be seen as inadequate for the description of meaning-in-interaction, both in written texts and in spoken. Items occurring in texts seemed to have meanings in context that extended greatly the 'core semantic' meaning, or which even contradicted or obscured those core meanings. For example, in a British service encounter such as leaving clothes to be cleaned, or films to be processed, a customer might well be asked *What was the name?*, where any meaning of 'pastness' is almost irrelevant to an account of the use of *was*, and the only sensible statement of 'meaning' is one which foregrounds institutional politeness and service conventions. It is this type of concern which discourse grammars address, building descriptions which attempt to incorporate language users, textual cohesion and coherence, and relevant features of context to explain usage.

In the field of written text, discourse grammar is epitomised in the work of Waugh (1991), who looks at the French *passé simple* ('simple past' or preterite) form. Waugh shows convincingly that the key to the meaning of the form rests in an investigation of its distribution in real discourse. When the form is scrutinised in its contexts of occurrence (e.g. novels, newspaper articles), pragmatic, textual, modal, discourse, expressive and referential meanings of the *passé simple* are all relevant and, Waugh concludes: 'None of these should be disregarded nor treated as derivative' (p. 241). One of the central points, she asserts, is the notion of detachment in written texts: texts such as novels, stories, historical works, tales, legends, newspaper and magazine articles, etc. 'are addressed to whom it may concern' (p. 243). It is this factor rather than the pastness of events *per se* which determines the use of the interpersonally detached *passé simple* form; in conversation, the same events would normally be expressed with the 'involving' present perfect tense form.

A similar, English example of written discourse-grammar is Zydattiss' (1986) study of 'hot news' texts, in which the typical textual pattern of initial scene-setting with the present perfect tense (which grabs the reader's attention) is followed by the details of the hot-news event, which are normally in past tense. McCarthy (1998: Chapter 5) shows how initial scene-setting and following-detail devices in news reports and literary narratives are not confined to present perfect and past tense, but operate in the same way in future reference with pairs such as *be to* plus *will*, and in past habitual reference with *used to* and *would*.

These kinds of studies attempt to re-define the purview of grammatical description and view grammatical meaning as interactively determined, rather than being inherently 'in' the structure under scrutiny. It is clear that such a view of grammar is well out of kilter with an idealised, sentence-based, Chomskian approach to language description or a Krashen-type model of SLA where grammatical morphemes are cognitively acquired with abstract meanings. On the other hand, it is ideally placed to serve a Vygotskian, socio-culturally embedded view of language use and language acquisition (see section 4.7.2), although such links have not been drawn explicitly or explored in any great depth to date. Discourse grammarians do not deny that past tense forms can have the meaning of pastness; it is just that pastness is one of the possible senses that may be foregrounded at any point in discourse, just as other senses may be too. In looking at isolated sentences, however, it may be that a detached, *referential* meaning such as pastness might be the only plausible mental contextualisation, since no interpersonal evidence is available. It is only in context that a sentence such as *I wanted to talk to you* gains its meaning either as a report of a past-time state of affairs, or as a present-time indirect/polite request.

Spoken discourse grammars operate in a similar way to written ones, with senders and receivers, and strategies of planning and sequencing playing the same central roles as in written discourse-based approaches.

Hughes and McCarthy (1998) look at several examples of grammatical features that require a new perspective when examined in their actual contexts, both spoken and written. They use corpus evidence, but their approach goes beyond statements of statistical distribution of items (see the discussion of corpus linguistics in Chapter 6) to qualitative interpretations of grammatical relations based on evidence across a range of texts (just as Waugh did with her studies of the French past tense). Hughes and McCarthy find, for instance, that conventional paradigms for arranging items such as demonstratives and pronouns (for an example, see sections 1.5.1 and 3.3.2 of this book) often fail to capture the real strategic choices reflected in discourse. They take the trio *it*, *this* and *that* and show that speakers (see also McCarthy 1994a; 1998: Chapter 4.2) select among the three items for various types of focussing upon topic entities:

[Conversation between a medical adviser and a patient]

Adviser:	Okay. So the same pharmaco-dynamics is going on with every medicine you take virtually.
Patient:	Mm.
Adviser:	But no **that** really isn't a problem. Okay. You can sometimes in the first week find your, your complexion, your skin's a bit more spotty.
Patient:	[wails] Agh. Oh I don't want **that**.
Adviser:	**That**'s the only risk though.
Patient:	Just the for the first week?
Adviser:	Yeah, usually **it**'s not a long-term problem. Again **this** is, initially tends to be an early thing which will settle itself down.

(CANCODE data)

The point Hughes and McCarthy make is that the conventional paradigms such as those of the subject and object pronouns on the one hand (where *it* is typically contrasted with *he* and *she*), and the demonstratives on the other (where *this*/*that* are in contrast only with *these*/*those*) in effect separate what should be brought together, and that, at the discourse-grammar level, the relevant paradigm consists of *it*, *this*, and *that* in opposition. In a similar way, Carter and McCarthy (1995) show how, in everyday conversational speech-reporting, speakers have a choice between past simple reporting verbs (*X said that* ...; *X told Y that* ...) and past continuous ones (*X was saying that* ...; *X was telling Y that* ...) as alternative ways of framing reports of the same events, with the difference residing in the status of the reported item as either 'report' (past simple reporting verb) or 'topic opener' (past continuous reporting verb).

Even more fundamentally, conversation analysts and corpus linguists present evidence for a re-assessment of the sentence as a viable unit of grammatical description. Well-formed sentences are the exception rather than the norm in many kinds of everyday conversation (e.g. casual talk, some service encounters), and the clause emerges as a better candidate for the base unit of description (see Miller 1995), which was noted as being Halliday's position, in section 3.6. What is more, the units of grammar are often co-created by participants, such that an element of one speaker's turn may only be grammatically coherent when seen as a continuation of another speaker's utterance. One such (attested) example is:

[The speakers have just come back from a swim, and are feeling good about their efforts to do some exercise]
A: I can feel that it was a good thing
B: ⌞To have done
A: Yeah
B: Mm

B's 'perfect infinitive' *to have done* only makes sense as a 'post-modifier' to A's nominal *a good thing*; the whole noun phrase is therefore an interactively created unit, not something constructed in isolation in the first speaker's head, even though that was clearly his meaning, as evinced by the *yeah* that follows. Speaker A need not have continued after *thing*; his utterance was perfectly 'well-formed' as it was, but it becomes a different, and equally well-formed utterance when B adds her piece. Similarly, Tao and McCarthy (in press) found that non-restrictive *which*-clauses could be added to a first speaker's utterance by a second speaker, as in the following example:

[Speakers are planning a family holiday, and discussing train and ferry times]
<speaker 1> It leaves, it gets in at ... I'm sure I said the night crossing
<speaker 2> You said 12 till 10
<speaker 1> No that's coming back 12 o'clock coming home midday but that one the one going out it gets in at 7 in the morning
<speaker 3> **Which is fine isn't it**
(CANCODE data)

Examples such as this one illustrate grammar as joint-construction, rather than just an encoding by one speaker and a decoding by another, and one is reminded of Farr and Rommetveit's (1995:265) admonition that 'when expression is ... equated with "encoding" and impression with "decoding" ... one has bought the language of the telecommunication engineer and one ends up with a totally artificial system of communication'. In their view, grammar would partake in that 'commonality' that is the hallmark of the discourse process, and 'commonality is established when two persons construct a temporarily shared world by engaging in dialogue' (*ibid.*: 271). The shared world is as much expressed in grammar as it is in lexical selection, and co-construction is one of its key manifestations.

Beyond-the-sentence investigations of grammatical choices suggest that discourse grammars do more than just add 'bolt-on-extras' to existing sentence grammars, and precipitate a complete re-assessment of how grammars are written, especially spoken ones. In the pedagogical domain, observations of real spoken data also underscore the need to re-evaluate many of the taken-for-granted rules as presented in course books and reference books. Kesner Bland (1988), for example, looks at progressive tense forms used with static verbs in attested utterances such as *I'm hating this weather* and *I'm really loving it*, forms which would normally be 'forbidden' in most text books and course books. Kesner Bland concludes that the existence of such forms in everyday conversation, and the useful communicative functions they perform, 'force us to reassess constantly the relationship between the grammar book and the language students are apt to encounter' (p. 67).

Celce-Murcia (1991) sees value in a discourse-based approach to grammar as stemming from a study of learners' communicative needs and the assembly of a corpus of material relevant to those needs; after these stages, and only then, should the decision be taken as to the most useful grammar to be taught. The teaching of the grammar then proceeds on the basis of the relevant discourse contexts and the texts that belong to them. Celce-Murcia shares with Larsen-Freeman (1991) a firm conviction that focussing on grammatical form without looking at its functional meanings in discourse paints only an impoverished picture of language for learners and fails to unite grammar with its uses in interaction. Grammatical errors too have been re-assessed from a discourse-grammar point of view: Zalewski (1993) argues that even apparently 'local' errors in L2 English such as wrong inflections of person and number can have global effects on comprehensibility in text, owing to the discourse-cohesive role such morphemes can often play.

Thus, discourse grammars force us to re-assess our pedagogy, in both the written and spoken media, while the latter, the spoken grammar, has yet to be fully articulated for a language such as English. Furthermore, the very metalanguage for talking about grammar can no longer be taken for granted. The example, noted above, of a choice in speech reporting between indirect reports with past simple (*X said that...*) and those with past continuous (*X was saying that...*) have no name in conventional grammars, and structural labels fail to capture the distinction between speech-oriented reports (past simple) and topic-oriented ones (past continuous). The problem is that there is no agreed metalanguage for talking about spoken grammars, and the applied linguistics profession, at the time of writing, still lacks one.[5] It is perhaps one of the most important tasks applied linguists face: to re-orientate our metalanguage so that our professional discourse reflects the changed landscape sketched out by exploratory studies of spoken grammar. As with everything else within our shared discourse, the effects of different perspectives on language, and the ways we talk about them, ultimately permeate our attitudes to teaching or whatever other applied domain our efforts occupy.

5.7 Language as genre

Much good research has been done on genres in more specialised varieties of written language (most notably Swales 1990; also Christie 1986; Reid 1987; Martin 1992). Most of this work emphasises the socially rooted nature of genres and their recognisability for participants within discourse communities. Swales in particular (*ibid.*) relates genres to the discourse communities that produce them (e.g. academics writing for one another and reporting their research, constructing and critiquing their discipline, etc.). But the fact that lay people, i.e. not expert linguists, can also label everyday written and spoken discourses with genre-names (e.g. a soap opera or documentary on television, or a joke-telling session) is clearly significant from the point of view of the recognisability of genres for participants themselves (see Walter 1988:6). You do not have to be a linguist to recognise a 'story' or 'an argument'. The degree to which genres are institutionalised is also an important factor, and is most obvious in highly regularised contexts such as academic writing, scientific and technical reports, literary genres such as the short story or the sonnet, and so on. Stubbs (1996:12) talks of the mutually defining nature of institutions and genres (though he alternates between 'genre' and 'text-type' to refer to typical modes of communication): as institutions evolve, so do the text-types that communicate their activities to those within and without the institution.

The question remains as to how we recognise the relevant linguistic features that typify different genres, how participants orient towards them and how they reveal their awareness of them. These questions are particularly salient in spoken language, where, apart from well-documented genres such as service encounters (Merritt 1976; Hasan 1985; Ventola 1987; Aston 1988a; Iacobucci 1990) and narratives (Labov 1972; Jefferson 1978; Polanyi 1981; Goodwin 1984), many of the everyday forms of talk we experience are still unclassified in generic terms. There have been a number of studies of *register*, i.e. the relationship between language features and their context of utterance (see Halliday 1978), many of which focus on formality and informality, interpersonal aspects of meaning, and spoken/written differences. Biber's (1988) seminal work on the distinguishing features of written and spoken texts and how significant language features cluster in different types of texts overlaps to a considerable extent with the study of genre. In his later work, Biber uses the term *register* for 'all aspects of variation in use' (Biber 1995:9), and his research covers aspects that are close to what in other research traditions is referred to as genre. Register studies contribute much to our understanding of the different factors that influence linguistic choice, but do not offer a clear model of what, for example, a personal narrative *is*, or how participants show their engagement in an activity such as joke-telling or having an argument.

5.8 Speech genres

The most notable early example of a study that pointed the way forward for describing spoken genres was Mitchell's (1957) observations of the language of trading at markets and shops in Cyrenaica (in what is present-day Libya). Mitchell was interested in how different features of the situation (the participants, their purposes, the setting, etc.) influenced the language that was used between vendors and purchasers so that there merged a recognisable, recurring form of discourse. Like later genre researchers such as Hasan (1985) and Ventola (1987), Mitchell identified *stages* in the service encounters he observed at first hand. Service encounters are interactions whose purpose is the transaction of goods, information and services, typically exemplified by conversations in shops, hotels, information bureaux, etc. Mitchell identified phases of the conversation, such as *salutation → enquiry as to the object of sale → investigation of the object of sale → bargaining → conclusion.* Within each phase, variation was possible (for example, influenced by different spatial conditions – open air market transactions displayed different patterns of interaction to those in closed markets).

Since Mitchell's day, the notion of spoken genre has been developed by various other linguists, including Hymes (1972), who describes genre as a higher-order feature of speech events. Hymes emphasises the dynamism of genres. Genre is something separate from the speech event itself: a genre *may* coincide with a speech event, but genres can also occur within speech events, and the same genre can show variation in different speech events. Since Hymes, debate has continued round the question of dynamism and variation in how genres are realised. Most linguists working in the area accept the notion of genre as norm-governed social activity that manifests linguistic and non-linguistic behaviour to varying degrees of institutionalisation. Coupland (1983) accepts this variability and offers the example of the difference between buying and selling something trivial like a stamp or a newspaper, and a large item of expenditure such as buying a holiday at a travel agency. Both are service encounters but the travel agents example is less likely to be ritualised or to follow a well-worn template, and is likely to offer more opportunites for interactional/relational talk (i.e. talk whose purpose is the establishment or reinforcing of social relations) alongside the transactional talk (i.e. the talk that gets the buying and selling business done). Bargiela-Chiappini and Harris (1995) make a similar argument in distinguishing between the more institutionalised participant roles in events such as service encounters compared with business meetings, where the interaction may be more fluid and prone to variation.

Ylänne-McEwen (1997) reveals in detail how transactional and relational features intermingle in service encounters (once again in the travel agency context) and shows persuasively that descriptions of genre that do not pay at least equal regard to the interactional/relational process as well as the transactional in typical encounters are inadequate. Similarly, Lindenfeld's (1990) account of small talk in urban French market places reveals that small talk does not occur randomly: vendors' small talk is directed mainly to utilitarian matters, while customers' small talk tends to focus on personal topics. Vendor and customer are both building and consolidating their social identities in the course of the conversation. Komter's (1991) study of job interviews also considers the small talk that typically occurs at the beginning of an interview as a significant phase in the interview process, and in an echo of Mitchell's (1957) original study, talks of the *phase structure* (p. 54) of the interview.

The building of personal relationships manifested in the discourse process have also been shown to be important in academic genres. Thompson (1997) studied university research presentations. She, too, stresses the work of building an appropriate relationship between speaker and audience and the participant roles as being an integral part of the oral research presentation genre. In such discourses, the presenter typically projects him or herself as 'the modest, self-deprecating expert' (p. 334) and engages in serious facework, that is to say attempts to protect him or herself *and* the listeners from threats to mutual esteem. Once again, studies such as Thompson's are important since they suggest that models of genre that consider relational elements (concerned with creating and consolidating social relations, in contrast to 'doing business') as secondary events which disturb the conventional flow of the transactional discourse are incomplete. Here I take the position that an approach to genre that pays equal attention to the relational elements is the most relevant kind of model for applications to the teaching of spoken language. Even learners with apparently strongly oriented transactional needs in spoken language usually also feel a desire to 'be themselves' and to relate in a human way to their interlocutors.

Some genre-type studies focus more on variability and mixing of activities. Duranti (1983) argues that the same genre can be realised in different ways according to the nature of the speech event, depending on who the speakers are, what their purposes are, etc. Walter (1988: 2–3), who investigates jury summations, also considers the setting in which speech occurs as an important variable. Fairclough (1995:167ff) underscores the way genres are sequenced and often intermixed. He takes broadcast political discourse as an illustration of how genres change over time, and in particular the process of 'conversationalisation' of public discourse. The sequencing of elements, distinguishing compulsory and optional elements, and how such elements are recognised amid the variation evident in genres is explored by Eggins and Slade (1997:230–5), who also acknowledge the importance of lexico-grammatical analysis as well as the analysis of elements beyond the sentence such as turn-taking or adjacency pairs.

Bakhtin (especially Bakhtin 1986) has been very influential in contributing to the overall understanding of genre. Bakhtin's concept of genre is based on the *utterance*, an abstract unit of talk which may vary in length from one speaker-turn to a whole monologue or (in written language) a whole novel. The utterance is defined by its termination at a point where an interlocutor may potentially respond.[6] For Bakhtin, utterances reflect specific conditions and goals of different types, not only by their lexical, grammatical and phraseological makeup, but by their 'compositional structure' (1986:60). Whilst utterances are locally determined and individual, 'each sphere in which language is used develops its own relatively stable types of these utterances' (*ibid.*), and these stable characteristics are what constitute genres. Interpersonal aspects are also important for Bakhtin: 'each speech genre in each area of speech communication has its own typical conception of the addressee, and this defines it as a genre' (*ibid.*: 95). The Bakhtinian perspective is taken further by Kelly Hall (1995), who explores the links between the institutionalised/socio-historical meanings of the generic resources available in interaction and the practical strategies interactants engage in in each new situation. The importance of Bakhtin's approach (and indirectly, too, that of Vygotsky; see Emerson 1983; Wertsch 1985) is that it breaks down the distinction between language as the product of the individual psyche and language as a social construct. Any theory of genre needs to include that perspective.

5.9 Goal-orientation

Conversational participants, especially in more casual settings, are social beings with practical goals, and it is their goals that drive the interaction forward, rather than some sense of obedience to institutional norms. However, goals need not be fixed or pre-ordained, and may emerge as the discourse progresses (i.e. they may become apparent as a result of the unfolding interaction, rather than predetermining it), and they may be multiple in number (Tracy and Coupland 1990). If we take a goal-orientation approach to genre, it becomes possible to integrate better the transactional features of conversations and the relational/interactional ones. Iacobucci (1990), for instance, shows how the relational aspects of customer calls to a phone company are not tangential or to be considered merely as 'side sequences', but are often purposefully directed towards fulfilling the transactional goals of the discourse more effectively and efficiently.

Casual conversation is possibly the prime example of how useful the study of goal-orientation can be. Casual conversation displays features which have led some to conclude that it is too vague a notion to qualify for the title of genre, or else that it is defined by the very fact that, in terms of genre-mixing, anything goes. But casual conversation, on closer scrutiny, is no less goal-driven than any other kind of talk, even though the goals may be multiple, may only emerge in real time and may be largely relational. Considering the relational goals can often assist in the understanding of casual conversation much more than the pursuit of notions such as 'topic' or 'matters under discussion'.

Nevertheless, one major problem in the study of goals in interaction is how one actually determines what the goals are, since these will very often not be explicitly stated by participants, and the evidence for the analyst is usually indirect, and available only in the shape of phenomena such as 'formulations', and other similar kinds of linguistic evidence. Formulations are paraphrases or summaries of positions reached in the ongoing talk, whereby participants externalise their perspectives on the directions and goals of the unfolding discourse (Heritage and Watson 1979), which the analyst can use as evidence for statements about the way the discourse is progressing. But it is only this kind of indirect evidence that is usually available, short of adopting a more ethnographic approach and using participants themselves as informants to tease out the goals of any given speech event.

Goal-orientation ties the notion of genre closely to action. Dolz and Schneuwly (1996) put forward the link between genres and social action as a defining characteristic of genres, and consider the ability to use the generic resources to pursue goals to be inseparable from the ability to act in the immediate social situation. However, once again, such notions are elusive in real data, and the analyst is working with only an indirect record, a trace of what actually took place as an event. But still, attempting to see things from the participants' viewpoint and to appreciate how they articulate their own understandings avoids at least the worst excesses of the imposition of structure and order by the linguist, using analytical frameworks that may not reflect in any way the reality of the conversation for those who were involved in it.

Comparisons of spoken texts from different settings and involving different participants often show up lexical and grammatical similarities that enable us to observe generic patterns wherein the local features of lexis and grammar correspond to global features of goal-type and types of participant relationship. By the same token, differences in lexical and grammatical features across texts may indicate different relationship-types as well as different goal-types. Biber and Finegan (1989) illustrate this well with differences between written and spoken texts that can be in many respects similar, but in key respects different. For example, in their data, personal letters often share features with non-conversational spoken genres, but are distinguished by a greater number of 'affect markers' (e.g. *I feel*; see Biber 1988:131–3 for further discussion).

Other dimensions may also be brought into play in the plotting of features in texts. Plotting texts in terms of their features and how they cluster and pattern enables us better to grasp the variation present in texts that share similarities at the global level, and enables us to make at least some links between higher-order features and the basic lexico-grammatical choices which speakers make in line with their goals and relationships in individual settings. The gradability of spoken genre features thus displayed is in line with Wikberg's (1992) arguments for the importance of gradience and variability in the classification of written genres, which are often subject to over-simplified text-typology labels. As Biber and Finegan (1991) state, genre study should include both a characterisation of typical texts as well as a characterisation of the potential range of variation.

A genre-based approach to the study of spoken and written texts has the potential to offer a highly relevant model for the applied linguist seeking a tangible level of generalisability in the design of syllabuses or the identification of skills as targets for language learning. It offers the possibility of using powerful categories to get a handle on the otherwise bewildering world of texts and their individuality. When we move away from the deterministic certainties of traditional, sentence-based grammars, genre studies offer access to a higher level of organisation that can regulate the apparently infinite variability of texts and contexts.

5.10 Conclusion

This chapter has explored further how different ways of approaching language have influenced applied linguistics and language pedagogy. It has examined the significant trend in recent years to examine language more and more in its real contexts of use and to bring to centre stage the participants and their social worlds. It has focussed on the idea of language as discourse rather than language as sentences, but that has also had implications for a more basic question of the nature of the evidence with which applied linguists work. The chapter has taken the line that speech and writing need to be looked at in their separate manifestations, and that separating them raises important questions for issues of description. But what has united written and spoken language in this chapter is that both media of communication can be studied in social contexts, and through real texts. This means, in terms of a theory of language, that the evidence is essentially external, existing in the social world, and not inside the linguist's head, in his or her intuition. This last point has profound resonances in the practical ways in which applied linguists conduct their own discourse, and in the final chapter we shall shift our focus away from language as an object of study for linguists and applied linguists, and look at applied linguistics itself as a 'discourse' with, as with any discourse, its contexts of activity, its methods and ways of doing, and, finally, with its own ways of talking about, and thus constructing, itself as a discipline.

Notes

1 By far the best source of further information on writing is Ehlich *et al.*'s (1996) *Bibliography on Writing and Written Language*. The papers in Coulmas and Ehlich (1983) are also important.
2 E.g. Halliday (1989).
3 See section 3.6 for Halliday's definition of 'functional'.
4 However, see the debate between Ghadessy and Carrell in the *TESOL Quarterly Forum* (Ghadessy 1985; Carrell 1985) as to whether 'world knowledge' or normal linguistic decoding is paramount in reading.
5 See also the discussion of 'left' and 'right' in Chapter 6 as another example of problems in the terminology of spoken grammars.
6 See Hasan (1992) for a critique of the ambivalence of some of Bakhtin's categories. Hasan is right to criticise Bakhtin's work as being difficult to operationalise. However, as long as one does not regard Bakhtin's ideas as a model or instrument of analysis, but rather as a thought-provoking set of theories, their value in assisting our understanding of and our ability to construct the nature of the spoken language remains intact.

6

Applied linguistics as professional discourse

6.1 Introduction

So far in this book we have characterised applied linguistics as different ways of approaching understandings of language in the service of addressing and possibly solving both theoretical and practical problems in language teaching. But applied linguists are, by definition, practical people working as a community, and it is their modes of practice and communicating with one another, as much as anything, which define them as a professional group. Although we may all be interested in language, and in the problems and issues of language teaching and learning, our approaches and methods, and the discourses we engage in to communicate those approaches and methods will be very different. So much has already been implicit (and often explicit) in everything we have said about different views on language in the previous chapters. In this chapter, we look at just some of the ways in which applied linguists practise their trade, position themselves and communicate with one another. We cannot hope to cover them all in detail, but we shall focus on some of the central types of activity that are currently shaping and influencing the profession. Although we shall somewhat artificially separate out the different types of applied linguistic activity, we should always bear in mind that many applied linguists, during their professional careers, engage in more than one type of practice, often simultaneously. It is this which, in part, characterises the humanistic nature of the applied linguistic enterprise, and which is one of the important ingredients in the cement that binds applied linguists within their professional community.

6.2 Research

Some applied linguists spend part of their career engaged in research. This is a professional profile most immediately associated with applied linguistics departments in colleges and universities, where, if one is fortunate, grant-funded projects can be the focus of important research questions concerning aspects of language teaching and learning. There is, however, no unified notion of what constitutes research. In the United States, the word *research* has been, for many, conventionally synonymous with experimental, empirical investigations into teaching/learning problems, usually accompanied by quantified statistical evidence validated by techniques associated with the harder sciences. Such investigations, or 'studies' as they are usually called, may take place in classrooms, or in laboratory-type settings (see section 4.5 for a discussion of the latter). The British tradition of applied linguistics tends to attach a wider scope to the word 'research', embracing activities such as corpus linguistics, textual analysis, historical research, lexicographical research, researching material for descriptive and pedagogical grammars, etc. This is perhaps an oversimplification, but the beginning applied linguist should not be surprised at encountering such different perceptions of the meaning of the term 'research' amongst his or her international peers. Indeed, in the excellent *Research Notes* section of the *TESOL Quarterly*, established under the able editorial eye of Diane Larsen-Freeman in Volume 10 of the journal in 1976, the definition of research was implicitly that which is synonymous with quantitatively oriented empirical studies.[1] Larsen-Freeman refers to the reporting of 'results' of studies (p. 347) in outlining the purpose of the nascent *Research Notes* section, and, during the late 1970s and the early years of the 1980s, the overwhelming majority of the research investigations reported are of the empirical/quantitative kind.

Recently, however, the emphasis on both sides of the Atlantic and internationally has shifted away from purely quantitative notions of research in applied linguistics towards qualitative research paradigms. Qualitative research focusses more on observation, close contact and cooperation with the target participants, case studies, critical insights, holistic interpretations, judgements, and so on (see Eisenstein 1986), or, put another way, 'identifying the presence or absence of something and with determining its nature or distinguishing features (in contrast to quantitative research, which is concerned with measurement)' (Watson-Gegeo 1988:576). Gaies (1983), referring to the 'recent' incorporation of qualitative research into language teaching and learning, points to the influence of research methods from related disciplines such as sociology and anthropology.

Still in the pages of the *TESOL Quarterly*, by 1986, we find Chaudron persuasively arguing the usefulness of both quantitative and qualitative research methods in classroom-based investigations, with an especially important link between the qualitative assessment of important variables and the quantitative exploration of them (Chaudron 1986). In the 1990s, qualitative research was now seen as embracing 'naturalistic inquiry, longitudinal case studies, educational ethnography, the ethnography of communication, discourse analysis, and other approaches that employ qualitative methods' (Johnson and Saville-Troike 1992:603), though debates were entered as to the reliability of qualitative research findings (*ibid.*). By the mid-1990s, the *TESOL Quarterly* was publishing guidelines for submissions both for quantitative and qualitative research, and these represent clear, definitive statements of the perception of at least this key journal in our field as to the important differences between the two research paradigms. Finally, the journal dedicated Volume 29, number 3, in the autumn of 1995, entirely to qualitative research, showing how the qualitative paradigm had definitely come of age in the language teaching research community, and how its status, side-by-side with the quantitative tradition, was now recognised.[2] This is a very clear example of the chronology of a many-voiced discourse that has shaped our present-day perceptions of how applied linguists 'do' applied linguistics.

A third type of activity (in addition to quantitative and qualitative research), perhaps not often thought of as research, but sharing in the fundamental investigative urge that fuels all research, is theory-building and model-building. This last type might seem, on the face of it, to be anything but 'applied' linguistics, and yet its practitioners, epitomised by figures such as Henry Widdowson (1979; 1980; 1984; 1990) and Bernard Spolsky (1968; 1990), have done much to map out the philosophical territory in which the practice of applied linguistics takes place and its independence from linguistics as a discipline (see section 1.2 for an example of the kind of modelling of the profession Widdowson has contributed). In a sense, too, applied linguist theorists such as Widdowson have honed the discourse of applied linguists, and often held us all to account as much for how we use or abuse our common language as for what we practise. This type of research is one of accumulating learning, wisdom, and experience in both practical and theoretical domains, and is, by definition, not associated with the beginner. These three broad notions of research (the quantitative, the qualitative and the theoretical) are seen by Wray *et al.* (1998:7–8), in their excellent practical manual of research projects in linguistics, as a natural consequence of the fact that the study of language spans the sciences and the humanities.

Whichever type of research applied linguists carry out, within language teaching and learning, the aim is normally to ameliorate something, whether it be our understanding of how vocabulary is incorporated into the mental lexicon, the design and use of materials and resources such as text books and dictionaries, selecting techniques for teaching and learning, an understanding of learners' personal experiences and their failures and successes, their affective responses, knowledge about the actual language we use as raw input, etc. Few would disagree that these are laudable research aims. However, considerable debate continues as to where and how research is carried out, as we saw in Chapter 4. Apart from the laboratory, there is the classroom as a natural arena for research, and here debates have arisen as to whether investigations are best carried out by dispassionate observation on the part of an extra observer, whether special lessons or activities should be staged and carefully controlled for experimental purposes, or whether teachers in their own environment are their own best researchers, and whether the normal lesson, with all its vagaries, is the best milieu for investigation (see Foster 1998). Thus, while much classroom research focuses on specific types of innovative pedagogical intervention to judge their effectiveness, other research investigations work more with the status quo. For example, Peirce *et al.* (1993) investigate the relationship between a relatively new practice – self-assessment – and objective measures of language proficiency. On the other hand, Jarvis and Robinson (1997) take what they assert to be the existing norm in many primary classrooms around the world (i.e. the teacher-fronted lesson with a large class), rather than investigating the effectiveness of any new methodology, and relate the normal teacher–pupil discourse to the theoretical postulates of a Vygotskian approach to language acquisition, itself a relatively recent growth-area in SLA (see section 4.7.2). Nunan (1990), meanwhile, sees classrooms and learners as providing vital research evidence for broader issues of curriculum development. Or the problem under investigation may simply be one that has always been there but neglected, as in Ellis's (1995a) study of vocabulary acquisition in the classroom arising from oral input (as opposed to, for example, reading, which has more often been the focus of vocabulary research), and which is then subjected to specific manipulation of the conditions of occurrence. Another apposite example comes from Dörnyei and Malderez (1997), who focus on group dynamics in the classroom, and how these have implications for success and failure in language learning. They bring a perspective from social psychology to bear upon the typical, now well-entrenched practice of present-day language teaching to get learners working and interacting in groups, and argue convincingly that awareness of the group dynamic factor is important for teachers.

Others would argue strongly that classrooms, and the kinds of data available there, are inadequate to the research aims of understanding educational processes such as language learning. Holliday (1996) offers a mordant critique of the way much ethnographic research 'emicises' verbal data (i.e. abstracts from it) without consideration of the wider cultural context of curriculum planning, educational management, and the wider cultures of communities and societies beyond the classroom. Holliday enjoins researchers to develop a 'sociological imagination', and the research community to integrate the ethical issues of research practice (such as invasion of privacy, empathy with those observed, cultural sensitivity, the observed having a voice, etc.) with a broader, more cosmopolitan perspective in the research environment. Such a view repositions the relationship between observer and observed and challenges the fairly narrow focus of much applied linguistic research in and out of classrooms. As such, it is another important voice in the ongoing discourse that shapes applied linguistics.

The third kind of research activity referred to above, theory-building, has also spawned many debates and questions in applied linguistics. In an article responding to a special issue of the journal *Applied Linguistics* devoted to theory construction in SLA (volume 14 (3), 1993), van Lier (1994) raises several issues that have wider implications for the kinds of theories applied linguists build. Firstly, there are questions of what the field of investigation is, whether a field such as SLA is part of linguistics, or education, or psychology, or whatever. Taking a stance on this basic question obviously influences the kinds of theories that are considered relevant and useful. Van Lier makes the important point that different theoretical foundations arise because our 'discourse worlds' (p. 330) are different. In other words, the very way we construct and communicate our professional activities shapes our theorising just as much as extant theories shape our practice.

Much of what has been said in this book so far concerning how theorists and practitioners work with and view language itself underscores this perspective: applied linguistics is essentially a discourse, an ongoing and shifting conversation among its adherents rather than a set of inscribed tablets that lay out the field and its spheres of activity. Difference and variation in theorising applied linguistics, van Lier argues, is not necessarily a sign that the profession has not yet matured (i.e. become a well-established discipline), but rather is a reflection of the different work to be done 'and all these kinds of work need theoretical and practical dimensions' (*ibid.*). Van Lier also proposes that theorising in a field such as SLA (and, one might extrapolate, for much of the rest of applied linguistics) must include addressing basic questions such as the nature of evidence, the adequacy of documentation and the relationship between explanation and understanding. In this last respect, van Lier sees the human sciences as quite different from the natural sciences. While in the natural sciences, causation might be a central feature of explanation, a human science such as SLA must seek for more: understanding, and understandings, says Van Lier, are dialogic processes, socially constructed, that is to say they are part of the professional *discourse* of applied linguists.

Van Lier's programme for theory in SLA is therefore one based on research of a humanistic kind, founded in intra-professional discourse, the rhetoric of academic argumentation, and a rationality that springs from human understanding rather than the positivism associated with the natural sciences. Once again, the work of an applied linguist-theorist like Widdowson would seem to fit squarely within such a research tradition. Widdowson (1990) also outlines a basically humanistic programme of theory appraisal for applied linguistics in stressing the importance of mediation, interpretation and evaluation, without which one cannot properly judge the usefulness of a theory to practical matters of pedagogy. It is indicative of the ongoing nature of the debate and the likelihood that it will never resolve itself into a cosy world of mutually back-patting applied linguists that Widdowson (2000) returns to the theme of what constitutes the discipline and how it should operate in the new-millennium edition of the journal *Applied Linguistics*. Here he takes to task corpus linguistics, a relatively recent development, one which, on the face of it, seems to replace the vagaries of intuition with 'objective' evidence, but which is doomed to be no more than 'linguistics applied' if it fails to subject itself to the mediating and relevance-constructing principles of applied linguistics.

Thus it is by no means universally accepted that theory in applied linguistics should be of the rationalist-positivist kind centred on causation and demonstration, and the research tradition in theory construction has an ever-growing humanistic character which reflects the discourse of our profession.[3] Nor is there agreement that applied linguists should unite around any particular theoretical stance. This lack of a unified consensus of criteria for theory-building is commented on by Ellis (1995b), who notes that 'theory evaluation is perhaps more an art than a science' (p.77); the value of theories in applied linguistics will usually be measured by their impact on the consumer, and can only properly be evaluated 'in relation to their intended purpose' (ibid.: 88).

One last point that needs to be raised in this brief discussion of theoretical research is the way theory communicates itself (or fails to do so), between theorist and consumer. We have already commented upon the unease that some practitioners have voiced concerning the discourse that does (or does not) take place between theorists and practitioners (e.g. Lennon 1988; Kirby 1991; see section 1.6). Van Lier (1994) quite rightly sees the problem of communication between theorists and practitioners as two-sided: theorists often have a 'fear of practice' (p.340), and practitioners often display a fear of theory and reflection/research. Van Lier takes the position that theorists justifiably react against the notion that everything should be transparently applicable, but that theory should be 'constrained by ordinary everyday goings-on' (ibid.). Equally, teachers under pressures of various kinds (time, peer suspicion, etc.) and displaying an understandable rejection of jargon-laden and obfuscating theory deserve an environment in which research is promoted and collaboration with theorists facilitated.

My own experience of communicating with teachers at professional conferences in more than 30 countries leaves me with the conclusion that, at the time of writing, yawning gulfs still separate what we 'research-oriented' applied linguists find interesting and what 'action-oriented' applied linguists (i.e. the teachers) find relevant. We can either shout across these Grand Canyons and hope to hear one another, or lower a few ropes on either side and meet and talk in the silent valleys that lie in between. What I have learnt (a lesson not always easy to apply) is that it is my ethical duty as an applied linguist to make my theoretical position clear and understandable and to mediate the theory of others. If I do the opposite, and make theory appear too complex and too hard for practitioners, I have failed. From my own perspective, at least, the discourse of applied linguistics should be plain and lucid.

6.3 Principle and practice: the case of corpus linguistics

It may seem odd to be turning our attention to a question of technology and methodology when the direction in which I have taken the debate in this chapter so far has been more towards applied linguistics as a discourse. However, the discourse of applied linguistics would have little grounding in reality if it could not be measured against change in method and practice (see, for example, how Rampton 1995 perceives criticality in terms of the concrete influences of socio-political forces). It so happens that corpus linguistics both represents cutting-edge change in terms of scientific techniques and methods, and presents us with dilemmas that arise from the humanistic contexts in which an (apparently) detached technology operates. Corpus linguistics probably also foreshadows even more profound technological shifts that will impinge upon our long-held notions of education, the roles of teachers, the cultural context of the delivery of educational services and the mediation of theory and technique as the twentieth century becomes history.

Corpus linguistics occupies an uncertain territory in applied linguistics. Its origins are in the search for objectivity about language use (e.g. see Halliday 1966 and Sinclair 1966 for early visions of its usefulness) by freeing the linguist from the subjectivity of intuition. It is based on the fundamental notion that external evidence, i.e. evidence of actual use, is a better primary source than internal evidence, i.e. the intuition of the native speaker. Its method, gathering large amounts of representative data, whether written or spoken, immerses it in the social, the world of texts and users, of producers and consumers. And as with all other aspects of applied linguistic activity, different ideological perspectives prevail. One way of doing corpus linguistics, for example, is simply to see it as an exercise in numbers, where the goal is to import as much language data as possible (say, a billion words of running text), from as wide a sweep of sources as one can practically manage (though this might include a fair dash of opportunism – if the data is on offer, grab it). Such data is then analysed dispassionately by the computer and its output is a series of statistics that tell us something about frequency of occurrence of word-forms, lexical items or structures, and frequency of combinations (collocations, phrases, etc.). These statistical data then become the yardstick for dictionaries, grammars, thesauruses, course books, and so on. In recent years, led by pioneers such as Sinclair and his COBUILD corpus team, successful and immensely useful and innovative practical products have been made available to language learners. Behind such an apparently mechanical operation, though, there lurk ponderous issues that relate to ideology, both in terms of views of language, what it is we 'apply' and wider social and cultural issues.

How one deals with the results of corpus analyses varies, and depends on one's aims and perspectives. Computers are good at presenting figures, and good at showing probabilities. This has led some, recently, to propose that grammars could be re-conceived on the basis of probabilities, rather than deterministic rules. A deterministic rule would be, for example, that the third person singular present simple form of English verbs ends in -s. A probabilistic rule, on the other hand, states what is most likely to be selected in a given set of contextual circumstances. In any language, structures which appear to belong to the same meaning sets, but which contrast with one another in some way (e.g. simple versus continuous/ progressive verb-forms in English), will often display quite different statistical distributions for those forms in a corpus (e.g. one form may be twice as frequent as its partner-form). These statistical facts can either be ignored as irrelevant to a description of the internal systems of a language, or they can be brought on board as part of the meaning of those forms, rather in the way that Firth argued that *dark* was part of the meaning of *night* because of the likelihood of their co-occurrence (Firth 1951/1957). Taking such statistical data into account enables grammarians to propose the construction of probabilistic grammars. In an early discussion of probability in grammar, Halliday (1961: 259), for example, pointed to the fundamental nature of language as probabilistic and not as 'always this and never that'. Halliday has recently turned to corpus linguistics to put flesh on this notion. He asserts that probabilities of occurrence are 'an essential property of the system – as essential as the terms of the opposition itself' (1991:31). Halliday (1992) argues further that the different probabilities of occurrence in different registers is also significant, since it is not likely that items in opposition will be equiprobable in a corpus reflecting any given register.

Probabilistic explanations of grammatical features necessarily open up the question *why?*, and answers can only be sought in social and contextual motivation. In this way, attention to statistics cannot be paid without equal attention to the social factors that produce them. This is one way of 'applying' corpus insights to, say, a pedagogical grammar. If one takes the line that learners might find it extremely useful to know that a particular structure is more probable than another in a given situation, all other things being equal, then the probabilities thrown up by a corpus might be as genuinely usable and helpful as the time-honoured practice of the teacher saying 'well, you could say it, but I don't think I personally would say it in that situation'. This last utterance is, as anyone who has taught a language that is not their first one well knows, even more difficult for the non-native-speaking teacher to make with confidence. So probabilistic grammars need not be just the academic indulgence of teams of applied linguist computer nerds remote from ordinary consumers. As with everything else we have discussed in this book, it largely comes down to how relevant teachers and learners perceive them to be.

Foremost in seeing even more profound implications of corpus linguistics for a radically different view of language as a whole has been Sinclair (1991). Sinclair's work represents the classic case of independent applied linguistics, in that he has come from practice to a new theory, not vice versa. This, I have argued, is one of the key ways in which applied linguistics carries out its discourse and defines itself (see also Sridhar 1993). Sinclair, engaged in the eminently practical pursuit of writing a learners' dictionary in the early 1980s, began to be aware more and more that certain dearly held principles of language study (e.g. the primacy of syntax, the unpredictability and 'irregularity' of lexis) were simply no longer tenable when faced with corpus evidence.[4] Lexis was far from irregular; regular vocabulary patterns appeared everywhere in the corpus. Idiomaticity, far from being a minor, or marginal affair in language, appeared to be ubiquitous and at least as important as syntax in the construction of meaning (1991:112). Idiomatic constructions were everywhere in the corpus Sinclair was working with, especially in the patterns formed by combinations of the most frequent words in the language (as opposed to the quaint, infrequent idioms often associated with language teaching manuals). This and other factors led Sinclair to posit a close bond between sense and structure, and to conclude that features such as collocation and particular idiomatic (in the sense of individual) but very frequently occurring combinations were the real cement that held texts together. Syntax was more, as it were, an emergency repair kit for filling the occasional gaps and cracks amid the flow of idiomaticity. Sinclair's proposal is radical, and many will find it problematic, but it stands as a good example of how a 'neutral' technology can throw up fundamental questions for theory, and how a practical, 'applied' problem, in this case writing a dictionary using computer evidence, can bounce back and challenge theory. We should not doubt that galloping technological change will bring many more such upheavals over the coming decades.

Neutral stands in scare quotes in the previous paragraph because profound ideological issues rear their heads at every turn in corpus work.

In my own work, for example, with my colleague Ronald Carter, on the CANCODE[5] spoken corpus, we have encountered difficulties with the metalanguage of corpus linguists that have forced us to re-think how we express ourselves. Our corpus is informal spoken language, and our initial interest was in features of spoken grammar (see Carter and McCarthy 1995a). One area that interested us was how speakers used the resources of the clause and word-order to focus on particular aspects of information and evaluation. We collected examples of the type *Jenny, you never know where you are with her*, and *He's a builder, **my brother***. Conventionally, the words in bold are known as 'left-' and 'right-dislocated' items, respectively (Ashby 1988; Geluykens 1992). And yet, clearly, spoken language has no 'left' or 'right'; it exists in time, not space. 'Left' and 'right' are page-driven metaphors, and even more narrowly, western-orthographic page-driven (other cultures write right-to-left, or vertically). *Left* and *right* are convenient to refer to the page-like output on the computer screen, or the page of a printout, but they dangerously metaphorise speech into writing – the very opposite of what Carter and I were attempting to do in our advocacy of the independence of spoken grammar. The best option for expressing the facts of spoken language seems to be to adopt temporal metaphors rather than spatial ones and to speak of 'pre-' and 'post-positioning', etc., rather than left or right. The point here is that apparently neutral technologies and the practices associated with them rarely are neutral, and that it is in the practice of those technologies that applied linguists are often obliged to return to the basics of metalanguage and the mutual discourse with which they define their activities. Corpus linguistics, with all its impartial hardware, is no exception to this.

Widdowson (2000) sees even greater dangers in the kind of reality that a corpus creates. For some, the technology dazzles, and the evidence of corpus analyses is seen as incontrovertible 'facts', which must trounce feeble intuition in the language classroom. The language of the corpus is, above all, real, and what is it that all language learners want, other than 'real' contact with the target language? But for Widdowson, the very act of freezing language in a computer database wrenches it from its original context and reality and renders the task of using such material as 'authentic' or 'real' in language teaching an impossibility. Widdowson rightly assails the tendency on the part of some to assume that because corpus language is 'real' (i.e. actually attested) it will do for injecting reality into the contrived world of the classroom. He touches a deep instinct in language teachers when he argues for the classroom to be seen not necessarily as a place into which the real world must be dragged at all costs, but as a place of 'created context, like a theatre' (*ibid.*: 8). He sees immense potential in the use of technology and in corpus insights, but for him, the pedagogical mediation, the 'applied linguistics' as opposed to the 'linguistics applied' side of things is paramount.

No one could really disagree with Widdowson, and if he falls into error at all, it is that he pushes too heavily against an open door. Very few applied corpus analysts (as opposed to descriptive ones) would ever advocate simply dumping large loads of corpus material wholesale into the classroom. Language teaching is a far more complex affair than simply the choice of texts to be used in the class. I and others have argued that there are potentially several ways of approaching corpora (McCarthy 1998:22; Tognini-Bonelli 1996). One can assume one knows it all already and just go to a corpus to find texts that demonstrate the known facts (the 'corpus-based' approach). One can do the opposite, and go with a completely open mind to a corpus, willing to be guided, illuminated by it in ways one could not dream of (a 'corpus-driven' approach). But one can also mediate the corpus, design it from the very outset and build it with applied linguistic questions in mind, ask of it the questions applied linguists want answers to, and filter its output, use it as a guide or tool for what you, the teacher, want to achieve (a 'corpus-informed' approach). It is this last approach that Widdowson (2000) fails to explore. Some examples of a corpus-informed approach could be the design of better and new kinds of reference materials (e.g. databased dictionaries on CD- or DVD-ROM, automated self-updating thesauruses to which new corpus material can be added by the user), the use of corpus evidence to (re-)prioritise the syllabus (for example, relegating structures prominent in writing but rare in speech to a secondary position in a syllabus for learners for whom writing is irrelevant or of lesser importance), using corpus evidence from 25 restaurant conversations recorded in target contexts to help you in the writing of one, typical restaurant dialogue, albeit concocted. In the real world of real applied corpus linguists, some of Widdowson's fears seem far removed from actual practice, though his voicing of the possible dangers and abuses serves an important function in the overall debate as to what applied linguists do and how they should be doing it.

Remaining with corpus linguistics, there are also some wider social and ideological implications that affect our professional identity. These relate to questions arising from technological potential and the choices that have to be made in exercising it. The CANCODE corpus, for instance, has been referred to by me and my colleagues, in the past, as a collection of data gathered in the British Isles, in order to reflect the inclusion of data from the Irish Republic, in an attempt to broaden the geographical and socio-cultural base. However, Irish applied linguists do not necessarily perceive their native island as a 'British' isle at all, and may interpret such nomenclature as a claim to British ownership of the English language and its culture in these islands that I inhabit. In our more recent presentations, we have therefore adopted the term 'the islands of Britain and Ireland' to describe our catchment area.[6] This is by no means an act of precious political correctness, but an acknowledgement that assembling a corpus is itself an ideologically embedded activity, where choices and perceptions are conditioned by the limitations of the world-view of the applied linguists who undertake the task.

Resource limitations usually forbid idealistic enterprises, and most corpus projects fall foul of the limitations of their own data. CANCODE is a spoken corpus of English, but, whose speech and whose English? Although its founders set out to break the hegemony of middle-class, southern-England English by including speakers from across the social and geographical spectrum of Britain and Ireland, this immediately raises the question of a) the viability of such a sample as a model of 'standard' English, and b) the usefulness of an old-world, northern European set of English dialects in a global community where English is multi-dialectal and includes many non-native dialects. In connection with the case of British and Irish English mentioned above, for example, Farr and O'Keeffe (2000) show how even the most frequent items in the grammar (in their case, modal verbs) can have quite different usages reflecting different cultural perspectives in British and Irish English corpora. Corpus linguistics can by no means, therefore, exclude itself from the broader debate on the status of different groups of native-speakers and of the ownership of a world language like English.

6.4 Should applied linguistics be a critical discipline?

In recent years there has also been considerable debate over the role of ideology in applied linguistics. This is a complex area, and one that does not resolve into a single, clear image, but in which common threads are apparent. 'Critical' approaches to language study are essentially concerned with the roles of ideology and power in views of language and of language use. A simplified characterisation might be to say that at one end of the spectrum is the stance that it is the business of linguists and applied linguists simply to describe language and to describe the processes of learning and teaching languages. At the other end is the view that language is never neutral, is always bound up with particular ways of seeing the world, and that applied linguists are always engaged in a politically and ideologically embedded activity. There are also, of course, many possible positions in between.

Kramsch (1995) offers us an insightful way into the debate when she refers to the historical change in the discourse community of language teaching professionals and consumers over recent decades. There has been a shift from language teachers seeing literature specialists as the guiding lights of language education, and a shift from a 'consensual discourse community of belletristically inclined students' (p. 44). Applied linguists have taken over the role formerly occupied by literature experts, and the learning community has become diverse, culturally heterogeneous and often without any clear internal identity. This broadening and demo- cratisation of what was, until relatively recently, a comfortable consensus, has brought with it new political awareness as well as new tensions and suspicions. Above all, it has created a multi-voiced discourse that provides a platform for widely opposing views as to what the ideology of the applied linguistic profession is or should be. All this reflects not merely the changes within educational institutions and shifts in relative power be- tween exponents of different disciplines (the usual historical process of the rise of new academic élites and the rout of the old), but also social changes that affect language use (e.g. the 'democratisation' of discourse itself in the wider world of mass media and global communications). In the case of English, the politics of language are inevitably tied up with the decline of British political dominance and the growth of English as the ordinary property of the global community, put crudely, an inexorable shift from English as associated with Shakespeare to English as more likely to be associated with the Internet or pop culture. In this democratic climate, ideological stances are inevitably more divisive and controversial, and to take the position that the role of language in our professional activity is unrelated to ideological and political concerns becomes harder and harder to sustain in a climate where it is politically incorrect to do so.

Two strands of debate stand out as relevant to our concerns in this chapter, the one centring around the notion of critical language study (epitomised in the field of critical discourse analysis, or CDA)[7] and the other around the broader notion of models of language in a culturally heterogeneous world of language education, which we shall address in section 6.5. The former involves (usually) the role of specific texts, the latter broader questions of applied linguistic methodology. The fact that this distinction is problematic and undesirable has not escaped the notice of those centrally involved in trying to define applied linguistics in recent years (e.g. Stubbs 1997).

Critical discourse analysis, represented in works such as Fairclough (1989; 1995) and Kress (1990), sees the task of the (applied) linguist as taking a critical stance towards language use, and as analysing texts in such a way as to illuminate and bring to the fore the ideology of their producers. Language is seen as ideologically embedded, and never neutral, and CDA analysts are interested in exposing acts of linguistic manipulation, oppression and discrimination through language and the use of language in the unjust exercise of power. Critical text analyses might, for instance, reveal how language choices such as transitive versus intransitive verb, or active versus passive voice, or particular choices of modal verbs or pronouns enable writers to manipulate the realisations (or concealment) of agency and power in the representation of action (see Fairclough 1997 for a brief exemplification). Or, in a similar vein, a critical analysis of a particular lexeme or set of lexemes might purport to show how shifts in meanings over time both reflect and construct ideological perspectives (see Stubbs 1997 for discussion of some relevant examples), or how particular speech-acts reflect power relations in unequal spoken encounters (e.g. Wodak 1997).

CDA is not without its critics, sternest among whom recently have been Widdowson (1995a and b; 2000) and Stubbs (1997), both of whom have taken it to task for its lack of rigour, its sometimes cavalier attitude to form-functional relations and (particularly from Stubbs) its faith in the usefulness of very small amounts of data. Equally, there is a whiff of political correctness in much of what CDA presents, and a middle-class left-wing bias and academic élitism which is often only thinly disguised behind the unquestioned caring for minorities and the oppressed which CDA practitioners sincerely possess. However, its voice within applied linguistics is a powerful one; it is part of our professional discourse, and its effects on the lives of those touched by the influence of applied linguistics will depend, as with other philosophies and stances described in this book, upon the persuasiveness of its rhetorical constructs and its perceived relevance to a practical pursuit such as language teaching.

Stubbs (1997), occupying a less opposed position than Widdowson, sees possibilities for CDA to speak with a more persuasive voice by adopting a corpus-based approach (see Chapter 6), a comparative methodology (across texts and across cultures) and more attention to the reception of texts (readers, intended audiences, etc.), rather than to the agenda of the analyst. Certainly, one can see the possibilities for a useful critique of the discourse of English language teaching within Stubbs' proposal. For example, over the more than three decades that I have been involved in ELT, there has been a largely unchallenged assumption that the world-view of learners should coincide with the ideological concerns of a benign middle-class. Thus teaching materials often display anodyne content resulting from passing through the concerned hands of authors, editors, reviewers, curriculum planners, etc. to an outcome guaranteed not to offend any bourgeois sensitivity wherever it might rear its head on the globe (see Dingle 1999). Or again, another interesting area for critical research is the (shifts in) the dominant metalanguage of language teaching research and methodology. Kramsch (1995) points to the metaphors of freedom and individuality (*natural approach, learner-centred instruction, learner needs,* etc.) which 'happen to fit nicely into a certain dominant democratic discourse that values learner autonomy and self-reliance, and views with distrust any artificial manipulation of a learner's interlanguage by social or political forces' (p. 50). But we are all prisoners of our times, and in the decades that I have been in English language teaching I have watched the metaphors of learning shift, from a rather Victorian notion that language learning was a hard slog rewarding only the disciplined and assiduous (notions such as 'drilling', course book titles such as *Practice and Progress*), through to the recent technological fetishism of metaphors such as 'processing' and course books with titles such as *Streamline* and *Interchange*. This is not to suggest that a conspiracy is afoot, but simply to sketch at least a couple of agenda items for a critical approach to the professional discourse of language teaching, nor is it to deny the excellent conference presentations of late which are beginning to question sexist, racist and culturist bias in teaching materials. Indeed, in the area of language testing, one might say that a healthy critical discourse has already developed which is asking many pertinent questions about the power relations immanent in tests and the ideological foundations of superficially 'objective' testing programmes (Shohamy 1994; 1997; McNamara 1997; 1998).

In truth, one of the most apparent pieces of evidence that applied linguistics has already been deeply influenced by critical approaches is the very growth of the scope of the profession. A decade ago, Candlin (1990) asked the question 'What happens when applied linguistics goes critical?' and answered by defining applied linguistics as both problem-oriented and socially oriented, and by claiming for it territory far wider than that of only language pedagogy. For Candlin, at that point in time, and one might remark still true to a great extent now, what was lacking in applied linguistics was a stance on 'what our relationship was with our under-standing of social structure, what our research methodology implied for those whose data we were glad to have, [and] what impact we might expect to have on language-related and language-sourced problems of our time' (p. 461). In the intervening decade, and very much influenced by figures like Candlin, we have seen applied linguistics spread its net more and more into the uses of language outside of the classroom, into other professional contexts, and into social domains such as ageing, literacy and counselling.

Rampton (1995) detects even more fundamental shifts in the political ecology of applied linguistics (in Great Britain at least), and makes a fascinating comparison between opposing models of literacy, as ex-pounded by Street (1984), and opposing paradigms of applied linguistics. In Street's work, two basic views of literacy are propounded. On the one hand it is 'neutral technology', a cognitive issue, a social advantage, related to writing, which is itself distinctive, and the object of politically neutral, objective research. This is the 'autonomous' model. It is opposed by the 'ideological model', wherein literacy is seen as value-laden and embedded in socio-political processes, where research is focussed on social rather than cognitive issues, where illiteracy is not seen as a disadvantage but as one of a set of social identities, and where writing has no special privilege. The parallels with changes in applied linguistics as a whole are striking. In the Britain of the 1980s, socio-political factors caused a shift in the dominant applied linguistic paradigm towards an 'ideological' model. Rampton cites Carter's co-operative work with practising school teachers on the Language in the National Curriculum (LINC) project in mother-tongue education as an example of the shift away from the autonomous, academy-dominated model for such research that had prevailed in earlier times (see Carter 1990 for an example of the products of this work).

Rampton's arguments underline the way a profession such as applied linguistics is or can become 'critical' in the broadest sense, even without paying homage to the trappings of a specific sub-discipline such as CDA.

What is very clear is that applied linguistics is an ongoing discourse and one which, in particular configurations of socio-political forces (in Britain's case, 1980s free-market Thatcherism) engages in a self-critique and embarks on new programmes of action that re-define it as a professional enterprise. We have come to an applied linguistics which is far beyond the rather simplistic notion of 'applying linguistics', the crow-bar approach where linguistic theory provides the tool to dislodge the obstinate problems of language teaching and learning. Seeing applied linguistics as a socio-politically embedded activity actually has the added advantage that it underpins the autonomous notion of the profession, defined by Phillipson (1992), as a 'scientific activity requiring the elaboration of its own theoretical base in relation to its intended applications' (p. 176). That theoretical base will flourish more independently when served by a critical consciousness than when the profession simply acts as a conduit for theories derived from linguistics. Corson (1997), for example, sees the ideal context for the social embedding of applied linguistics in 'critical realism', a body of theory originating in the philosophy of science that values as real and valuable the non-human properties of the social world, including people's reasons and accounts of their experiences. For Corson, too, applied linguistics should not just borrow its discourse from linguistics.

What emerges from the debates over 'criticality' in applied linguistics is the common thread of socio-political awareness of the status of applied linguistics and its practices, whether directly in its day-to-day encounters with language (CDA) or more diffusely in its general ethics and self-positioning vis-à-vis linguistic theory and the societies and practitioners that support its existence as a professional activity. Applied linguists, in short, are not just people who apply linguistics; they are 'applied' in the sense of 'social practice', and they exist and work in the language teaching community, or whatever professional or social community their work bears upon.

6.5 Texts and users

Corpus investigations work with texts, selected however imperfectly from the spoken and written production of target populations, and it is tempting for the applied corpus linguist to believe that the texts in a corpus will be a good resource for language teaching, which, in most of its present-day manifestations, considers the use of texts important. Critical discourse analysts also have texts as their central resource. Once again, large ideological questions loom. Some of the questions include:

- How representative are the texts in the corpus of the target culture? Written corpora often include literary texts and newspaper texts. How many people read literature as opposed to newspapers? Should a British written corpus, for instance, contain 10 times more popular, tabloid newspapers than quality broadsheet ones, to represent sales and dissemination?[8] Are literary texts useful in second language pedagogy anyway?
- Should texts be taken without editing from the corpus and imported 'raw' into the classroom? Does editing a corpus text destroy its naturalness and status as a piece of 'real' language (see the discussion in section 6.4 above)?
- Is the fact that something is a real sample of language the same as saying that it is *authentic* as a sample for language learning?
- Can any texts (especially spoken ones) be wrenched from their cultural context and dealt with mechanistically by corpus analysis and still yield useful teaching material (Widdowson 2000)?

All of these questions are ideological ones and, as always, one's stance towards questions of language itself, the status of teachers and learners in the teaching/learning process, and one's view of how learning should ideally occur affect how we frame our answers to the questions.

In one sense, of course, all texts 'represent' their culture, since texts both reflect and construct cultures, but for language teachers and learners the question is a more pressing one concerning cultural biases and cultural relevance to the local situation. That even our most neutral texts are culture-laden should not be in doubt, and one of the services CDA might perform is to spotlight cultural bias. But often it is only the perspective of history that enables us to see just how culture-laden language teaching texts can be. If we take an example of a British-based text for English as a foreign language teaching from as recently as the 1930s (Figure 12), we can see in it a culture many of us would nowadays abhor and react to with embarrassment. It is by no means certain that the consumers of the text in the 1930s would have felt anything was wrong with it or that it was abnormal as a piece of text for reading comprehension:

BREATH-TAKING ADVENTURES AMONG
CANNIBALS

I. I presume you have heard of James Chalmers, a missionary in New Guinea, who was eaten by cannibals?

J. Yes. I have heard the story. He was the son of an Aberdeen stone-mason, and seems to have imbibed the passion for roaming with the first breath of sea air he drew.

I. He was sent to the far South Seas as a missionary, and after many years in New Guinea he met a tragic end. One day he visited the natives of Gearibari Island along with a friend. He knew that the natives he was to visit were among the most bloodthirsty in all New Guinea.

J. I suppose he was courteously received by the islanders.

I. Yes, and escorted to the neighbouring village. On the way, without a moment's notice, cowardly blows were rained on the head of Chalmers and his friend. Both fell senseless.

J. What happened next?

I. Their heads were instantly cut off, and their bodies given to the women to cook for the expected banquet.

J. When I was a missionary there I performed the bravest act of my life.

I. You took part in a cannibal brawl?

J. That is so. A native girl had run away to escape an unwelcome marriage, and an attempt to bring her back by force led to a fierce fight between her sympathisers and those of the would-be bridegroom.

I. Did you frighten the natives off with your rifle?

J. I was without firearms. The girl was in the centre of a wild-eyed surging throng, and was in danger of being pulled limb from limb. I came single-handed to her rescue.

I. Did you use your walking-stick on the heads of the fanatics?

J. I grasped a stout stick, and rushing amid a hail of arrows and stones, I forced my way through the crowd. I took the girl, who had fainted, in one arm and charged the mob, hitting right and left with the other. Never had I looked on death more closely. I expected every moment to be my last.

Figure 12: From Wenlock (1937:49–50)

It is easy to laugh at such an obviously contrived text, but we should not do so, for it is certain that our successors will find equally ridiculous many of the texts we present learners with today, however well-meaning and politically correct we may consider ourselves. We cannot escape the cultural confines of our language, and only the most insipid sentences can hope to escape reference to the culture in which they exist. Modern-day corpora are full of equally culture-bound texts, and the applied linguist who would apply them to pedagogy must always have this in mind. In this respect, applied corpus linguists are not immune from the general debate as to whether the teaching of English as a second language can distance itself from the political, cultural, racial, gender and power issues raised by the dominance of English in the present-day world, as convincingly laid out by Pennycook (1999).

One option when faced with the problem of how to use the contents of a corpus is simply to let the corpus decide, that is to say, to take the 'corpus-driven' approach mentioned in section 6.4, where no preconceptions are allowed as to what the corpus will throw up, whether in form or content (Tognini-Bonelli 1996). Another option is to attempt some sort of editing, or to simply use the corpus as a source of guidance for the creation of authentic-looking texts or for extracting lexico-grammatical information, what I have called a 'corpus-informed' approach, which admits of common-sense and experience in editing texts so that they are not off-putting or counter-productive in the pedagogical context. These two options are no mere practical issues, but involve ideological stances with regard to faithfulness to external evidence versus the intervention (some would say interference) of internal evidence (intuition, experience), as well as the political and cultural issues mentioned above.

A further problem arises, though, and one which Widdowson (1998) points to. Authenticity is not an objective characteristic of texts, but one which users bring to texts by their ability and willingness to re-contextualise them, to re-create the world of their original utterance. Widdowson takes the line that so-called 'real' language in the classroom (such as corpus-driven materials) can hardly be experienced as authentic in the sense that original participants experienced their creation: 'The classroom cannot replicate the contextual conditions that made the language authentic in the first place' (p. 715). Widdowson has a point. But his weakness is that he tends to see the problem solely from the viewpoint of the savant applied linguist. What we really need to test authenticity and relevance is learners' own reports. If learners find such texts fascinating and a challenge to the imagination (or at least as fascinating and challenging as Widdowson's alternative – a piece of literary text), then what is *relevant* is not the texts' claim to be real samples of the language, but their claim to be more socially and culturally engaging than bland and lifeless sentences and drills. I am constantly struck by the way many L2 learners of English report to me how useful they perceive TV soap operas in English to be in their learning experience (and I can vouch for the same in my attempts at learning Swedish). Learners, in the main, are imaginative folk, and quite as capable of immersing themselves in the world of a conversational transcript as they are of doing so in a piece of literary fiction.

Literary texts are not mentioned idly here, for an important branch of pedagogical applied linguistics uses literary texts as vehicles for language learning. The work of Carter and Long (1991) and McRae (Carter and McRae 1996) is at the forefront of a movement passionately committed to the value of literary texts as a source of language awareness and of productive activity in the language classroom. Such work is a reaction against both the belletristic approach to the reading of literature that passes as language teaching in many quarters in the world, as well as against the banal and dumbed-down world of shopping and vacations that informs the content of so much language teaching elsewhere these days. Carter and his associates (see Carter and Simpson 1989; Carter, Walker and Brumfit 1990) exploit the analytical resources of discourse analysis, modern pragmatics and other types of language analysis to make our understanding of literary creation as relevant as possible to our understandings of text production and reception in general. Theirs is an applied linguistic discourse that attempts to bridge the gulf that grew up between the old, belletristic tradition of academic literary studies and the rejection and suspicion with which the communicative approach confronted it in the 1970s and 1980s. It is an ideology founded in a humanistic view of language and language acquisition; as such it can be accused of being a mere act of faith in an unproven methodology (see Edmondson 1997 for a robust attack), but it is an important part of our applied linguistic discourse, since literature teaching is still a significant element in the delivery of language education in many parts of the world.

The use of texts, from whatever source, is a central aspect of language pedagogy, but it raises issues of cultural ownership, and of the authority of producers, too – a question that will re-surface in the next section.

6.6 Native speakers, expert users

One question that arises in any language teaching context is that of a standard or norm for the target language. Traditionally, this has been associated with the native speaker and, in the case of English, with old-world educated native speakers and, even more narrowly, with writing emanating from those sources (see Honey 1997 for examples of this view). However, the reality of its target domains in many parts of the world militates against the usefulness of such a model of standard English. Examples to be considered are the role of English as a language of 'development' rather than as a cultural vehicle in Modern India, as described by Dasgupta (1993), or as a language of spoken business negotiations between non-native users, as evidenced in the work of Firth (1995). The picture is further complicated by the fact that written English, in its many manifestations in the world, displays far less variety than spoken English. When writing, users orientate towards standard norms; when speaking they are as likely to orientate towards and accommodate to one another, and to express themselves in one of the myriad English accents and dialects, whether native or non-native. This raises an ideological problem for corpus-designers. Should corpora play safe and stick to written data, or should we plunge wholeheartedly into the kaleidoscope of spoken language? The answer will depend on one's ideological stance, rather than some objective notion of representativeness based on statistico-metrics. Carter and McCarthy (1995a) and McCarthy and Carter (1997) opt for an informal spoken corpus, on the basis of what we can learn about spoken language *per se* rather than any particular dialect, and place their faith in the universality of spoken features such as indirectness, topicalisation, modality, etc., even though realisations might differ from corpus to corpus, depending on where it is sourced.

Another ideological issue is raised by using a spoken corpus of native speakers, such as the CANCODE corpus. If the range of speakers is demographically representative, then clearly many levels of competence (whether linguistic or communicative) will be apparent among the speakers in the corpus, just as in writing. Traditionally, the great and the good in written languages have been accepted as those defined by the academic canons of university literature departments (itself a process not without huge ideological bias, e.g. the exclusion of women writers). We have no such list of the great and the good for spoken language, especially ordinary, everyday communication. The spoken corpus will include many speakers who seem intuitively able, clear, communicative and expressive; it will also include those who stumble, who make a poor fist of getting their meanings over, who display eccentric usages, and so on. Many of the native speakers in a corpus will be less proficient than many non-native speakers known to us.[9] The automatic claim of the native speaker to be the target user is therefore questionable. Seen from a communicative point of view (and in many cases also from the point of view of grammatical accuracy vis-à-vis standard grammars), there will be expert and inexpert native speakers, and expert and inexpert non-native speakers. The ideological shift required is one that takes us from the notion of the native speaker to the notion of the expert user, in the knowledge that both may be rather difficult to define within our present discourse-frameworks. As a programme for research within applied linguistics, identifying criteria for expert use of a language like English in different cultural contexts is an urgent one, and one which will be necessary if we are to develop a notion of standard that is not tied to old-world, written norms and perceived as another manifestation of linguistic imperialism (see Rajagopalan 1997 for further discussion). The alternative is probably unattainable: to assemble a database that is truly representative of all the thousands of types of spoken English that occur in thousands of contexts around the world, 24 hours of every day.[10]

Alongside all of these questions is the issue of local accountability: a grammar or lexicon, or speech-act inventory even founded with the best of intentions on expert-user based international research will need to show its relevance to local contexts. We should bear in mind Kramsch's (1993) powerful vision of the learner as someone struggling not just with lexico-grammar and pronunciation, but making the long and arduous journey from one cultural context (the classroom) to another (the target culture), crucially seeking that third place in between, where a transformed identity is forged. The texts (whether spoken or written) that learners are exposed to are voices from the target culture; we necessarily owe it to teachers and learners to identify target cultures in a relevant and usable way. Corpora have the potential to build cultural bridges; they also have the potential to reinforce cultural barriers. Local contexts are all-important, but they may be unable to have their voices heard because of lack of technological resources. In issues of technology, as in so many other respects, applied linguistics suffers from the unequal weight of the influence of the westernised industrial societies, and technological imperialism often goes hand in hand with linguistic and cultural dominance and insensitivity. A new discourse is badly needed, one in which the perceptions of technology and usefulness and real needs in local contexts is embraced, one which requires a shift in the modes of dissemination of applied linguistic professional discourse and a shift in level of awareness within our profession.[11]

Corpus linguistics, then, cannot bury its head in the sand and ignore the ideological issues its growth has spawned. In its desire to get at real language use and to reflect what ordinary users do with language, it has disturbed a hornet's nest of issues that pull in questions of standards, of the status of native speakers, of cultural and technological imperialism, and of how it expresses its own conceptual world in its metalanguage. It is not special in these respects, as I have tried to argue throughout this book.

No view of language or way of approaching language is neutral; but corpus linguistics, with its commitment to the world of linguistics and to the 'world-out-there', epitomises so many of the issues in one go.

6.7 Conclusion

This chapter has attempted to home in on applied linguistics as a kind of discourse. All discourse takes place in a social context, and applied linguistics, because of its very definition as an applied, problem-oriented discipline, cannot confine its discourse to within the walls of the ivory towers of academe. I have argued that applied linguistic discourse is, and should be, multi-voiced, and that the process of forming a disciplinary identity is enacted on many levels, in theory, research practices, methods and technologies, and in the day-to-day fabric of our professional conversations. The main risks to the healthy growth of the organism are ones touched on in this chapter and elsewhere in this book: an over-enthusiasm to tie up loose ends, get us all in line and singing from the same hymn-sheet, a lack of awareness and sensitivity towards our ethical responsibilities to our language-teacher peers and to language learners, a lack of awareness of the social, political and cultural contexts that condition our activities, a cosiness that comes from working in a narrow circle that excludes so many of our peers from less privileged parts of the world, an over-inflated sense of our importance in the world of language teaching, and a lack of self-criticality.

The strengths of our profession are its willingness to engage in cross-disciplinarity, the fact that a good many applied linguists are either still in, or not too far away from, the classroom and the field to remember why the profession exists, the fact that we are talking to one another, that universities and governments are slowly coming to realise the value of applied linguistics and are prepared to accord it validation as a discipline and to fund its efforts, and the fact that we are, generally speaking, curious people always interested to look at something new.

Setting out to write an introduction to applied linguistics is, in many ways, a fool's errand, and one over which I have vacillated and procrastinated many times during the long period of gestation of this book. One thing is for certain: there is no one introduction to issues in applied linguistics that will cover everything and please everyone. Some will find this book full of gaps, perhaps because their own area of applied linguistics has received scant or no attention; others will find in me nought but bias and self-justification. If I have a bias, and if you have not already found comfort in it or been enraged by it, it is in my belief that, because we are responsible to society in a unique way, we owe it to our interlocutors to make sense of language as a social phenomenon. We also have a duty, wherever we can, to mediate scientific explanations of its psychological and cognitive aspects, but without a social sense, such explanations are merely interesting. I have attempted to do much, but, as the Irish writer James Stephens said, 'Nothing is perfect. There are lumps in it'.[12]

Notes

1 The *Research Notes* had a predecessor in the journal in the *Recent Research in TESOL* column inaugurated by Spolsky in 1968, where, again, the 'research study' was the centre of focus.

2 See also Edge and Richards (1998) for an interesting discussion of the basis of qualitative research in applied linguistics.

3 For example, chaos and complexity theory has recently been explored as an alternative scientific paradigm for SLA, in which causality and linearity no longer occupy a central position (Larsen-Freeman 1997). And this is by no means only applied linguistic theorising at the level of the academy. At the time of writing, at least one group of hard-headed chalk-face language teachers are involved in serious investigation of chaos and complexity theory and its practical implications, in the city of Nagoya, Japan, centring round the JALT (Japan Association for Language Teaching) Chapter.

4 I speak from personal experience here, having had the privilege of working as an 'apprentice' with Sinclair in the 1980s at the University of Birmingham. I and other colleagues watched with admiration as he progressively rewrote the ground rules for interpreting linguistic data.

5 CANCODE stands for Cambridge and Nottingham corpus of Discourse in English. It is a 5-million word corpus of everyday conversation assembled in the islands of Britain and Ireland, and forms part of the Cambridge International Corpus. The corpus was established at the School of English Studies at the University of Nottingham, UK, with funding from Cambridge University Press, with whom the sole copyright resides. For a full account of the corpus and its construction, see McCarthy (1998).

6 I am grateful to Anne O'Keeffe of Mary Immaculate College/University of Limerick, Ireland, for pointing out this problem to me and for suggesting a more appropriate alternative.

7 Fairclough (1997:4) says of CDA that he assumes it 'to be part of applied linguistics', though, in his case, an applied socio-cultural linguistics rather than pedagogical linguistics.

8 I am grateful to Henry Widdowson for raising this particular, very pertinent question (personal communication).

9 This relates back to our question in section 4.3, as to whether non-native speakers should be seen as users of other languages rather than as 'failed monolinguals' (Cook 1997).

10 English, as usual, is the subject of argumentation here, though it should be noted that similar problems exist in choosing models of multi-national languages such as French and Spanish. North American universities will often adhere to the spoken model of metropolitan France rather than that of the near-neighbour, French Canada, and publishers will vet language teaching materials for use in Latin America in terms of their faithfulness to Castilian Spanish norms.

11 It is well-known, for instance, that the major journals in our field tend overwhelmingly to disseminate views emanating from the technologically advanced English-speaking centres (see Block 1996 for a discussion).

12 James Stephens (1882–1950) *The Crock of Gold*.

References

Abbs B and Freebairn I 1980 *Developing Strategies*. London: Longman

Abraham W 1991 (ed) Discourse particles across languages. *Multilingua* 10 (1/2)

Agard F and Dunkel H 1948 *An Investigation of Second-Language Teaching*. Boston: Ginn

Aijmer K 1984 Go to and will in spoken English. In Ringbom H and Rissanen M (eds) *Proceedings for the Second Nordic Conference for English Studies*. Åbo: Åbo Akademi, 141–57

Aiking-Brandenburg M, James A and Meijs W 1990 Suffixation and second language acquisition: morphological derivation in the English of Dutch secondary school pupils. *ITL* 87–8: 65–93

Aitchison J 1994 *Words in the Mind: An Introduction to the Mental Lexicon*. Second Edition. Oxford: Basil Blackwell

Alexander L G 1988 *Longman English Grammar*. London: Longman

Altieri F 1725 *Italian-English and English-Italian Grammar*. London

Anderson J M 1971 *The Grammar of Case: Towards a Localistic Theory*. Cambridge: Cambridge University Press

Anzilotti G 1982 The rhetorical question as an indirect speech device in English and Italian. *Canadian Modern Language Review* 38 (2): 290–302

Arnold T 1718 A new English grammar, or, A short, but clear and sure direction for the true pronunciation, accentuation and compleat acquisition of the English tongue together with the chiefest English idioms by Theodore Arnould. Hanover: Printed for Nicholas Förster, 1718

Artigal J 1992 Some considerations on why a new language is acquired by being used. *International Journal of Applied Linguistics* 2: 221–40

Ashby W 1988 The syntax, pragmatics, and sociolinguistics of left- and right-dislocations in French. *Lingua* 75: 203–29

Aston G (ed) 1988 *Negotiating Service: Studies in the Discourse of Bookshop Encounters*. Bologna: Editrice CLUEB

Aston G 1995 Say 'thank you': some pragmatic constraints in conversational closings. *Applied Linguistics* 16 (1): 57–86

Atkinson J and Heritage J (eds) 1984 *Structures of Social Action*. Cambridge: Cambridge University Press

Austin J L 1962 *How to Do Things with Words*. Oxford: Oxford University Press

Ausubel D 1964 Adults vs children in second language learning: psychological considerations. *Modern Language Journal* 48: 420–4

Baily A 1758 *An Introduction to Languages, Literary and Philosophical; Especially to the English, Latin, Greek and Hebrew: Exhibiting at one View their Grammar, rationale, Analogy and Idiom*. In 3 Parts. London: Rivington

Baker A and Goldstein S 1990 *Pronunciation Pairs*. Cambridge: Cambridge University Press

Bakhtin M 1986 *Speech Genres and Other Late Essays*. C Emerson and M Holquist (eds). Austin: University of Texas Press

Bar-Lev Z 1986 Discourse theory and 'contrastive rhetoric'. *Discourse Processes* 9 (2): 235–46

Baret J 1580 *An Alvearie or Quadruple Dictionarie, Containing Foure Sundrie Tongues: Namelie English, Latine, Greeke and French*. London: Henry Denham

Baret J 1573 *An Alveare or Triple Dictionarie, in Englishe, Latin and French*. London: Henry Denham

Bargiela-Chiappini F and Harris S 1995 Towards a generic structure of meetings in British and Italian managements. *Text* 15 (4): 531–60

Barnes W 1854 *A Philological grammar, Grounded upon English, and Formed from a Comparison of more than sixty Languages*. London: J R Smith

Bate J 1756 An Hebrew grammar: formed on the usage of the words by the inspired writers: being, an attempt to make the learning of Hebrew easy. By Julius Bate, A M Dublin

Bauer L 1983 *English Word-Formation*. Cambridge: Cambridge University Press

Bauhr G 1992 Sobre el futuro cantaré y la forma compuesta voy a cantar en español moderno. *Moderna Språk* 86 (1): 69–79

Béal C 1994 Keeping the peace: a cross-cultural comparison of questions and requests in Australian English and French. *Multilingua* 13 (1/2): 35–58

Beaugrande R de 1997 Theory and Practice in Applied Linguistics: Disconnection, Conflict, or Dialectic? *Applied Linguistics* 18 (3): 279–313

Beaugrande R de and Dressler W 1981 *Introduction to Text Linguistics*. London: Longman

Benson M and Benson E 1993 *Russian-English Dictionary of Verbal Collocations (REDVC)*. Amsterdam: Benjamins

Berry M 1975 *An Introduction to Systemic Linguistics*. London: Batsford

Biber D 1988 *Variation Across Speech and Writing*. Cambridge: Cambridge University Press

Biber D 1995 *Dimensions of Register Variation*. Cambridge: Cambridge University Press

Biber D and Finegan E 1989 Styles of stance in English: lexical and grammatical marking of evidentiality and affect. *Text* 9 (1): 93–124

Biber D and Finegan E 1991 On the exploitation of computerized corpora in variation studies. In Aijmer K and Altenberg B (eds) *English Corpus Linguistics*. London: Longman, 204–20

Bilmes J 1988 The concept of preference in conversation analysis. *Language in Society* 17: 161–81

Block D 1996 Not so fast: some thoughts on theory culling, relativism, accepted findings and the heart and soul of SLA. *Applied Linguistics* 17 (1): 63–83

Bloomfield L 1933 *Language*. New York: Holt, Rhinehart and Winston

Blum-Kulka S 1989 Playing it safe: the role of conventionality in indirectness. In Blum-Kulka S, House J and Kasper G (eds) *Cross-Cultural Pragmatics: Requests and Apologies*. Norwood: Ablex, 37–70

Boden D and Zimmerman D H (eds) 1991 *Talk and Social Structure: Studies in Ethnomethodology and Conversation Analysis*. Cambridge: Polity Press

Bolinger D 1976 Meaning and memory. *Forum Linguisticum* 1 (1): 1–14

Bongaerts T, van Summaren C, Planken B and Schils E 1997 Age and ultimate attainment in the pronunciation of a foreign language. *Studies in Second Language Acquisition* 19: 447–65

de Bot K and Weltens B 1995 Foreign language attrition. *Annual Review of Applied Linguistics* 15: 151–64

Bougard M-T and Bourdais D 1994 *The French Experience 1*. London: BBC Books

Boyer A 1694 *The Compleat French-Master for Ladies and Gentlemen*. London: Tho. Salisbury

Bradford B 1988 *Intonation in Context*. Cambridge: Cambridge University Press

Brazil D C 1985 Phonology: Intonation in discourse. In Van Dijk T A (ed) *Handbook of Discourse Analysis*. Volume 2. London: Academic Press, 57–75

Brazil D C 1997 *The Communicative Value of Intonation in English*. Cambridge: Cambridge University Press

Bridel E P 1797 An introduction to English grammar: intended also to assist young persons in the study of other languages, and to remove many of the difficulties which impede their progress in learning. London: printed and sold by James Phillips & Son, for Ed. P Bridel

Brinsley J 1647 The posing of the parts, or, A most plain and easie way of examining the accidence and grammar by questions and answers arising directly out of the words of the rules [microform]: the tenth edition corrected and inlarged. London: Printed by M F and J Y and Andrew Hebb

Broeder P, Extra G, van Hout R and Voionmaa K 1993 Word formation processes in talking about entities. In Purdue C (ed) *Adult Language Acquisition: Cross-Linguistic Perspectives. Volume II*. Cambridge: Cambridge University Press, 41–72

Brooks F and Donato R 1994 Vygotskian approaches to understanding foreign language learner discourse during communicative tasks. *Hispania* 77: 262–74

Brown H D 1980 *Principles of Language Learning and Teaching*. Englewood Cliffs NJ: Prentice-Hall

Brown P and Levinson S 1987 *Politeness: Some Universals in Language Usage*. Cambridge: Cambridge University Press

Brumfit C J 1980 Being interdisciplinary – some problems facing applied linguistics. *Applied Linguistics* 1 (2): 158–64

Brumfit C J 1991 Applied linguistics in higher education: riding the storm. *BAAL Newsletter* 38: 45–9

Bygate M 1987 *Speaking*. Oxford: Oxford University Press

Campbell G L 1991 *Compendium of the World's Languages*. London: Routledge

Cancino H, Rosansky E and Schumann J 1978 The acquisition of English negatives and interrogatives by native Spanish speakers. In Hatch E (ed) *Second Language Acquisition: A Book of Readings*. Rowley, Mass: Newbury House, 207–30

Candlin C 1990 What happens when applied linguistics goes critical? In Halliday M A K, Gibbons J and Nicholas H (eds) *Learning, Keeping and Using Language. Selected papers from the 8th World Congress of Applied Linguistics. Sydney, 16–21 August 1987*. Volumes I and II. Amsterdam: John Benjamins, II: 461–86

Carrell P 1983 Some issues in studying the role of schemata, or background knowledge, in second language comprehension. *Reading in a Foreign Language* 1: 81–92

Carrell P 1985 Response to Ghadessy. *TESOL Quarterly* 19 (2): 382–90

Carter R A 1987 *Vocabulary: Applied Linguistic Perspectives*. London: Allen and Unwin

Carter R A (ed) 1990 *Knowledge about Language*. London: Hodder and Stoughton

Carter R A, Hughes R, and McCarthy M J 1995 Discourse context as a predictor of grammatical choice. In Graddol D and Thomas S (eds) *Language in a Changing Europe*. Clevedon: BAAL/Mutilingual Matters, 47–54

Carter R A and Long M (1991) *Teaching Literature*. Harlow: Longman

Carter R A and McCarthy M J 1988 *Vocabulary and Language Teaching*. London: Longman

Carter R A and McCarthy M J 1995a Grammar and the spoken language. *Applied Linguistics* 16 (2): 141–58

Carter R A and McCarthy M J 1995b Discourse and creativity: bridging the gap between language and literature. In Cook G and Seidlhofer B *Principle and Practice in Applied Linguistics. Studies in Honour of H G Widdowson*. Oxford:

Oxford University Press, 303-21

Carter R and McCarthy M J 1999 The English *get*-passive in spoken discourse: description and implications for an interpersonal grammar. *English Language and Linguistics*: 3 (1): 41-58

Carter R A and McRae J (eds) 1996 *Language, Literature and the Learner: Creative Classroom Practice*. London: Longman

Carter R A and Simpson P (eds) 1989 *Language, Discourse and Literature: An Introductory Reader in Discourse Stylistics*. London: Routledge

Carter R A, Walker R and Brumfit C (eds) 1996 *Literature and the Learner: Methodological Approaches*. Basingstoke: Macmillan

Castro J 1751 *Grammatica Anglo-Lusitanica and Lusitanica Anglica; or a New Grammar English and Portuguese and Portuguese and English*. 2nd edition. London

Celce-Murcia M 1991 Grammar pedagogy in second and foreign language teaching. *TESOL Quarterly* 25 (3): 459-80

Celce-Murcia M, Dörnyei Z and Thurrell S 1997 Direct approaches in L2 instruction: A turning point in communicative language teaching? *TESOL Quarterly* 31 (1): 141-52

Chafe W 1982 Integration and involvement in speaking, writing and oral literature. In Tannen D (ed) *Spoken and Written language: Exploring Orality and Literacy*. Norwood NJ: Ablex, 35-54

Channell J 1981 Applying semantic theory to vocabulary teaching. *English Language Teaching Journal* 35 (2): 115-22

Channell J 1994 *Vague Language*. Oxford: Oxford University Press

Chapelle C 1990 The discourse of computer-assisted language learning: Toward a context for descriptive research. *TESOL Quarterly* 24 (2): 199-225

Chaudron C 1986 The interaction of quantitative and qualitative approaches to research: A view of the second language classroom. *TESOL Quarterly* 20 (4): 709-17

Cheng W and Warren M 1999 Inexplicitness: what is it and should we be teaching it? *Applied Linguistics* 20 (3): 293-315

Chitoran D 1981 Contrastive remarks on English and Romanian intonation from the point of view of pragmatics. In Kuhlwein G, Thome G and Wilss W (eds) *Kontrastive Linguistik und Ubersetzungswissenschaft*. Munich: Fink, 18-24

Chomsky N 1957 *Syntactic Structures*. The Hague: Mouton

Chomsky N 1959 A review of B. F. Skinner's *Verbal Behavior*. *Language* 35, 26-58

Chomsky N 1965 *Aspects of the Theory of Syntax*. Cambridge Mass: MIT Press

Chomsky N 1966 *Cartesian Linguistics: A Chapter in the History of Rationalist Thought*. Lanham MD: University Press of America

Chomsky N 1968 *Language and Mind*. New York: Harcourt Brace

Christie F 1986 Writing in schools: generic structures as ways of meaning. In

Couture B (ed) *Functional Approaches to Writing Research Perspectives*. London: Frances Pinter, 221–39

Cohen A and Swain M 1976 Bilingual education: The immersion model in the North American context. *TESOL Quarterly* 10 (1): 45–53

Collier R 1991 Multi-language intonation synthesis. *Journal of Phonetics* 19 (1): 61–73

Colsoni F 1695 *A New and Accurate Grammar; whereby the French and Italian, the Spaniard and Portuguese May Learn to Speak English Well; with Rules for the Learning of French, Italian and Spanish*. London: printed for S Manship

Comrie B 1981 *Language Universals and Linguistic Typology: Syntax and Morphology*. Oxford: Basil Blackwell

Coningham C G 1894 *Practical Business Conversation*. Yokohama: Kelly & Walsh Ltd

Connor U 1987 Research frontiers in writing analysis. *TESOL Quarterly* 21 (4): 677–96

Cook G 1989 *Discourse*. Oxford: Oxford University Press

Cook V J 1979 *Using Intonation*. London: Longman

Cook V J 1997 Monolingual bias in second language acquisition research. *Revista Canaria de Estudios Ingleses* 34: 35–49

Cooper C 1685 Grammatica linguæ Anglicanæ [microform]. Londini: Typis J Richardson, impensis Benj. Tooke

Corder S P 1967 The significance of learners' errors. *International Review of Applied Linguistics* 5: 161–9

Corson D 1997 Critical realism: an emancipatory philosophy for applied linguistics? *Applied Linguistics* 18 (2): 166–88

Coulmas F and Ehlich K (eds) 1983 *Writing in Focus*. Berlin: Mouton Publishers

Coulthard R M 1985 *An Introduction to Discourse Analysis*. London: Longman

Coupland N 1983 Patterns of encounter management: further arguments for discourse variables. *Language in Society* 12: 459–76

Coupland N, Coupland J and Giles H 1991 *Language, Society and the Elderly: Discourse, Identity and Ageing*. Oxford: Blackwell

Cowie A P 1988 Stable and creative aspects of vocabulary use. In Carter R A and McCarthy M J (eds) *Vocabulary and Language Teaching*. London: Longman, 126–39

Cruse D A 1977 The pragmatics of lexical specificity. *Journal of Linguistics* 13: 153–64

Crystal D 1981 *Directions in Applied Linguistics*. London: Academic Press

Crystal D 1969 *Prosodic Systems and Intonation in English*. Cambridge: Cambridge University Press

Cummins J 1991 Interdependence of first- and second-language proficiency in bilingual children. In Bialystock E (ed) *Language Processing in Bilingual Children*. Cambridge: Cambridge University Press

Cummins J and Swain M 1986 *Bilingualism in Education: Aspects of Theory, Research, and Practice*. London: Longman

Dasgupta P 1993 *The Otherness of English: India's Auntie Tongue Syndrome*. New Delhi/Newbury Park: Sage

De Vere M 1853 *Outlines of Comparative Philology, with a Sketch of the Languages of Europe, Arranged upon Philologic Principles etc*. New York: Putnam

Dingle J 1999 Why are materials so anodyne? Conference paper. MATSDA Conference on 'Restraints and Creativity', Trinity Institute, Dublin, 15–16 January 1999

Di Pietro R 1977 The need to be practical. In Makkai A, Becker V and Heilmann L (eds) *Linguistics at the Crossroads*. Lake Bluff, Illinois: Jupiter Press, 3–12

Dolz J and Schneuwly B 1996 Genres et progression en expression orale et écrite. Éléments de réflexions à propos d'une expérience romande. *Enjeux* 37/38: 49–75

Dörnyei Z and Malderez A 1997 Group dynamics and foreign language teaching. *System* 25 (1): 65–81

Downing A and Locke P 1992 *A University Course in English Grammar*. London: Prentice Hall

Dressler W U 1986 Explanation in natural morphology, illustrated with comparative and agent-noun formation. *Linguistics* 24: 519–48

Drew P 1984 Speakers' reportings in invitation sequences. In J Atkinson and J Heritage (eds) *Structures of Social Action*. Cambridge: Cambridge University Press, 129–51

Drew P and Holt E 1988 Complainable matters: the use of idiomatic expressions in making complaints. *Social Problems* 35 (4): 398–417

Drew P and Holt E 1995 Idiomatic expressions and their role in the organisation of topic transition in conversation. In Everaert M, van der Linden E-J, Schenk A and Schreuder R (eds) *Idioms: Structural and Psychological Perspectives*. Hillsdale NJ: Lawrence Erlbaum Associates, 117–32

Dunbar R 1982 Discourse pragmatics and contrastive analysis: some parallel constraints on German and English subordinate clauses. In Lohnes W and Hopkins E (eds) *The Contrastive Grammar of English and German*. Ann Arbor: Karoma, 152–61

Dunn W and Lantolf J 1998 Vygotsky's zone of proximal development and Krashen's ['I + 1']: Incommensurable constructs; incommensurable theories. *Language Learning* 48 (3): 411–42

Duranti A 1983 Samoan speechmaking across social events: one genre in and out of a 'fono'. *Language in Society* 12: 1–22

Dušková L 1984 Similarity – an aid or hindrance in foreign language learning. *Folia Linguistica* XVIII (1–2): 103–15

Eclectikwn E 1846 *Language in Relation to Commerce, Missions and Government. England's Ascendancy and the World's Destiny.* Manchester: printed by A Burgess and Co

Edge J 1989 Ablocutionary value: on the application of language teaching to linguistics. *Applied Linguistics* 10 (4): 407–17

Edge J and Richards K 1998 May I see your warrant, please?: Justifying outcomes in qualitative research. *Applied Linguistics* 19 (3): 334–56

Edmondson W 1997 The role of literature in foreign language learning and teaching: some valid assumptions and invalid arguments. *AILA Review* 12: 42–55

Eggins S and Slade D 1997 *Analysing Casual Conversation.* London: Cassell

Ehlich K, Coulmas F and Graefen G (eds) 1996 *A Bibliography on Writing and Written Language.* Berlin: M de Gruyter

Eiler M A 1986 Thematic distribution as a heuristic for written discourse function. In Coutoure B (ed) *Functional Approaches to Writing Research Perspectives.* London: Frances Pinter, 49–68

Eisenstein M 1986 Alternatives in second language research: Three articles on the state of the art. Introduction. *TESOL Quarterly*, 20 (4): 683–7.

Ellis R 1988 The effects of linguistic environment on the second language acquisition of grammatical rules. *Applied Linguistics* 9: 257–74

Ellis R 1994 *The Study of Second Language Acquisition.* Oxford: Oxford University Press

Ellis R 1995a Modified oral input and the acquisition of word meanings. *Applied Linguistics* 16 (4): 409–34

Ellis R 1995b Appraising second language acquisition theory in relation to language pedagogy. In Cook G and Seidlhofer B *Principle and Practice in Applied Linguistics. Studies in Honour of H G Widdowson.* Oxford: Oxford University Press, 73–89

Ellis R 1999 Item versus system learning: Explaining free variation. *Applied Linguistics* 20 (4): 460–80

El Sayed A 1990 Politeness formulas in English and Arabic. A contrastive study. *ITL* 89–90: 1–23

El-Hassan S 1988 The intonation of questions in English and Arabic. *Papers and Studies in Contrastive Linguistics* 22: 97–108

Elphinston J 1756 *The Analysis of the French and English Languages. With their Roots and Idioms.* 2 Volumes. London: P Vaillant

Emerson C 1983 The outer world and inner speech: Bakhtin, Vygotsky and the internalization of language. *Critical Inquiry* 10 (2): 245–64

Evans G 1980 Pronouns. *Linguistic Inquiry* 11: 337–62

Fairclough N 1989 *Language and Power*. London: Longman

Fairclough N 1995 *Critical Discourse Analysis*. London: Longman

Fairclough N 1997 Discourse across disciplines: discourse analysis in researching social change. *AILA Review* 12: 3–17

Fanselow J 1987 *Breaking Rules*. New York: Longman

Farr F and O'Keeffe A 2000 Hedging the issues of language corpora and language varieties: as you would! Paper presented at the Second North American Symposium on Corpus Linguistics and Language Teaching, Flagstaff AZ, Northern Arizona University, March 31–April 2 2000

Farr R M and Rommetveit R 1995 The communicative act: an epilogue to mutualities in dialogue. In Marková I, Grauman C and Foppa K (eds) *Mutualities in Dialogue*. Cambridge: Cambridge University Press, 264–74

Farrar F W 1870 *Families of Speech*. London: Longmans Green and Co.

Fillmore C 1968 The case for case. In Bach E and Harms R (eds) *Universals in Linguistic Theory*. New York: Holt, Rinehart and Winston, 1–88

Firbas J 1992 *Functional Sentence Perspective in Written and Spoken Grammar*. Cambridge: Cambridge University Press

Firth A (ed) 1995 *The Discourse of Negotiation: Studies of Language in the Workplace*. Oxford: Pergamon

Firth J R 1935 The technique of semantics. *Transactions of the Philological Society*: 36–72

Firth J R 1951/1957 Modes of Meaning. In *Papers in Linguistics*. Oxford: Oxford University Press, 190–215

Fisiak J 1983 Present trends in contrastive linguistics. In Sajavaara K (ed) *Cross-Language Analysis and Second Language Acquisition*. Jyväskylä: University of Jyväskylä, 9–38

Fleming D 1995 The search for an integrational account of language: Roy Harris and conversational analysis. *Language Sciences* 17 (1): 73–98

Fontenelle T 1994 Towards the construction of a collocational database for translation students. *META* 39 (1): 47–56

Foster P 1998 A classroom perspective on the negotiation of meaning. *Applied Linguistics* 19 (1): 1–23

Fox B 1987a Morpho–syntactic markedness and discourse structure. *Journal of Pragmatics* 11: 359–75

Fox B 1987b *Discourse Structure and Anaphora*. Cambridge: Cambridge University Press

Fox R 1970 The relative clause in three languages. *TESOL Quarterly* 4 (2): 131–6

Francis G 1989 Thematic selection and distribution in written discourse. *Word* 40 (1–2): 201–21

Francis G and Hunston S 1992 Analysing everyday conversation. In Coulthard R (ed) *Advances in Spoken Discourse Analysis*. London: Routledge 123–61

Fraser B 1990 An approach to discourse markers. *Journal of Pragmatics* 14: 383–95

Fredborg K M 1980 Universal grammar according to some 12th-century grammarians. In Koerner K, Niederehe H-J and Robins R H *Studies in medieval Linguistic Thought*. Amsterdam: John Benjamins, 69–84

Fries P 1983 On the status of theme in English: arguments from discourse. In Petöfi J S and Sözer (eds) *Micro and Macro Connexity of Texts*. Hamburg: Helmut Baske, 116–52

Gaies S 1983 The investigation of language classroom processes. *TESOL Quarterly* 17 (2): 205–17

García C 1992 Responses to a request by native and non-native English speakers: deference vs. camaraderie. *Multilingua* 11 (4): 387–406

Gass S and Selinker L (eds) 1993 *Language Transfer in Language Learning*. Amsterdam: John Benjamins

Geisler C, Kaufer D and Steinberg E 1985 The unattended anaphoric 'this'. *Written Communication* 2 (2): 129–55

Gellerstam M 1992 Om aktiva enspråkiga ordböcker. *Tijdschrift voor Skandinavistiek* 13 (2): 59–66

Geluykens R 1992 *From Discourse Process to Grammatical Construction: on Left-dislocation in English*. Amsterdam: John Benjamins

Genesee, F 1987 *Learning Through Two Languages: Studies of Immersion and Bilingual Education*. Cambridge Mass.: Newbury House.

Gethin A 1990 *Antilinguistics. A Critical Assessment of Modern Linguistic Theory and Practice*. Oxford: Intellect

Gethin A 1999 *Language and Thought*. Exeter: Intellect

Ghadessy M 1985 Word knowledge and world knowledge. *TESOL Quarterly* 19 (2): 375–82

Giacobbe J 1992 A cognitive view of the role of L1 in the L2 acquisition process. *Second Language Research* 8: 232–50

Giacobbe J and Cammarota M 1986 Learners' hypotheses for the acquisition of lexis. *Studies in Second Language Acquisition* 8: 327–42

Gill A 1619 *Logonomia Anglica*. Facsimile edition 1972 (eds B Danielsson and A Gabrielson). Stockholm: Almqvist and Wiksell

Givón T (ed) 1979 *Syntax and Semantics. Volume 12. Discourse and Syntax*. New York: Academic Press

Givón T 1984 *Syntax: A Functional-typological Introduction. Volume 1*. Amsterdam: John Benjamins

Goodwin C 1984 Notes on story structure and the organisation of participation. In Atkinson J and Heritage J (eds) *Structures of Social Action: Studies in Conversation Analysis*. Cambridge: Cambridge University Press, 225–46

Gregg K 1984 Krashen's monitor and Occam's razor. *Applied Linguistics* 5: 79–100

Gregg K, Long M, Jordan G and Beretta A 1997 Rationality and its discontents in SLA. *Applied Linguistics* 18 (4): 538–58

Grice H P 1975 Logic and conversation. In Cole P and Morgan J (eds) *Syntax and Semantics, Volume 9: Pragmatics*. New York: Academic Press, 41–58

Grimes J 1975 *The Thread of Discourse*. The Hague: Mouton

Haegeman L 1983 Be going to, gaan, and aller: some observations on the expressions of future time. *International Review of Applied Linguistics in Language Teaching* XXI (2): 155–7

Haegeman L 1989 Be going to and will: a pragmatic account. *Journal of Linguistics* 25 (2): 291–317

Halle M 1977 Morphology in a generative grammar. In Makkai A, Becker Makkai V and Heilmann L (eds) *Linguistics at the Crossroads*. Lake Bluff, Illinois: Jupiter Press, 120–30

Halliday M A K 1961 Categories of the theory of grammar. *Word* 17: 241–92

Halliday M A K 1966 Lexis as a linguistic level. In Bazell C E, Catford J C, Halliday M A K and Robins R H (eds) *In Memory of J R Firth*. London: Longman, 148–62

Halliday M A K 1967 *Intonation and Grammar in British English*. The Hague: Mouton

Halliday M A K 1974 *Learning How to Mean: Explorations in the Development of Language*. London: Edward Arnold

Halliday M A K 1977 Language as social semiotic: Towards a general sociolinguistic theory. In Makkai A, Becker Makkai V and Heilmann L (eds) *Linguistics at the Crossroads*. Lake Bluff, Illinois: Jupiter Press, 13–41

Halliday M A K 1978 *Language as Social Semiotic*. London: Edward Arnold

Halliday, M. A. K. 1985 *An Introduction to Functional Grammar*. London: Edward Arnold.

Halliday M A K 1989 *Spoken and Written Language*. Oxford: Oxford University Press

Halliday, M A K (1991). Corpus studies and probabilistic grammar. In Aijmer, K & Altenberg B (eds) *English corpus linguistics*. London: Longman. 30–43.

Halliday, M. A. K. (1992). Language as system and language as instance: the corpus as a theoretical construct. In Svartvik, J. (ed) *Directions in corpus linguistics*. Berlin: Mouton de Gruyter. 61–77.

Halliday M A K and Hasan R 1976 *Cohesion in English*. London: Longman

Halm W and Ortiz Blasco C 1988 *Contact Spanish (English Edition)*. Student's Book.

Cambridge: Cambridge University Press

Hamayan E 1995 Approaches to alternative assessment. *Annual Review of Applied Linguistics* 15: 212–26

Hancock M 1997 Behind classroom code switching: Layering and language choice in L2 learner interaction *TESOL Quarterly* 31 (2): 217–35

Harris J 1751 *Hermes, or, a Philosophical Inquiry Concerning Universal Grammar.* London

Harris R 1990 On redefining linguistics. In Davis H and Taylor T (eds) *Redefining Linguistics.* London: Routledge, 18–52

Harris Z 1946 From morpheme to utterance. *Language* 22: 161–83

Harris Z 1952 Discourse analysis. *Language* 28: 1–30

Hasan R 1984 Coherence and cohesive harmony. In Flood J (ed) *Understanding Reading Comprehension.* Newark, Delaware: International Reading Association, 181–219

Hasan R 1985 The structure of a text. In Halliday M A K and Hasan R *Language, Context and Text: Aspects of Language in a Social-semiotic perspective.* Oxford: Oxford University Press, 52–69

Hasan R 1992 Speech genre, semiotic mediation and the development of higher mental functions. *Language Sciences* 14 (4): 489–528

Hatch E 1992 *Discourse and Language Education.* New York: Cambridge University Press

Haverkate H 1988 Toward a typology of politeness strategies in communicative interaction. *Multilingua* 7 (4): 385–409

Hawkins J 1991 Language universals in relation to acquisition and change: a tribute to Roman Jakobson. In Waugh L and Rudy S *New Vistas in Grammar: Invariance and Variation.* Amsterdam: John Benjamins, 473–93

Hayashi T 1978 *The Theory of English Lexicography.* Amsterdam: John Benjamins

Hedard M 1989 Langues voisines, langues faciles? *Studi Italiani di Linguistica Teorica e Aplicata* 18 (1/2): 225–31

Heid U and Freibott G 1991 Collocations dans un base de données terminologique et lexicale. *META* 36 (1): 77–91

Heritage J and Watson D 1979 Formulations as conversational objects. In Psathas G (ed) *Everyday Language.* New York: Irvington Press, 123–62

Hewes J 1624 *A Perfect Survey of the English Tongue, taken According to the Use and Analogie of the Latine.* London: printed by E All-de for Wm Garret

Hewings M and Goldstein S 1998 *Pronunciation Plus: Practice through Interaction.* Cambridge: Cambridge University Press

Hilles S 1991 Access to universal grammar in second language acquisition. In Eubank L (ed) *Point counterpoint: Universal Grammar in the Second Language.* Amsterdam: Benjamins, 305–38

Hoey M 1983 *On the surface of Discourse*. London: Allen and Unwin

Hoey M P 1991a *Patterns of Lexis in Text*. Oxford: Oxford University Press

Hoey M P 1991b Some properties of spoken discourse. In R Bowers and C Brumfit (eds) *Applied Linguistics and English Language Teaching*. Basingstoke: Macmillan/MEP

Hofmann T R 1989 Paragraphs, and anaphora. *Journal of Pragmatics* 13: 239–250

Holliday A 1996 Developing a sociological imagination: expanding ethnography in international English language education. *Applied Linguistics* 17 (2): 234–55

Holliday A 1999 Small cultures. *Applied Linguistics* 20 (2): 237–64

Honey J 1997 *Language is Power: The Story of Standard English and its Enemies*. London: Faber

Hopper P and Thompson S 1993 Language universals, discourse pragmatics, and semantics. *Language Sciences* 15 (4): 357–76

House J 1985 Contrastive discourse analysis and universals in language usage. *Papers and Studies in Contrastive Linguistics* 20: 5–14

Howarth P 1998 Phraseology and second language proficiency. *Applied Linguistics* 19 (1): 24–44

Howatt A 1984 *A History of English Language Teaching*. Oxford: Oxford University Press

Howell J 1660 *Lexicon Tetraglotton. An English-French-Italian-Spanish Dictionary*. London: printed by J G for Cornelius Bee

Hudson R 1988 Some issues over which linguists can agree. In N Mercer (ed) *Language and Literacy*. Vol 1. Milton Keynes: The Open University

Huebner T 1985 System and variability in interlanguage syntax. *Language Learning* 35: 141–63

Hughes G 1988 *Words in Time: A Social History of the English Vocabulary*. Oxford: Basil Blackwell

Hughes R 1996 *English in Speech and Writing*. London: Routledge

Hughes R and McCarthy M J 1998 From sentence to discourse: discourse grammar and English Language Teaching. *TESOL Quarterly*, 32 (2): 263–87

Hughes S 1986 Salutary lessons from the history of linguistics. In Bjarkman P and Raskin V (eds) *The Real-World Linguist: Linguistic Applications in the 1980s*. Norwood: Ablex, 306–22

Huish A 1663 Priscianus nascens, or, A key to the grammar school [microform]. London: Printed for William Garret, and are to be sold by Timothy Garthwait

Hulstijn J 1997 Second Language Acquisition research in the laboratory: possibilities and limitations. *Studies in Second Language Acquisition* 19 (2): 131–43

Hunston S and Francis G 1998 Verbs observed: a corpus-driven pedagogic grammar. *Applied Linguistics* 19 (1): 45–72

Hunt R W 1980 *The History of Grammar in the Middle Ages*. Amsterdam: John Benjamins

Hymes D 1964 Towards ethnographies of communication. In Gumperz J and Hymes D (eds) *The Ethnography of Communication. American Anthropologist* 66 (6): 1–34

Hymes D 1967 Models of the interaction of language and social setting. *Journal of Social Issues* 23 (2): 8–28

Hymes D 1972 Models of the interaction of language and social life. In Gumperz J and Hymes D (eds) *Directions in Sociolinguistics: The Ethnography of Communication*. New York: Rinehart and Winston Inc, 35–71

Iacobucci C 1990 Accounts, formulations and goal attainment strategies in service encounters. In Tracy K and Coupland N (eds) *Multiple Goals in Discourse*. Clevedon: Multilingual Matters Ltd, 85–99

Itkonen E 1991 *Universal History of Linguistics*. Amsterdam: John Benjamins

Jakobson R 1968 *Child Language, Aphasia and Phonological Universals*. The Hague: Mouton

James C 1980 *Contrastive Analysis*. London: Longman

James C 1986 What is applied linguistics? In In Bjarkman P and Raskin V (eds) *The Real-World Linguist: Linguistic Applications in the 1980s*. Norwood: Ablex, 17–32

Jarvis J and Robinson M 1997 Analysing educational discourse: An exploratory study of teacher response and support to pupils' learning. *Applied Linguistics* 18 (2): 212–28

Jefferson G 1978 Sequential aspects of storytelling in conversation. In Schenkein J (ed) *Studies in the Organisation of Conversational Interaction*. New York: Academic Press, 219–48

Jespersen O 1922 *Language: Its Nature Development and Origin*. London: George Allen and Unwin Ltd

Johnson D and Saville-Troike M 1992 Validity and Reliability in Qualitative Research on Second Language Acquisition and Teaching: Two researchers comment. *TESOL Quarterly* 26 (3): 602–05.

Jones L 1984 *Functions of English. Student's Book*. New edition. Cambridge: Cambridge University Press

Jones S 1999 *Investigating Antonymy in Text*. Unpublished PhD dissertation. University of Liverpool

Jonson B 1640 *The English Grammar*. Facsimile edition 1972. Menston: Scolar Press

Jordan M P 1984 *Rhetoric of Everyday English Texts*. London: Allen and Unwin

Källgren G and Prince E F 1989 Swedish VP-topicalisation and Yiddish verb-topicalisation. *Nordic Journal of Linguistics* 12: 47–58

Kaplan R B 1966 Cultural thought patterns in intercultural education. *Language Learning* 16: 1–20

Kaplan R B (ed) 1983 *Annual Review of Applied Linguistics. 1982.* Rowley MASS: Newbury House

Katz J J and J Fodor 1963 The structure of a semantic theory. *Language* 39: 170–210

Katz J J 1972 *Semantic Theory.* New York: Harper and Row

Keenan E L 1976 Towards a universal definition of 'subject'. In Li C N (ed) *Subject and Topic.* New York: Academic Press, 303–33

Keijsper C E 1983 Comparing Dutch and Russian pitch contours. *Russian Linguistics* 7 (2): 101–54

Kellerman E 1986 An eye for an eye: Crosslinguistic constraints on the development of the L2 lexicon. In Kellerman E and Sharwood Smith M (eds) *Crosslinguistic Influence in Second Language Acquisition.* Oxford: Pergamon Press, 35–48

Kellerman E 1995 Crosslinguistic influence: Transfer to nowhere? *Annual Review of Applied Linguistics* 15: 125–50

Kelly Hall J 1995 (Re)creating our worlds with words: a sociohistorical perspective of face-to-face interaction. *Applied Linguistics* 16 (2): 206–32

Kennedy G 1987a Expressing temporal frequency in academic English. *TESOL Quarterly* 21 (1): 69–86

Kennedy G 1987b Quantification and the use of English: a case study of one aspect of the learner's task. *Applied Linguistics* 8 (3): 264–86

Kesner Bland S 1988 The present progressive in discourse: Grammar versus usage revisited. *TESOL Quarterly* 22 (1): 53–68

Khanittanan W 1988 Some observations on expressing politeness in Thai. *Language Sciences* 10 (2): 353–62

King A and Lansdell G 1979 *Adult French Course. Student's Book.* Harlow: Longman

Kirby J P 1991 Applied linguistics and the teacher: across the divide. *ITL* 93–94: 71–83

Kjellmer G 1990 On some characteristics of the English Lexicon. *Studia Linguistica* 44 (2): 126–54

Kniffka H, Blackwell C and Coulthard M (eds) 1996 *Recent Developments in Forensic Linguistics.* Frankfurt am Main: P. Lang

Komter M 1991 *Conflict and Cooperation in Job Interviews: A Study of Talk, Tasks and Ideas.* Amsterdam: John Benjamins

Kramsch C 1993 *Context and Culture in Language Teaching.* Oxford: Oxford University Press

Kramsch C 1995 The applied linguist and the foreign language teacher: Can they talk to each other? In Cook G and Seidlhofer B *Principle and Practice in Applied Linguistics. Studies in Honour of H G Widdowson*. Oxford: Oxford University Press, 43–56

Krashen S 1981 *Second Language Acquisition and Second Language Learning*. New York: Pergamon

Krashen S 1982 *Principles and Practice in Second Language Acquisition*. Oxford: Pergamon Press

Krashen S 1985 *The Input Hypothesis: Issues and Implications*. London: Longman

Krauss R, Fussell S and Chen Y 1995 Coordination of perspective in dialogue: intrapersonal and interpersonal processes. In Marková I, Grauman C and Foppa K (eds) *Mutualities in Dialogue*. Cambridge: Cambridge University Press, 124–45

Kress G 1990 Critical discourse analysis. *Annual Review of Applied Linguistics* 11: 84–99

Kullova J 1987 Algunos aspectos de los medios entonativos en español. *Revista de Filología Española* 67 (1/2): 19–34

Kunin A V 1970 Anglijskasa frazeologija. Moscow: Izdat'elstvo 'Vyssajaskola'

Kuno S 1982 Principles of discourse deletion – case studies from English, Russian and Japanese. *Journal of Semantics* 1 (1): 61–93

Labov W 1972 *Language in the Inner City*. Oxford: Basil Blackwell

Lambert W and Taylor D 1996 Language in the lives of ethnic minorities: Cuban American families in Miami. *Applied Linguistics* 17 (4): 477–500

Lantolf J 1996 Second language acquisition theory building: 'Letting all the flowers bloom!' *Language Learning* 46: 713–49

Lantolf J and Pavlenko A 1995 Sociocultural theory and second language acquisition. *Annual Review of Applied Linguistics* 15: 108–24

Larsen-Freeman D 1991 Teaching grammar. In Celce-Murcia M (ed) *Teaching English as a Second or Foreign Language*. Second edition. New York: Newbury House, 279–96

Larsen-Freeman D 1997a Impressions of AILA 1996. *AILA Review*, 12 (1995–6): 87–92

Larsen-Freeman D 1997b Chaos/complexity science and second language acquisition. *Applied Linguistics* 18 (2): 141–65

Leech G N 1983 *Principles of Pragmatics*. London: Longman

Lehrer A 1969 Semantic cuisine. *Journal of Linguistics* 5: 39–56

Lehrer A 1974 *Semantic Fields and Lexical Structure*. Amsterdam: North Holland

Lehrer A 1978 Structures of the lexicon and transfer of meaning. *Lingua* 45: 95–123

Lehrer A 1985 Is semantics perception-driven or network-driven? *Australian Journal of Linguistics* 5: 197–207

Lehrer A 1993 Semantic fields and frames: are they alternatives? In Lutzeier P R (ed) *Studies in Lexical Field Theory*. Tübingen: Max Niemeyer Verlag, 149–62

Lehtonen J and Sajavaara K 1983 From traditional contrastive linguistics towards a communicative approach: theory and applications within the Finnish-English cross-language project. In Sajavaara K (ed) *Cross-Language Analysis and Second Language Acquisition*. Jyväskylä: University of Jyväskylä, 81–94

Lennon P 1988 The linguist and the language teacher: love at first sight or the end of the honeymoon. *English Teaching Forum* 2

Lepetit D 1989 Cross-linguistic influence on intonation: French/Japanese and French/English. *Language Learning* 39 (3): 397–413

Lepschy G 1982 Linguistic historiography. In Crystal D (ed) *Linguistics Controversies: Essays in linguistic theory and practice in honour of F.R.Palmer*. London: Edward Arnold, 25–31

Levend Nederlands 1984. Foreword by J L Trim and J F Matter. Department of Linguistics, University of Cambridge. Cambridge: Cambridge University Press

Lewis M 1993 *The Lexical Approach: The State of ELT and a Way Forward*. Hove UK: LTP

Lewis M 1997 *Implementing the Lexical Approach: Putting Theory into Practice*. Hove UK: LTP

Lightbown P and Spada N 1993 *How Languages are Learned*. Oxford: Oxford University Press

Lindenfeld J 1990 *Speech and Sociability at French Urban Market Places*. Amsterdam: John Benjamins

Lindstrom O 1978 *Aspects of English Intonation*. Göteborg: Acta Universitatis Gothoburgensis

Long B 1919 English vs Esperanto as a world language. *English* 1: 19 etc.

Long M H 1983 Native speaker/non-native speaker conversation and the negotiation of comprehensible input. *Applied Linguistics* 4: 126–41

Longacre R 1983 *The Grammar of Discourse*. New York: Plenum Press

Lowth R 1762 *A Short Introduction to English Grammar*. Facsimile edition 1967. Menston: The Scolar Press

Lyons J 1977 *Semantics*. 2 Volumes. Cambridge: Cambridge University Press

Makkai A 1972 *Idiom Structure in English*. The Hague: Mouton

Makkai A, Becker Makkai V and Heilmann L (eds) 1977 *Linguistics at the Crossroads*. Lake Bluff, Illinois: Jupiter Press

Malmkjaer K 1991 *The Linguistics Encyclopedia*. London: Routledge

Malmkjaer K 1997 Translation and language learning. *AILA Review* 12 (1995/6): 56–61

Manes J and Wolfson N 1981 The compliment formula. In Coulmas F (ed) *Conversational Routine*. The Hague: Mouton, 115–32

Mann W and Thompson S 1988 Rhetorical structure theory: toward a functional theory of text organization. *Text* 8 (3): 243–81

Mansfield G 1983 Discourse intonation in English and Italian: a first contrastive analysis. *Analysis. Quaderni di Anglistica* 1 (1): 179–89

Marinova-Todd S, Bradford Marshall D and Snow C 2000 Three misconceptions about age and L2 learning. *TESOL Quarterly* 34 (1): 9–34

Marmaridou S 1988 Contrastive analysis at discourse level and the communicative teaching of languages. *Papers and Studies in Contrastive Linguistics* 22: 123–32

Martin J 1992 *English Text: System and Structure*. Amsterdam: John Benjamins

Matthews P 1979 Deep structure. In Allerton D J, Carney E and Holdcroft D (eds) *Function and Context in Linguistic Analysis*. Cambridge: Cambridge University Press, 148–58

Mauger C 1679 Claudius Mauger's French grammar [microform]:the ninth edition/ corrected and enlarged by the author. London: Printed by S. Roycroft for John Martyn, and are to be sold at the sign of the Bell

Mauger C and Festau P 1690 *A New Double Grammar, French-English and English-French*. Leiden. Also The Hague (1693): A Moetjens

McCarthy M J 1984 A new look at vocabulary in EFL. *Applied Linguistics* 5 (1): 12–22

McCarthy M J 1988 Some vocabulary patterns in conversation. In Carter R A and McCarthy M J (eds) *Vocabulary and Language Teaching*. London: Longman, 181–200

McCarthy M J 1990 *Vocabulary*. Oxford: Oxford University Press

McCarthy M J 1991a *Discourse Analysis for Language Teachers*. Cambridge: Cambridge University Press

McCarthy M J 1991b Morphology. In Malmkjaer K (ed) *The Linguistics Encyclopaedia*. London: Routledge, 314–23

McCarthy M J 1994a It, this and that. In Coulthard M (ed) *Advances in Written Text Analysis*. London: Routledge, 266–75

McCarthy M J (ed) 1994b *Word Routes. Français-Anglais*. Cambridge: Cambridge University Press

McCarthy M J (ed) 1995 *Word Routes. Inglese-Italiano*. Cambridge: Cambridge University Press

McCarthy M J 1998 *Spoken Language and Applied Linguistics*. Cambridge: Cambridge University Press

McCarthy M J and Carter R A 1994 *Language as Discourse: Perspectives for Language Teaching*. London: Longman

McCarthy M J and Carter R A 1997 Octopus or Hydra? *IATEFL Newsletter* 137: 16–17

McCarthy M J and O'Dell F 1994 *English Vocabulary in Use. Upper Intermediate and Advanced*. Cambridge: Cambridge University Press

McCarthy M J and O'Dell F 1999 *English Vocabulary in Use. Elementary*. Cambridge: Cambridge University Press

McCawley J 1986 What linguists might contribute to dictionary making if they could get their act together. In Bjarkman P and Raskin V (eds) *The Real-World Linguist: Linguistic Applications in the 1980s*. Norwood: Ablex, 3–18

McGroarty M 1998 Constructive and constructivist challenges for applied linguistics. Paper presented at the *Language Learning* 50th Jubilee Symposium, Ann Arbor Michigan, September 18–19 1998

McLaughlin B 1978 *Second Language Acquisition in Childhood*. Hillsdale NJ: Lawrence Erlbaum Associates

McLaughlin B 1990 'Conscious' versus 'unconscious' learning. *TESOL Quarterly* 24 (4): 617–34

McNamara T 1997 'Interaction' in second language performance assessment: Whose performance? *Applied Linguistics* 18 (4): 446–66

McNamara T 1998 Policy and social considerations in language assessment. *Annual Review of Applied Linguistics* 18: 304–19

McNeill D 1966 Developmental psycholinguistics. In Smith F and Miller G (eds) *The Genesis of Language: A Psycholinguistic Approach*. Cambridge Mass: MIT Press, 15–84

Meara P 1984 The study of lexis in interlanguage. In A Davies, C Criper and A Howatt (eds) *Interlanguage*. Edinburgh: Edinburgh University Press, 225–35

Meara P 1980 Vocabulary acquisition: a neglected aspect of language learning. *Language Teaching and Linguistics: Abstracts* 13: 221–46

Merritt M 1976 On questions following questions in service encounters. *Language in Society* 5: 315–57

Miller G A 1956 The magical number seven, plus or minus two: Some limits on our capacity for processing information. *Psychological Review* 63: 81–97

Miller G A 1978 Semantic relations among words. In Halle M, Bresnan J and Miller G A *Linguistic Theory and Psychological Reality*. Cambridge MASS: MIT Press, 60–118

Miller J 1995 Does spoken language have sentences? In Palmer F R (ed) *Grammar and Meaning*. Cambridge: Cambridge University Press, 116–35

Mitchell T F 1957 The language of buying and selling in Cyrenaica: a situational statement. *Hespéris* XLIV: 31–71

Mitchell T F 1975 *Principles of Firthian Linguistics*. London: Longman

Mohan B 1985 *Language and Content*. Reading MA: Addison-Wesley

Molino J 1985 Où en est la morphologie? *Langages* 78: 5–40

Monaghan J (ed) 1987 *Grammar in the Construction of Texts*. London: Frances Pinter

Moon R 1997 Vocabulary connections: multi-word items in English. In Schmitt N and McCarthy M J (eds) 1997 *Second Language Vocabulary: Description, Acquisition and Pedagogy*. Cambridge: Cambridge University Press, 40–63

Moon R 1998 *Fixed Expressions and Idioms in English*. Oxford: Clarendon Press

Moskovit L 1983 When is broad reference clear? *College Composition and Communication* 34: 454–69

Mutsu H 1894 *A Japanese Conversation Course*. Tokio [sic]: Z P Maruya & Co

Nádasdy A 1995 Phonetics, phonology and applied linguistics. *Annual Review of Applied Linguistics* 15: 63–80

Nation I S P 1990 *Teaching and Learning Vocabulary*. New York: Newbury House

Nattinger J R and deCarrico J S 1992 *Lexical Phrases and Language Teaching*. Oxford: Oxford University Press

Newman A 1988 The contrastive analysis of Hebrew and English dress and cooking collocations: some linguistic and pedagogic parameters. *Applied Linguistics* 9 (3): 293–305

Nida E 1975 *Componential Analysis of Meaning*. The Hague: Mouton

Nyyssönen H 1992 Lexis in discourse. In Lindeberg A-C, Enkvist N E and Wikberg K (eds) *Nordic Research on text and Discourse*. Akademis Förlag, 73–80

Nunan D 1989 *Understanding Language Classrooms: A Guide for Teacher Initiated Action*. London: Prentice Hall

Nunan D 1990 Using learner data in curriculum development. *English for Specific Purposes* 9 (1): 17–32

O'Brien T 1995 Rhetorical structure analysis and the case of the inaccurate, incoherent source-hopper. *Applied Linguistics* 16 (4): 442–82

O'Connor J D and Arnold G F 1961 *Intonation in Colloquial English*. London: Longman

Odlin T 1989 *Language Transfer: Cross-linguistic Influence in Language Learning*. Cambridge: Cambridge University Press

Offelen H 1686/1687 *A Double Grammar for Germans to Learn English; and for English-men to Learn the German Tongue*. London: N Thompson *et al.*

Okell J 1994 *Burmese: An Introduction to the Spoken Language Book 1*. Southeast Asian Language Text Series. Northern Illinois University: Center for Southeast Asian Studies

Oller J W Jr 1977 On the relation between syntax, semantics and pragmatics. In

Makkai A, Becker Makkai V and Heilmann L (eds) *Linguistics at the Crossroads*. Lake Bluff, Illinois: Jupiter Press, 42–53

O'Neill R and Kingsbury R (1974) *Kernel Lessons Plus. Teacher's Book*. London: Longman

Özbek N 1995 *Discourse Markers in Turkish and English: A Comparative Study*. Unpublished PhD thesis. University of Nottingham: School of English Studies

Palmer H 1924 *A Grammar of Spoken English*. Cambridge: W Heffer and Sons Ltd

Peirce, B, Swain, M. and Hart, D. 1993 Self-assessment, French immersion and locus of control. *Applied Linguistics* 14 (1): 25–42

Pennycook A 1999 Introduction: Critical approaches to TESOL. *TESOL Quarterly*. 33 (3): 329–48

Peters A 1983 *The Units of Language Acquisition*. Cambridge: Cambridge University Press

Phillipson R 1992 *Linguistic Imperialism*. Oxford: Oxford University Press

Pica T 1988 Interlanguage adjustments as an outcome of NS-NNS negotiated interaction. *Language Learning* 38: 45–73

Polanyi L 1981 Telling the same story twice. *Text* 1 (4): 315–36

Politzer R 1980 Requesting in elementary school classrooms. *TESOL Quarterly* 14 (2): 165–74

Pomerantz A 1984 Agreeing and disagreeing with assessments: some features of preferred/dispreferred turn shapes. In Atkinson J and Heritage J (eds) *Structures of Social Action*. Cambridge: Cambridge University Press, 57–101

Pomerantz A and Fehr B J 1997 Conversation analysis: An approach to the study of social action as sense making practices. In van Dijk T A (ed) *Discourse as Social Interaction*. London: Sage, 64–91

Priestley J 1761 *The Rudiments of English Grammar*. Facsimile edition 1969. Menston: The Scolar Press

Psathas G (ed) 1979 *Everyday Language: Studies in Ethnomethodology*. New York: Irvington Publications, Inc.

Quirk R, Greenbaum S, Leech G and Svartvik J 1985 *A Comprehensive Grammar of the English Language*. London: Longman

Rajagopalan K 1997 Linguistics and the myth of nativity: Comments on the controversy over 'new/non-native Englishes'. *Journal of Pragmatics* 27 92): 225–31

Rampton B 1995 Politics and change in research in applied linguistics. *Applied Linguistics* 16 (2): 233–56

Rampton B 1999 Dichotomies, difference and ritual in second language learning and teaching. *Applied Linguistics* 20 (3): 316–40

Reddick R 1986 Textlinguistics, text theory and language users. *Word* 37 (1–2):

31–43

Reid I (ed) 1987 *The Place of Genre in Learning: Current Debates*. Victoria: Deakin University Press

Richards J 1980 Conversation. *TESOL Quarterly* XIV (4): 413–32

Richards J 1994 *Interchange: Intro*. Cambridge: Cambridge University Press

Ringbom H 1985 The influence of Swedish on the English of Finnish learners. In Ringbom H (ed) *Foreign Language Learning and Bilingualism*. Åbo: Åbo Akademi

Roberts C and Street B 1997 Spoken and written language. In F Coulmas (ed.) *The Handbook of Sociolinguistics*. Oxford: Blackwell, 168–86

Roberts J 1983 Teaching with functional materials: the problem of stress and intonation. *ELT Journal* 37: 213–20

Robins R H 1979 Functional syntax in mediaeval Europe. In Allerton D J, Carney E and Holdcroft D (eds) *Function and Context in Linguistic Analysis*. Cambridge: Cambridge University Press, 196–205

Robins R H 1951 *Ancient and Medieval Grammatical Theory*. London: G Bell and Sons

Robins R H 1990 *A Short History of Linguistics*. London: Longman

Robins R H 1980 *General Linguistics: An Introductory Survey*. 3rd edition. London: Longman

Robins R H 1993 *The Byzantine Grammarians: Their Place in History*. Berlin: Mouton de Gruyter

Roget P 1852–1899 *Thesaurus of English Words*. 8 volumes. London: Longman, Brown, Green and Longmans

Romportl M 1973 *Studies in phonetics*. Prague: Czechoslovak Academy of Sciences

Rosch E H 1973 On the internal structure of perceptual and semantic categories. In Moore T E (ed) *Cognitive Development and the Acquisition of Language*. New York: Academic Press, 111–44

Rowland M. 1999. *The Body in Mind*. Cambridge: Cambridge University Press

Rudzka B, Channell J, Ostyn P and Putseys Y 1981 *The Words You Need*. London: Macmillan

Rumelhart D 1977 Toward an interactive model of reading. In Dornic S (ed) *Attention and performance*. Volume 6. Hillsdale NJ: Lawrence Erlbaum, 33–58

Sacks H, Schegloff E A and Jefferson G 1974 A simplest systematics for the organisation of turn-taking for conversation. *Language* 50 (4): 696–735

Sampson G 1979 The indivisibility of words. *Journal of Linguistics* 15: 39–47

Saussure F de 1916/1959 *Course in General Linguistics*. New York: McGraw-Hill

Sayce A H s.d. *An Elementary Grammar of the Assyrian Language*. London: Samuel

Bagster and Sons Ltd

Scarcella R and Brunak J 1981 On speaking politely in a second language. *International Journal of the Sociology of Language* 27: 59–75

Schachter J 1986 In search of systematicity in interlanguage production. *Studies in Second Language Acquisition* 8: 119–34

Schaffer D 1983 The role of intonation as a cue to turn-taking in conversation. *Journal of Phonetics* 11: 243–57

Schaffer D 1984 The role of intonation as a cue to topic management in conversation. *Journal of Phonetics* 12: 327–44

Schegloff E A and Sacks H 1973 Opening up closings. *Semiotica* 8 (4): 289–327

Scherer G and Wertheimer M 1966 *A Psycholinguistic Experiment in Foreign Language Teaching.* New York: McGraw-Hill

Schiffrin D 1987 *Discourse Markers.* Cambridge: Cambridge University Press.

Schmid H-J 1993 Cottage and Co: can the theory of word-fields do the job? In Lutzeier P R (ed) *Studies in Lexical Field Theory.* Tübingen: Max Niemeyer Verlag, 107–20

Schmitt N and Meara P 1997 Researching vocabulary through a word knowledge framework. *Studies in Second Language Acquisition* 19: 17–36

Schreuder R and Weltens B (eds) 1993 *The Bilingual Lexicon.* Amsterdam: John Benjamins

Schweda Nicholson N 1995 Translation and interpretation. *Annual Review of Applied Linguistics* 15: 42–62

Scuffil M 1982 *Experiments in Comparative Intonation: a Case Study of English and German.* Tübingen: Niemeyer

Searle J R 1969 *Speech Acts.* Cambridge: Cambridge University Press

Selinker L 1972 Interlanguage. *International Review of Applied Linguistics* 10: 209–31

Selinker L 1992 *Rediscovering Interlanguage.* London: Longman

Selting M 1992 Intonation as a contextualisation device: case studies on the role of prosody, especially intonation, in contextualising story-telling in conversation. In Auer P and Di Luzio A (eds) *The Contextualisation of Language.* Amsterdam: Benjamins, 233–58

Shettor W Z 1994 *Dutch: an Essential Grammar.* London: Routledge

Shirai Y 1992 Conditions on transfer: A connectionist approach. *Issues in Applied Linguistics* 3 (1): 91–120

Shohamy E 1994 The use of language tests for power and control. In J Alatis (ed) *Georgetown University Round Table on Language and Linguistics.* Washington DC: Georgetown University Press, 57–72

Shohamy E 1997 Critical Language Testing and Beyond. Plenary lecture, American Association of Applied Linguistics (AAAL) Annual Conference, Or-

168 · References

lando Florida, March 1997

Sinclair J McH 1966 Beginning the study of lexis. In Bazell C E, Catford J C, Halliday MAK and Robins R H (eds) *In Memory of J R Firth*. London: Longman, 410–30

Sinclair J McH 1991 *Corpus, Concordance, Collocation*. Oxford: Oxford University Press

Sinclair J McH and Coulthard R M 1975 *Towards an Analysis of Discourse*. Oxford: Oxford University Press

Skehan P 1989 *Individual Differences in Second Language Learning*. London: Edward Arnold

Skinner B F 1957 *Verbal Behavior*. New York: Appleton, Century, Crofts

Smith P D 1970 *A comparison of the cognitive and audiolingual approaches to foreign language instruction*. Philadelphia: Center for Curriculum Development

Soars J and Soars L 1987 *Headway. Intermediate/Upper-Intermediate. Student's Books*. Oxford: Oxford University Press

Spolsky B 1968 Linguistics and language pedagogy – Applications or implications? In J E Alatis (Ed.) *Twentieth Annual Round Table Meetings on Languages and Linguistics*. Washington DC: Georgetown University Press, 143–155

Spolsky B (1989) *Conditions for Second Language Learning*. Oxford: Oxford University Press

Spolsky B 1990 Introduction to a colloquium: The scope and form of a theory of second language learning. *TESOL Quarterly* 24 (4): 609–616

Sridhar S 1993 What are applied linguists? *International Journal of Applied Linguistics* 3 (1): 3–16

Stackhous T 1731 *Reflections on the Nature and Property of Languages in General, and on the Advantages, Defects and Manner of Improving the English Tongue in Particular*. [no data on publisher or place]

Stern H 1970 *Perspectives on Second Language Teaching*. Toronto: Ontario Institute for Studies in Education

Street B 1984 *Literacy in Theory and Practice*. Cambridge: Cambridge University Press

Stubbs M 1980 *Language and Literacy. The Sociolinguistics of Reading and Writing*. London: Routledge and Kegan Paul

Stubbs M 1996 *Text and Corpus Analysis*. Oxford: Blackwell

Stubbs M 1997 Whorf's children: critical comments on critical discourse analysis (CDA). In Ryan A and Wray A (eds) *Evolving Models of Language*. Clevedon: British Association for Applied Linguistics in association with Multilingual Matters Ltd, 100–16

Swain M and Lapkin S 1990 Aspects of the sociolinguistic performance of early and late French immersion students. In Scarcella R, Andersen E and

Krashen S (eds) *Developing Communicative Competence in a Second Language.* New York: Newbury House, 41–54

Swales J 1990 *Genre Analysis.* Cambridge: Cambridge University Press

Swan M and Smith B 1987 *Learner English: A Teacher's Guide to Interference and Other Problems.* Cambridge: Cambridge University Press

Sweet H 1899 *The Practical Study of Languages. A Guide for Teachers and Learners.* London: J M Dent and Sons

Takashima H 1989 How Japanese learners of English answer negative yes–no questions – a case of language transfer. *International Review of Applied Linguistics in Language Teaching* XXVII (2): 113–24

Tao H and McCarthy M J In press Understanding non-restrictive *which*-clauses in spoken language, which is not an easy thing. *Language Sciences*

Tarone E 1988 *Variation in Interlanguage.* London: Edward Arnold

Tarone E, Swain M and Fathman A 1976 Some limitations to the classroom applications of current second language acquisition research. *TESOL Quarterly* 10 (1): 19–32

Taylor J 1647 A new and easie institution of grammar [microform]. London: Printed by J. Young for R. Royston

Thomas J 1995 *Meaning in Interaction: An Introduction to Pragmatics.* London: Longman

Thomas P 1993 Choosing headwords from language-for-special-purposes (LSP) collocations for entry into a terminology data bank (term bank). In Sonneveld H and Loening K (eds) *Applications in Interdisciplinary Communication.* Amsterdam: Benjamins, 43–68

Thompson S E 1997 *Presenting Research: A Study of Interaction in Academic Monologue.* Unpublished PhD Dissertation. University of Liverpool

Tognini-Bonelli E 1996 *Corpus: Theory and Practice.* Birmingham: TWC

Tracy K and Coupland N 1990 (eds) *Multiple Goals in Discourse.* Clevedon: Multilingual Matters

Trevise A 1986 Is it transferable, topicalisation? In Kellerman E and Sharwood-Smith M (eds) *Cross-Linguistic Influence in Second Language Acquisition.* New York: Pergamon, 186–206

Trim J L M 1988 Some contrastive intonated features of British English and German. In Klegraf J and Nehls D (eds) *Essays on the English Language and Applied Linguistics on the Occasion of Gerhard Nickel's 60th Birthday.* Heidelberg: Julius Groos, 235–49

Trosborg A 1995 *Interlanguage Pragmatics: Requests, Complaints and Apologies.* Berlin: Mouton de Gruyter

Van Dijk T A 1972 *Some Aspects of Text Grammars.* The Hague: Mouton

Van Dijk T A 1980 *Macrostructures: an Interdisciplinary Study of Global Structures in*

Discourse, Interaction and Cognition. Hillsdale, New Jersey: Erlbaum

van Els T, Bongaerts T, Extra G, van Os C and Janssen-van-Dieten A 1984 *Applied Linguistics and the Learning and Teaching of Foreign Languages*. Translated by R van Oirsouw (First published 1977). London: Edward Arnold

van Lier L 1989 Reeling, writhing, drawling, stretching, and painting in coils: Oral proficiency interviews as conversation *TESOL Quarterly* 23 (3): 489–508

van Lier L 1994 Forks and hope: Pursuing understandings in different ways. *Applied Linguistics* 15 (3): 328–46

Ventola E 1987 *The Structure of Social Interaction: A Systemic Approach to the Semiotics of Service Encounters*. London: Frances Pinter

Voegelin C F and Voegelin F M 1977 *Classification and Index of the World's Languages*. New York: Elsevier

Vygotsky L 1978 *Mind in Society: The Development of Higher Psychological Processes*. Cambridge Mass: Harvard University Press

Wagner E 1992 The older seecond language learner: A bibliographic essay. *Issues in Applied Linguistics* 3 (1): 121–9

Wales M L 1983 The semantic distribution of aller + infinitive and the future tense in spoken French. *General Linguistics* 23 (1): 19–28

Walker W 1717 Some improvements to the art of teaching, especially in the first grounding of a young scholar in grammar-learning: the eighth edition, very much corrected. By William Walker, London: printed by H Meere, for G Sawbridge, and sold by A Bettesworth

Walter B 1988 *The Jury Summation as Speech Genre*. Amsterdam: John Benjamins

Watson-Gegeo K 1988 Ethnography in ESL: Defining the essentials. *TESOL Quarterly* 22 (4): 575–92.

Watts R J 1989 Taking the pitcher to the 'well': native speakers' perception of their use of discourse markers in conversation. *Journal of Pragmatics* 13: 203–37

Watts R 1999 The social construction of Standard English: Grammar writers as a 'discourse community'. In Watts R and Bex T (eds) *Standard English: The Widening Debate*. London: Routledge, 40–68

Waugh L 1991 Tense-aspect and hierarchy of meanings: pragmatic, textual, modal, discourse, expressive, referential. In Waugh L and Rudy S (eds) *New Vistas in Grammar: Invariance and Variation*. Amsterdam: Benjamins, 241–59

Wenlock R 1937 *Preparatory English Course for Foreign Students*. London: Macmillan

Werlich E 1976 *A text grammar of English*. Heidelberg: Quelle and Meyer

Wertsch J 1985 The semiotic mediation of mental life: L. S. Vygotsky and M. M. Bakhtin. In Mertz E and Parmentier R (eds) *Semiotic Mediation: Sociocultural and Psychological Perspectives*. London: Academic Press, 49–71

White B (ed) 1932 *The Vulgaria of John Stanbridge and the Vulgaria of Robert Whittinton*. London: Kegan Paul, Trench, Trubner and Co Ltd

Wikberg K 1992 Discourse category and text type classification: procedural discourse in the Brown and the LOB corpora. In Leitner G (ed) *New Directions in English Language Corpora*. Berlin: Mouton de Gruyter, 247–61

Widdowson H G 1979 *Explorations in Applied Linguistics 1*. Oxford: Oxford University Press

Widdowson H G 1980 Models and fictions. *Applied Linguistics* 1 (2): 165–70

Widdowson H G 1984 *Explorations in Applied Linguistics 2*. Oxford: Oxford University Press

Widdowson H G 1990 *Aspects of Language Teaching*. Oxford: Oxford University Press

Widdowson H G 1995a Discourse analysis: a critical view. *Language and Literature* 4 (3): 157–72

Widdowson H G 1995b Review of Fairclough *Discourse and Social Change*. *Applied Linguistics* 16 (4): 510–16

Widdowson H G 1998 Context, community and authentic language. *TESOL Quarterly* 32 (4): 705–16

Widdowson H G 2000 On the limitations of linguistics applied. *Applied Linguistics* 21 (1): 3–25

Wierzbicka A 1985 A semantic metalanguage for a cross-cultural comparison of speech acts and speech genres. *Language in Society* 14 (4): 491–514

Wilhelm K 1999 Building an adult ESL knowledge base: An exploratory study using an expert system. *Applied Linguistics* 20 (4): 425–59

Wilkins D 1976 *Notional Syllabuses*. Oxford: Oxford University Press

Wilkins D 1982 Dangerous dichotomies in applied linguistics and language teaching. In Crystal D (ed) *Linguistics Controversies: Essays in linguistic theory and practice in honour of F.R.Palmer*. London: Edward Arnold, 221–30

Winter E O 1977 A clause-relational approach to English texts: a study of some predictive lexical items in written discourse. *Instructional Science* 6 (1): 1–92

Winter E O 1982 *Towards a Contextual Grammar of English*. London: Allen & Unwin

Wodak R 1997 Critical discourse analysis and the study of doctor-patient interaction. In B-L Gunnarsson, P Linell and B Nordberg (eds) *The Construction of Professional Discourse*. London: Longman, 173–200

Wray A, Trott K and Bloomer A 1998 *Projects in Linguistics*. (With S Rea and C Butler) London: Arnold

Yang L and Givón T 1997 Benefits and drawbacks of controlled laboratory studies of second language acquisition. *Studies in Second Language Acquisition* 19: 173–93

Ylänne-McEwen V 1997 Relational processes within a transactional setting: An investigation of travel agency discourse. Unpublished PhD dissertation. University of Wales, Cardiff

Zalewski J 1993 Number/person errors in an information-processing perspective: Implications for form-focused instruction. *TESOL Quarterly* 27 (4): 691–703

Zobl H 1980 The formal and developmental selectivity of L1 influence on L2 acquisition. *Language Learning* 30: 43–57

Zydatiss W 1986 Grammatical categories and their text functions – some implications for the content of reference grammars. In Leitner G (ed) *The English Reference Grammar: Language and Linguistics, Writers and Readers.* Tübingen: Max Niemeyer Verlag, 140–55

Index

Page references followed by *n* refer to notes. Italicised terms refer to journal titles